Praise for
Between the Two Rivers

"From the first page of *Between the Two Rivers*, your attention will be captured. Readers won't be able to put the book down. You will hiss at the villains and cheer for the underdogs."
—Carol Hoyer, PhD, for Reader Views

"With this writing, Kouyoumjian joins authors Thea Halo and Peter Balakian, whose finely penned accounts of family members' survival of the Ottoman atrocities are essential reads for the understanding of these genocides."
—Elissa Mugianis, ForeWord Reviews

"Aida Kouyoumjian's rich memories of her mother will be a source of great fascination to anyone interested in the Armenian Genocide."
—Dawn MacKeen, Award-Winning Freelance Journalist

"The book reads like a chapter from *One Thousand and One nights*. An absorbing account that confirms the adage, 'Truth is stranger than fiction' … The author's visual descriptions touch the senses."
—Mary Terzian, Author of *The Immigrants' Daughter*

"Anyone who has traveled in the Middle East will recognize the authenticity of Aida Kouyoumjian's voice. This story is told with the deep cultural understanding of one born, raised and educated within sight of the minarets of Baghdad. Aida's writing launches the reader into the exotic land of pre-Saddam's Iraq, overflowing with vibrant colors, sights, sounds—and dangers."
—Joyce O'Keefe, Writer and former Foreign Service Officer

"Mannig's spirit, resourcefulness and courage captivate the reader."
—Genie Dickerson, Journalist, Washington, D.C.

"I am impressed with how you have woven personal history with solid research. BRAVO!"
—Helene Moussa, Retired scholar of Coptic art/Author of *Legacy to Modern Egyptian Art*, Toronto, Canada

"I cannot put it away. I knew the story would be incredible. But that is just part of it. The book is also masterfully written, in a very direct and honest manner. It is both touching and thought provoking at the same time. The characters are so alive they seem to have become part of my life. The book is clearly a winner."
—Artak Kalantarian, son of celebrated Armenian author Artashes Kalantarian and Manager, Seattle Armenians Yahoo Group

"I was absolutely fascinated! Your descriptions put such vivid images in my mind, as though I were there next to your mother, hearing and seeing everything. But you left me so hungry for more information ... What a marvelous tribute to a remarkable woman, and yes—a remarkable man!"
—Kelly Givens, Mt. Vernon, Washington

"I feel like I'm there in Mosul in 1918 as a ten-year-old girl, shivering and bloated with hunger ... Family is everything in this book. The fact that Aida Kouyoumjian can retell her mother's story so convincingly is the value of memory ... Her stories teach us how to live and not give up under atrocious circumstances.

"Aida Kouyoumjian moved to America in 1952. The fact that this novel is written in English is a testament to her intellect and very vibrant voice. The book depicts Arabic and Armenian traits and it weaves a carpet for me to get a glimpse of what life was like back then ... Growing up in the '50s, I remember my parents telling me to finish the food on my plate with 'Remember the starving Armenians.' "
—Deborah Cooke, Retired editor/published writer travel

"This is a brutally honest story—nothing seems to be exaggerated or glossed over in this true story—which makes more of an impact on the reader. Kouyoumjian did an amazing job at keeping the authenticity of the subject while writing a novel with great literary value on its own."
—Hasmik Kalantarian, Seattle, Washington

"Aida Kouyoumjian paints in minute details the vivid memories of her mother's daily experiences. We smell, taste, see, hear ... feel, cry and laugh alongside the hero. The powerful depiction of imagery painted in a colorful

palette, reminds one of an oriental style painting, we are entertained by exotic places, people, and even humor in the middle of a tragic story."
—Sona Stewart, Retired Art Critic, Issaquah, Washington

"My mind staggers at the disruption of simple human life by the whims and obsessions of others. This is a great book for you to revisit how you see other human beings on the verge of violent and disruptive behavior by those who do not have the right to do so. I just love your book ... It is a labor of love but worth every ounce of your heart and mind you poured into it. You are very gifted as a storyteller."
—Dr. William Rice, Professor of economics at California State University at Fresno.

"Thank you so much for sharing your mother's story with the world. You are a wonderful writer. I feel richer knowing you and your family's story."
—Vicki Heck, Librarian, Mercer Island Library, Washington

"What a great writer you are! Such rich detail, so evocative and emotional, such passion and feeling! Certainly your mother couldn't have told you ALL of this? And although you didn't dwell on the horrors of the Genocide, I was happy to read your book, which still contained so much hope. I can't wait for the sequel—and also wonder when Hollywood will film it?
—Bruce Greeley, Library Systems Analyst, Seattle, WA

"Your Haji-Doo's words: 'If it is written in the heart it will be written by the hand,' certainly became the heart of your ability to write such an important book. Many thanks ... and may God continue to give you that grand voice to write another related book."
—Mary Hall, Mercer Island

"I was instantly pulled into a world of anguish, despair, perseverance, resourcefulness, devotion, hope and pride. It touched me and, in many ways, changed my life forever. I first wanted to thank you for sharing her story, your story and the Armenian story ...."
—Shana Schreiber, student of Dr. Mary Johnson (Columbia College, South Carolina) researching the Armenian Genocide

"It is amazing to think that someone so young had such determination. I loved *Between the Two Rivers* and I want to know more. I highly recommend this book as a good read and great story."
—Catherine, Registered Nurse, Bellevue, Washington

"This book is a valuable and personal account of what many went through at the hands of the Turks at the time. I have sent copies to my daughter, cousin and nieces so that they may also know. Thank you for undertaking this effort."
—Hratch Kouyoumdjian, Architect, San Francisco

"I read your book straight through in a couple of days (a record time for me). I enjoyed it all and had to keep going from page to page. Some girl! Some woman! Some mother! You are a great writer. Keep it up."
—Dr. John Lindberg, retired physician, Mercer Island

"A powerful read—I couldn't put it down. Read it in two and half days and for me that is a 'Wow!' A history lesson for me, too. The book deserves another visit."
—Carole Tye, retired teacher, Mercer Island

"Your unique writing style kept me enthralled throughout the book. I especially liked the last few chapters about how Mannig and Mardiros fell in love and got married."
—Kyle Shanafelt, senior at Mercer Island High School

Beyond the Two Rivers

Beyond the Two Rivers

The Continuing Story of Mannig
the Heroine of Between the Two Rivers
Following the Armenian Genocide

AIDA KOUYOUMJIAN

coffeetownpress
Seattle, WA

Coffeetown Press
PO Box 70515
Seattle, WA 98127

For more information go to: www.coffeetownpress.com
armenianstory.coffeetownpress.com/

All rights reserved. No part of this book may be reproduced or transmitted in any form or by any means, electronic or mechanical, including photocopying, recording, or any information storage and retrieval system, without permission in writing from the publisher.

This is a work of nonfiction. Some names have been changed.

Cover design by Sabrina Sun

Beyond the Two Rivers
Copyright © 2014 by Aida Kouyoumjian

ISBN: 978-1-60381-151-4 (Trade Paper)
ISBN: 978-1-60381-152-1 (eBook)

Library of Congress Control Number: 2013948826

Printed in the United States of America

About the Cover

Dinner following the church wedding of the daughter of Eldorado and her groom, circa 1932. Mardiros is lower left; Mannig, second from left. "Eldorado" was the nickname of Hovannes Kouyoumdjian, who owned a photography studio located on Al-Rashid Street in Bagdhad and who was designated to photograph the Iraqi Royal Family. Hovanness was the son of the second son of Haroutyun Kouyoumdian, who was considered the patriarch of the Kouyoumdjian family since 1790, when records were first maintained.

The correct spelling of the family name is "Kouyoumdjian." Aida, her sister Maro, and their mother Mannig changed the spelling to Kouyoumjian upon coming to the United States, to make it easier to pronounce.

Sunset on the Tigris River, Baghdad. Eldorado Photo.

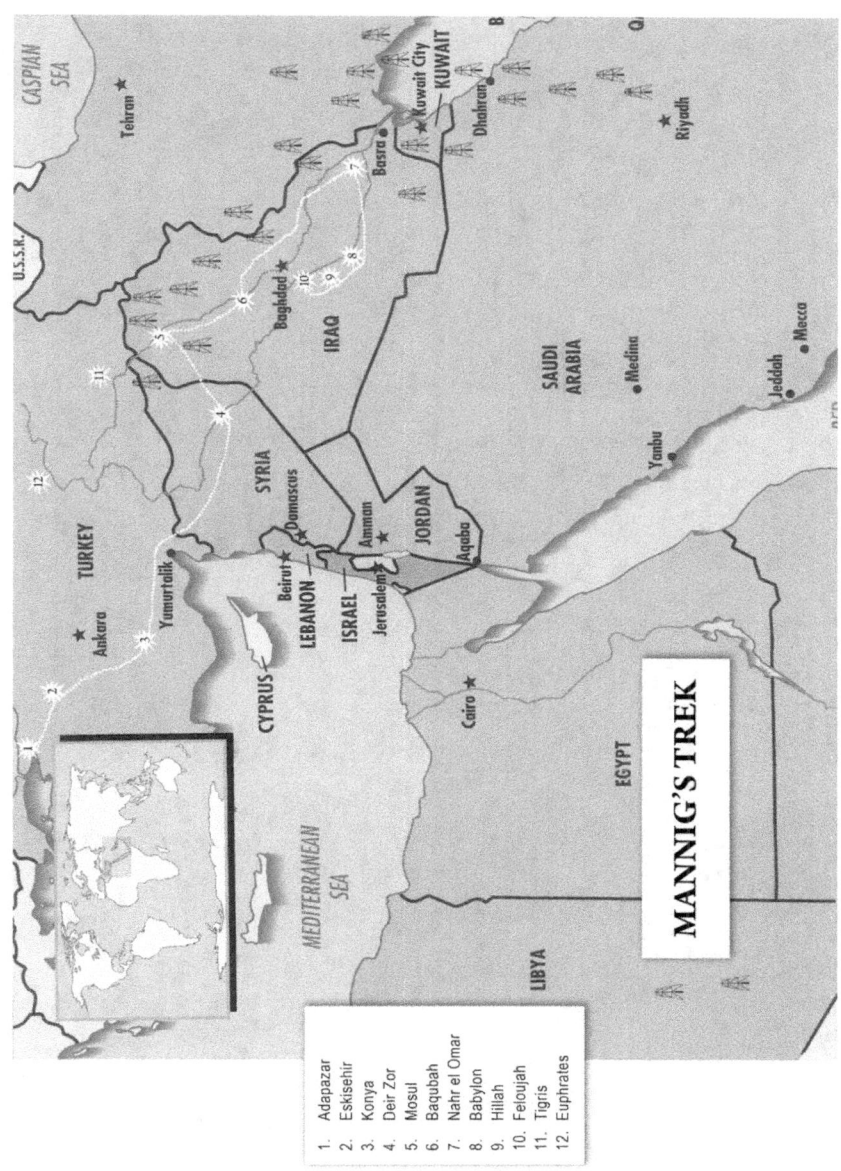

Route Followed by Young Mannig in *Between the Two Rivers*

Contents

About the Cover — ix

Chapter 1 — 1
What's in the Heart Shows in the Eyes

Chapter 2 — 5
The Massacre of the Royal Family

Chapter 3 — 15
Nuri el-Said

Chapter 4 — 21
Tea for the King

Chapter 5 — 31
The Jews are Leaving—Again

Chapter 6 — 37
Adriné's Visit

Chapter 7 — 43
Family Ties

Chapter 8 — 49
From Riches to Rags

Chapter 9 — 53
The Swallow's Nest

Chapter 10	61
Who's Who	
Chapter 11	69
The *Qasr* at a Glance	
Chapter 12	75
Hanim-*Effendi*	
Chapter 13	83
Supper on the Veranda	
Chapter 14	91
The Soirée	
Chapter 15	97
La fille aux cheveux de lin	
Chapter 16	103
The Haircut	
Chapter 17	111
Mistaken Identity	
Chapter 18	117
Good News, Good News	
Chapter 19	121
Escape from the *Qasr*	
Chapter 20	131
"The Word Is …."	

Chapter 21	135
The New Moon	
Chapter 22	141
Not Foreseen	
Chapter 23	147
Abu Ghraib and Beyond	
Chapter 24	153
The Taming of Mannig	
Chapter 25	159
Flowers for the King	
Chapter 26	167
Trite Concerns	
Chapter 27	171
A Vagabond Life	
Chapter 28	177
Escape from Felloujeh	
Chapter 29	183
The 1941 coup d'état	
Chapter 30	187
A Fireball in the Sky	
Chapter 31	193
Settling in Baghdad	

Chapter 32	197
The Thieves of Baghdad	
Chapter 33	203
Echoes of the War	
Chapter 34	207
Departures	
Epilogue	213
Glossary	221
Who's Who	225
What Makes an Armenian?	227

Chapter 1

What's in the Heart Shows in the Eyes

Mannig lived well. Ah, but to breathe free…. That's a different story. Her craving for family life emerged with her marriage. Following the Armenian Genocide that claimed all her family except her sister Adriné, she had clung to the Anatolian territories of Turkey. After World War I and three years at the orphanage, she led a life of comfort, surrounded by a slew of the Kouyoumdjian family in Felloujeh and Baghdad. She stepped lightly in affluence for thirty-six years.

Now in 1958, settled in the capital of Iraq, she was awakened in her bed on their roof by the first peddlers' sing-song wafting from the street. "*Sammoon haar! Sammoon haar!*" Ahmed, the Arab teenager, chanted out "hot bread." He was as deft as his father at balancing stacks of the flat rounds piled on a tray of palm-tree fronds atop his head. His—or more often his dad's—voice made alarm clocks unnecessary.

Such an early rising fit Mannig's plans to complete the housekeeping chores before the noonday July heat. Meanwhile her husband Mardiros would be getting ready for his day at the office downtown on Al Rashid Street.

While Mardiros plodded his sixty-eight-year old body downstairs, Mannig grabbed her robe. She wrapped it tightly around her mignon figure and finger-combed her dark hair, cut stylishly short. She dashed outside their fenced yard to catch the baker's son before he scurried to the next door.

She bought many loaves of the tiny, hot bread. Nibbling the crispy crust, she relished its tarragon flavoring. "Today's batch is *moomtaaz*—very tasty."

"*Shukran!*" The boy smiled and jingled the fifty fils into the pocket of his *dizhdasha* robe.

"Why isn't your father carrying the *Sammoon* this morning?"

"His friends came at dawn and took him someplace," the boy said, hurrying to the next house.

Soon, a matronly woman bellowed, "*Haaleeb! Haaleeb!*" while tethering her cow to the fence. Mannig handed her a metal bowl and studied the milkmaid's knack for finger-squeezing the cow's udder—lest she catch the woman sneaking water from a bottle tucked inside her flowing sleeve.

The garage door rattled open, startling the cow and provoking profanities from the milk woman.

Mardiros shrugged his shoulders apologetically and eyed Mannig, who stared at him, baffled by his early departure to work. *Before breakfast? Before indulging in his wake-up ritual of Turkish coffee?*

"Don't linger outside too long," he urged Mannig in Armenian, making sure she heard him. He hopped into his Jeep.

Why in Armenian? He must have sensed the need to resort to their mother tongue for privacy. She wondered why he was taking such a precaution.

He seemed compelled to rush away, and Mannig followed his Jeep with her eyes until it was out of sight.

He had donned his khaki shorts and shirt, his usual attire while engineering in the Mesopotamian lands for thirty years. Now that he was on loan by the Iraqi Irrigation Department to the American Development Board in Baghdad, she would rather he discard his desert uniform and wear a decent suit, like other office personnel at the headquarter of Tippets, Abbett and McCarthy.

She was happy for Mardiros that he could finally apply his college education. The timing of this job had been opportune, for the Kouyoumdjian clan had disbanded its sibling cooperative that earned them a living off their farmlands in Felloujeh. The couple was ecstatic when he was offered an engineering position with the Iraqi Irrigation Ministry, even though becoming a salaried employee was against the family tradition, especially in the eyes of his five brothers who themselves hired professionals in keeping with their ancestral customs.

His irrigation expertise often sent him to remote junctures of the Iraqi kingdom—wherever there was a dam to be built or a canal to be excavated. Mannig, their three children and her piano trekked with him across the lands of the Bedouin. A year or two in Abu-Ghraib, next to Felloujeh, then on to Wadi Tharthar, Tikrit, Kut, Hillah and Hindiyeh Barrage—isolated destinations—until their eldest daughter Aida was ten years old. Mannig insisted they settle in Baghdad so that all three children—Maro was seven and Setrak five—would receive proper educations in schools, the formal instruction she herself had been deprived of during the Ottoman persecution of the Armenians.

They rented several homes in diverse locations in Baghdad until building their current home in the residential suburb of Bustan al-Khass—literally, "Garden of Lettuce"—in its heyday, the epicenter for the Romaine variety.

The neighborhood consisted of two- or three-story residences, fenced apart, for middle and some upperclass Christian, Chaldean, Muslim, Jewish and Armenian families, a compound of cooperative religions. Mannig's neighbors to the left and right were Armenian; across the paved street were two Jewish, one Baha'i, and two Muslim households. The children played together and some attended the same schools.

They all knew one another and were ready to help out if the need arose. Almost always, if one family grilled shish-kebab in the backyard, the neighbors were alerted long before the aroma of charcoal and allspice permeated the air. The announcement inspired many to slake their own appetites by roasting their suppers.

Closing the front door with one hand and clutching the bowl of milk in the other, Mannig noticed unfamiliar men milling in and out of one of the Muslim homes. About to retreat inside, she froze at the sound of screeching tires of a black Mercedes.

The car parked haphazardly in front of the other Muslim house and two men dashed indoors, shouting the resident's name. Mannig didn't dwell on the goings-on at either home—she had to boil the milk then cool it before storing it in the ice-box.

She hoped the ice-man would deliver the block earlier than his usual 8 or 9 a.m. time. She wanted to prepare the custard to be layered on the sponge cake she intended to serve at their bridge party the next evening.

What a privilege to live in Bustan al-Khass, she thought. She didn't have to go to the *souq* for daily staples. Men peddled fresh vegetables and fruits to her front door at sunrise, and later on, women bartered eggs and chickens—a trade considered degrading to men. The major problem was haggling for a price that would not be underbid by another housewife, making one fodder for gossip. On occasion, someone would deny having bought a staple to avoid this fate.

Past ten in the morning and the ice-man hadn't come yet. Mannig was on the verge of calling her husband to buy a block from the factory and bring it with him at lunchtime when she heard the doors rattling.

She rushed out to the trellised pathway from their house. Seeing Mardiros jump off the Jeep made her come to a standstill.

"Get back inside," he shouted. Then, lightning quick, he lowered the garage door and padlocked it.

Sweat dripped from his forehead down to his neck, staining his khaki collar. His ragged breathing slowed his progress toward the house. Haggard, disheveled and distraught, he was not the same man who had left for work earlier that morning.

She did not need to ask the reason for his anxiety. Clearly he must have gotten tangled up in a horrendous incident or heard some dire forecast.

Another day of anxiety in 1941 in Felloujeh flashed before her eyes. He had dashed home unexpectedly, made her pack one suitcase for the two of them, another for the three children, and driven them off to Baghdad.

It turned out to be just in the nick of time. They had escaped the battleground between British forces and the Gaylani-Nazi sympathizing insurgency in Iraq—a skirmish that lasted barely a month. But their home, the sole residence on the western bank of the Euphrates River, had been ransacked by the advancing Gurkha forces defending British occupied territories. They had looted everything they could carry, smashed the gramophone and records, and thrown the books Mardiros had collected since his college days onto the riverbank. They chopped up anything they were unable to carry. Mannig hadn't wept for anything since the weeping meetings at the orphanage, but the sight of the axed keys of her piano opened the floodgates of her tears. She mourned its mutilation as if one of her children had been maimed.

On this day she worried about pressing Mardiros for details, least of all at this moment. Forcing him to rehash his experience might make him even more emotionally agitated.

"Are we caught up in another war?" she asked with a palpitating heart.

"This one is a *revolution*," Mardiros panted.

Chapter 2

The Massacre of the Royal Family

"I, myself, d-d-don't really understand what has happened," Mardiros stammered, wiping a smear of saliva off the edge of his lip. "I left for work this morning earlier than usual because I refused to believe what I heard on the radio. I-I-I didn't even finish shaving."

"What did you hear? And … and why didn't you say something to me?" This behavior was unusual for Mardiros; for the last thirty-six years of their married life he had always confided in her. It didn't matter that occasionally he ignored her suggestions.

"Yes, I did," he said, swallowing a lump. "I c-c-cautioned you …. I told you to go inside. B-b-but I didn't really know why myself." He looked at the wall-to-wall picture window overlooking the neighbor's porch then dashed over to draw the embroidered white linen curtains that Mannig had put in place for the long summer months.

She followed his lead, closing the rest of the draperies and blocking exposure to the outside world. Devoid of the winter Persian carpeting, the brown of the polished-stone floor reflected a dank paleness. Mannig had carefully supervised the professional carpet-packers, seeing that they sprinkled plenty of naphthalene mothballs before rolling each carpet in a separate gunnysack and storing the lot in the cellar. Without woolen flooring or heavy draperies, the hot summer temperatures of the outside world couldn't strike the shadowy indoors—at least, not with a vengeance.

Mardiros pulled his reading chair from its permanent position by the ochre ceramic hearth over to the free-standing Blau Punkt radio. Plopping into the chair, he tuned the radio to a Baghdadi station.

"Revolution! Revolution!" The man bellowed through the speaker.

Mannig gestured to reduce the volume to a whisper while she flipped the switch on for the ceiling fan to cool the room. She pulled a chair for herself beside the radio's carved mahogany pedestal.

"That's what I heard when I was getting dressed," he said. "I couldn't accept it. I assumed some prankster had gotten ahold of the station and was playing tricks with the listeners, blaring how so-and-so in the government was assassinated, so on, and so forth. Well, that was not an April Fool's joke. The first thing the revolutionaries did was to raid and seize the broadcasting station. And now, I c-c-cannot erase what I saw down on Al Rashid Street. It is an insurrection—a revolution of the worst kind."

"Revolution?" Mannig repeated. "Like the Bolshevik Revolution?"

"You might say that." He threw her a pensive glance. As usual, she had instantly connected a current event with an historical one. "That's exactly what they've d-d-done to our c-c-country." He coughed, choked, then stood up to clear his throat, a chronic habit due to his nicotine damaged lungs. Only a few years earlier, his doctor insisted he stop smoking lest he commit involuntary suicide. He had complied with the prescription, starting to chew gum instead. Mannig objected, comparing him to a masticating bull. He increased his intake of extra-sweetened Turkish coffee and sucked on sweet-and-sour candy balls. Consequently he gained an extra twenty pounds, way too much for his previously slender 5'11" frame. Now, it seemed, he would always be plagued with bouts of choking and coughing.

To give him quick relief, Mannig slapped his back firmly. She then dashed to the kitchen, racing back with water, bits of yesterday's ice clicking in the glass.

He sipped and recovered from the attack, back to normal. "A general in the army," Mardiros whispered, crunching onto a chip, "and his military cohorts, apparently have been secretly plotting with the Soviets for quite a while. At dawn this morning, that general dispatched his troops to attack the *Qasr* al-Zuhur palace. On the pretext that a helicopter would carry the royal family and its entourage to safety, the combatants directed them to the courtyard. When the king, the regent, the princess, the grandmother and the rest—all sixteen of them—gathered outside, the soldiers ordered them to face the fenced walls and machine-gunned them to death."

"What?" Mannig screamed. She was hunched over, shaking.

Mardiros touched his lips with his finger to hush her. His eyes were veiled in grief. "That was the humane part," he mumbled. "The real brutality came later, downtown, on Al-Rashid Street, b-b-beside my office …."

AS USUAL, MARDIROS HAD PARKED his Jeep in his slot in a side alley off the main thoroughfare that meandered with the Tigris River along its eastern bank. He headed northward to the newest five-story building of the Development

H.M. King Faisal II stands before a painting of his grandfather, H.M. King Faisal I. From Land of the Two Rivers: The Crown, The People, And The Country, Issued by The Director-General of Guidance and Broadcasting, 1957.

Board, a few blocks from the first of four bridges connecting the east and west riverbanks of the city. He cast a habitual glance at the minaret, piercing the crystal blue sky, silent as always that time of day. As usual, he passed a row of government buildings on his right. On occasion, he would turn into the Armenian Apostolic Church, emerging on to the alley of the *souq* to look at carpets—but not today. If he wanted more information about the news he'd heard on the radio, that would not be the best place to get feedback. Most of the ethnic communities of Baghdad pursued their trade or business without getting involved in politics.

He bypassed the smaller alleys—one *souq* for butchers, another for artisans and others for tradesmen, coppersmiths or silver smelts—each already filling the air with smells of melting metals and the sounds of pounding.

Curious about the shouts and ululation wafting beyond the curve of the four-lane boulevard, he stepped to the curb between the concrete columns that supported the second-story structures and apartment balconies above.

He noticed the residents of the apartments across the street leaning over their balconies and gazing toward the south end of Al-Rashid Street. He stepped into the street. Before he realized it, he was swept into the fervent crowd. Jostled by the mob, he was surrounded by blood-pumped faces, men hopping about in white *dizhdasheh* tunics, twirling and swirling their *keffiyeh* headgear in time to the hypnotic phrases.

"Y'allah!" "Y'allah!" "Y'allah!" "*Jamhuriya!*"

"With God!" "With God!" "A Republic."

"We got them!" "We've done it!" "Long live the Republic!"

Mardiros barely escaped being trampled. Shaken, he stumbled back to the sidewalk, scraping his left bare knee. Ignoring the blood oozing down his khaki knee-high socks, he crawled behind a column. He pulled himself up, pressed his back against the locked-down corrugated gate of a store, and blended into the background of bystanders. He had escaped the onslaught of frenzy but not his own panic, now flooding his sensibilities. Mesmerized, he observed the progress of a viciously ecstatic demonstration—a boisterous spectacle on Al-Rashid Street, the hub that defined the cultural, historical and political establishments of Iraq. The sounds and sights of the roused mob made his stomach churn, and bile coated his throat.

Jubilant screams became deafening as they neared.

Hordes of men of all ages tramped, shouting and waving the Iraqi flag.

Collaborators flailed daggers and leapt as high as they could with joy.

Trailing behind the jubilant mob, a nag plodded, drawing a manure-wagon. Soldiers with rifles cocked accompanied the putrid load, hitched to the back of the cart. Simultaneously, *Allah-u-Akbar* reverberated from the minaret, blending with the riotous cacophony winding down Al-Rashid Street.

Mardiros stood still.

It was not noon yet, so the *mu'edhin* should not be chanting his prayer. Fear gripped him then, for the clergy must be in cahoots with the demonstrators. His lungs tightened and his chest squelched his heart as his widened eyes focused on the two corpses being dragged by the manure wagon.

Four feet tied up to the rear of the wagon plank, their muddied soles facing the heavenly blue sky (a sacrilege for Muslims). The two men, naked except for white briefs, were dragged side-by-side, their torsos riddled with gunshots, their heads doused in blood.

Through a narrow opening between sidewalk onlookers, he spied a sheet of newspaper tied to the neck of each corpse with a string. *The Baghdad Times?* The one and only local publication in English. He squinted to read the huge scribbling in red blood, in English and in Arabic. One corpse was labeled KING FAISAL II, the other, ABDUL ILAH, the regent.

Mardiros' breathing stopped. He felt faint. He cocked his head and forced himself to inhale and exhale. *They've butchered the monarchy.* His heart boomed against his ribs. *Get out of here.*

He crouched into the first open shop and stayed absolutely still—as vulnerable and petrified as the owner. A tumultuous noise surged down the street with the *mu'edhin* booming his, *Allah-u-Akbar.* The mob jostled hither and lunged thither, flailing and gyrating high and fierce.

Mardiros couldn't remember how long he remained petrified before he realized the last of the barbarous demonstrators had dispersed beyond the northern bend of the street. The disappearance of the unruly throng left a suffocating silence amid the onlookers. The prayer chanter's voice dissipated; the asphalt of the wide Al-Rashid Street glistened, empty in the daylight sun; the radiating July heat overwhelmed the breeze from the Tigris River. The onlookers, mostly ashen and speechless, either milled into a *chai-khana* tea house or retreated into their own stores.

Mardiros pulled out his handkerchief to wipe his bloodied knee, but then hurriedly hid it inside his pocket, lest the English monogram betray his westernized leanings. He dusted his khaki, shortsleeved shirt and eyed the store owner. With only a nod, he stepped out into the sidewalk.

A pedestrian ahead of him grabbed the arm of his companion, "I don't want to lock up and go home …. There will be no one to thwart looters."

"I must call my family," another muttered.

"I wouldn't use the telephone these days," another cautioned. "Those demonstrators have probably tapped all the phones in Baghdad."

It behooved Mardiros, rather than going to his office, to beat a stealthy retreat and get home as fast as he could.

MARDIROS HAD SHARED NONE OF these grisly details with his wife. "I wish I had not driven the Jeep," he said, facing Mannig while keeping his ear glued to the silvery façade of the radio. "Any other car but a Jeep. That damn red machine radiates *America*, a symbol to all westernized nations. I'm grateful you didn't hear the mob screaming anti-West profanities."

He had avoided driving on the main thoroughfare in downtown, crossed the nearest bridge to the residential areas of the west bank. From there, he took side alleys, crossed another bridge, and headed back on the east bank toward Bustan al-Khass. He arrived home in one piece—physically, that is—his mind and emotions in a state of chaos.

"Listen! Do you hear the yelling on the radio?" Mardiros stared at Mannig. "They're not going to stop yelping rhetoric until they get their way … all the way to Moscow. A b-b-bloody, m-m-murderous c-c-coup d-d-d'état. That's what it is—an absolute and treacherous military takeover."

He railed and fired off his predictions without noticing Mannig's impatience for details about the demonstration downtown. He knew well her limited understanding of the Arabic language being broadcast. She spoke the vernacular and got by in the *souq*, but she struggled to understand the scholarly vocabulary used in newspapers, books and broadcasts—least of all the slogans yelled on the radio.

"Are you going to tell me what happened?" She sounded rattled. "Anything? Or do I have to call someone to find out—"

"Don't you dare telephone anyone!" he growled, rising to his feet.

The gravity of his voice startled her and she too jumped up.

"All right!" he coughed his words. "All right!" he repeated, raising his voice a few decibels. "I saw things downtown too horrendous to re-tell. I don't want to upset you any more than necessary."

"Don't you keep secrets from me, Mardiros." She poked his chest with her finger. "Don't you dare try to protect me. There's no place for that now."

Mardiros sipped on a bit of water. "You saw me leave early this morning," he said. "I heard on the radio something about a military take-over, but I didn't believe it. I wanted to get the truth at the office, and as quickly as possible."

"Revolution! Revolution!" The words reverberated throughout their living room.

"Wake up, Iraqis!" pounded in their ears.

"We have a new country!" "Celebrate our noble cause." "Stand up high, Iraqis!" "Applaud our new government."

The background chanting and ululations trilled in the vacuum of their solitude.

"The king is dead! The royal family annihilated!" These phrases were hollered over and over again, as Mardiros repeated them in Armenian.

Mannig stood petrified. "They killed our king? The little boy? He's not even twenty-three yet! He just got engaged."

"He *was* a boy," Mardiros interrupted her, trying to provide some perspective. "He has been on the throne for only five years. But for those revolutionaries, that's enough time for a king to claim Iraqi independence from the British. Not His Majesty—God save his soul. Apparently he shadowed

Abdel Ilah, the Regent, the man who those butchers accuse of being the tool to succumb to Western Powers by letting them rule over Iraq since 1939."

"Who are those revolutionaries?" Mannig asked, pulling her chair closer to his.

"A General Brigadier in the military," he said, blowing his nose. "Colonel Abdul Karim Qassum—a Soviet sympathizer. They say he received the blessings of the Russians to instigate the coup d'état. If you listen to the people in the streets, you'd conclude everyone expects the Bolsheviks to show up at our front door."

"Are we going to pack and escape again?" Mannig whispered. "Like we did in Felloujeh?"

"I pray not," Mardiros' calm voice lacked the power of assurance. "But I'm sure that this day of July 14th, 1958—as Roosevelt said for WWII—'will live in infamy.' Yes, our monarchy has been vaporized, but I hope anarchy isn't on the horizon."

Mannig sat still, thickening the silence between wife and husband. Not even the broadcaster's vocal cords disturbed it.

She was jolted from her seat. "We must hide the piano," she screeched. "I can't withstand another mutilation. I don't want to see the keys of my piano hacked with an axe again, as it happened in Felloujeh. You know how much I love my piano. Now that our children have grown, it has become my fourth child. Come, let's roll it out of the parlor …." She grabbed his hand and dragged him to the upright Baldwin.

He hesitated. "Where do you think you can hide this big thing?"

"In our bedroom closet," she said determinately and pushed the piano while he pulled it. In the bedroom, she dashed to the closet and pulled everything out—linens and towels stacked on a wardrobe. She emptied the drawers, strewing lingerie and shirts across their bed. "Come Mardiros. We must pull this out first."

"This is all very heavy stuff for us," he said, straightening his back. "Setrak should be doing all this. Where is he, anyway?"

"Oh, Setrak! Goodness gracious," Mannig panted. "How your story distracted me. I even forgot about him." She dashed back into the hall, to the kitchen and into the pantry and kicked open the back door. "Setra-a-a-k? Setra-a-a-k? Setra-a-a-k?" She called across the neighborhood at the top of her voice, elongating the second syllable Set/ra-a-a-k, as one did when searching for children.

One neighbor stuck her neck out of her second-story window. "I don't see him down our street."

Mardiros rushed into the front yard, poked his head over the fence and scanned up and down their street. Even though no one was around, he opened his mouth and decided to let out a quiet yell of a barely audible, "Set-rak?"

Mannig called him in. "Mardiros. Come back in. He'll come home, soon. He always does."

Mardiros shook a nervous head. "I'm glad our t-t-two d-d-daughters are out of the c-c-country," he stuttered, betraying his distress. "I wish Setrak were gone, too. What does he do all day long, anyway?"

"He's p-p-probably swimming," Mannig stammered, surprised by her own speech impediment. Setrak was past twenty-two and unemployed. Unlike his older sisters, Aida and Maro, who had both earned scholarships to attend universities in the United States, their son, Setrak was considered a slow learner. He had failed several grades, prompting his parents to bribe the school principal to maintain his enrollment until he was semi-qualified to earn a facsimile of a diploma.

During this summer of 1958, Setrak had been dilly-dallying around with Hakim, his buddy from a block away. They usually biked in their neighborhood to pass the time, and played backgammon almost daily at a nearby *chai-khana* along the Tigris River bank. Throughout the summer, they dipped in the tawny water and swam across to a park on a sand-spit midway across the river. Mannig counted her blessings each day when he came home without having gotten into some sort of trouble like idle boys often do—at least, she didn't know of any, especially since his exit from school two years earlier.

"He mustn't go here or there anymore," Mardiros wagged his finger. "And you shouldn't go out at all. I will do the shopping from now on … and the errands you need done. I won't drive that Jeep, either. Thank God, I can still walk."

The two returned to pulling the wardrobe out of the closet and rolling the piano into its place. Mannig scattered sheets and towels all over the musical instrument. After they were done, she was barely able to shut the closet. "Now let's push this piece of furniture against these doors. Help me stack these towels to hide the existence of anything behind it—completely."

"Our bedroom shrunk," Mardiros joked, eyeing the narrow strip between their bed and the jutting wardrobe.

"You'll get used to it," she said, reorganizing the contents of the drawers.

The two sat at the edge of their bed panting, staring at each other as if to say, "What now?"

Mardiros broke the silence. "I don't think it will come to this. We're far out in the suburbs; the murderers are downtown. Let's see what else they're jubilating over on the radio."

The broadcaster was still yelling his revolutionary slogans. "The king is dead! Abdel Ilah is dead! Every member of the royal family is dead!" he shouted. A sudden pause in his voice gave rise to the rustle of paper. "It says here ..." more paper shuffling, "it says ... *Allah-u-Akbar*, the minister of defense is dead! *Y'allah, Y'allah*! The minister of the interior, too. Y'allah! Y'allah! All the ministers are dead. Long live the *Jamhuriya*! The Republic is our future. All the ministers are dead .... No, wait. Not all. They can't find one minister ... but who? It looks like one traitor got away! Hey, new Iraqis! We must find the rascal. The traitor! Aha! The prime minister got away ...."

Both Mannig and Mardiros jumped to their feet, ashen.

"That snake slithered out of our hands!" the voice shouted. "Nuri el-Said is somewhere in Baghdad, in our beautiful Baghdad .... He will defile our beautiful Baghdad. Our beautiful Baghdad will reek like his *khara* shit. We must save Baghdad. Find that pig. Kill him ...."

"What did he say about Nuri el-Said?" Mannig asked.

Mardiros could hardly utter a word; Mannig couldn't take another breath. The news so far had impacted them only externally, superficially. Hearing the name Nuri el-Said petrified them.

Nuri el-Said was a friend of the Kouyoumdjians—a frequent bridge partner in their circle of friends.

They were jolted from their absorbed stance by a heavy thump-thumping in their backyard, followed by scurrying steps in their pantry.

Setrak, breathless, faced them in the hallway. "There's a tank on Hakim's street."

Chapter 3

Nuri el-Said

"What do you mean a *tank*?"

"A tank, Baba," Setrak said between short breaths. "Tank, you know. The boom, boom, boom kind, like a war tank."

"I'm going to see for myself," Mardiros said and swung around toward the door.

Mannig grabbed his sleeve. "You can't leave us alone," she shrieked. "A tank is a tank. You've already seen enough blood for one day. Stay here … for our sake."

Mardiros held his breath and, freeing his arm curbed his momentum. "All right! If I must, I'll control my anxiety." Approaching Setrak, he asked, "What is a tank doing on Hakim's street? Why were you there yourself?"

"The chai-khana owner booted us out," Setrak explained. "He closed his tea-shop in a snap and hurried home. 'Go home!' he yelled at us. It's dangerous to stay in public places, he told us. So, we came back and that's when we saw the tank … and … and … it sounded like a war, Baba. Like the movies … but like a real battle. Soldiers dashing in and out of houses, women screaming and children cowering; we didn't know what was happening. We were scared. We hid behind some onlookers. Someone next to Hakim said, 'The soldiers are looking for the prime minister.' "

"You don't mean, Nuri el-Said?" Mannig said in a shaky voice, naming their partner at bridge games.

"The soldiers found him on Hakim's street," Setrak continued. "They got out of the tank and rushed into that one house and then boom, boom, boom … the machine guns fired. We crouched. I was trembling. They quickly came out, dragging a woman … I don't know … I thought it was a woman … but it turned out it was a MAN—dressed like a woman. They dragged her-him out.

He-she was shot to death, blood all over her-him. Her headgear came loose and so we saw it was a man. They dumped his body on the tank ... fired in the air, yelling, "We got him! The stooge for the British! Nuri-el-Said—the *gawad*/traitor." They drove out of Hakim's street. So I ran home. I was scared. The boom, boom, boom was awful. They fired forty rounds .... No! More than fifty rounds of boom-booms at that man."

Nuri el-Said, the prime minister, had disguised himself as a woman and hid in different homes in residential enclaves, planning to arrange for an escape from Iraq. Word of mouth had betrayed his intent and whereabouts. He was caught and shot in Bustan al-Khass, his corpse desecrated and dragged down Al-Rashid Street throughout Baghdad.

Mannig dreaded her family's fate had the prime minister sought refuge in their home. What providence had protected them from such calamity?

Murderers. Murderers! The words echoed in her head. She grew weak in the knees, squatting in the hallway. Mardiros, her husband, had seen the mutilated bodies of the royal family, and Setrak, her son, the body of the prime minister—horrors to haunt them for the rest of their lives. *Who would be next?* She dreaded living through more atrocities, as she had during the genocide that massacred six members of her family. And that was not too long ago, a mere forty years earlier—during WWI in the lands of the Ottomans.

Mardiros rushed back to the radio in the living room.

A different baritone was reading declarations with staccato yet lyrical gusto. "Down with the monarchy! Long live our Republic! Death to royalty! Cheers to the people. Down with Britain's cronies. Forever our Republic!" Then he urged his audience to stand in attention to the national anthem.

Not recognizing it, both Mannig and Mardiros raised their shoulders.

So did Setrak. He shook his head. "Are we supposed to memorize this from now on? And sing before we sit at the cinema?"

"Cinema?" both Mardiros and Mannig yelled at Setrak, and Mannig wagged her finger at him. "No one is going to any cinema. Not unless we say so."

The broadcaster's voice interrupted the parental chastising.

"Long live Brigadier General Abdul Karim Qassim. The brave general of our army; the daring patriot of our free nation; the hero of our independent country ... of our beautiful city; of Baghdad! Baghdad *Ya Balad el-Rashidi*." As soon as his voice stopped, the national anthem—the new one—was repeated, again and again.

Setrak grabbed a pencil and reached for the issue of *Life Magazine* within his immediate reach. He jotted down whatever words he could, erasing, rewriting and continuing all along its white margins. He then tore the back page, folded it and put it in the pocket of his shorts.

Original Caption: "His Excellency Nuri es-Said, Prime Minister of Iraq, one of the principal architects of Iraq's present stability and future potential and a corner-stone of the constitution; soldier, diplomat, world statesman; one of the most outstanding personalities in Arab history." From *Land of the Two Rivers: The Crown, The People, And The Country*, Issued by The Director-General of Guidance and Broadcasting, 1957.

Mannig pulled the paper out. "Are you crazy?" She poked his chest with her finger. "You won't go anywhere with an American page on your person!"

During the instant lull following her explosive warning, she strove to calm herself, physically at least. The broadcaster's voice pounded above all other sounds. "We've got them! The regent, the king, the royal family! Everyone in Palace el-Zuhur is dead …." Suddenly the broadcaster's voice faded. The silence brought Mannig to her feet. "Why did he stop?" she asked Mardiros, but before she ended her question, the broadcaster was yelping again.

"It seemed he just got word that Nuri el-Said is now dead, too," Mardiros said, translating to Armenian.

"We knew that before them." Mannig snickered at the new regime's authority, while she watched Mardiros, who was pushing a chair. He jutted it against the west wall and stood on it, reaching for the framed black-and-white photographs.

"We must hide these, too," he said. "Unlike your piano, these pictures could incriminate us, for no other reason than for our associations." He removed the one of King Faisal I, a commercial photograph of the first king of Iraq; and a second one taken when His Majesty was visiting the Kouyoumdjians in Felloujeh. Then he pushed the chair to the next wall and removed two copies of historical photographs: one of Aida, their older daughter, giving a bouquet of flowers to King Ghazi—the son of King Faisal I—and the other of Mannig standing next to the fiancée of King Faisal II, the current king, now murdered at the age of twenty-two.

Mannig hugged the four glass-cooled pieces of memorabilia close to her chest. "I must wrap each with a towel before you figure out where to hide them."

"Inside the p-p-p-piano, of course," he said. As he stepped down, he faltered and lost his balance. Attempting to prevent his fall, Mannig grabbed his arm, at the same time dropping the framed photographs. The raucous crash spilled broken glass across the tile floor. Mardiros fell on his backside with a loud "Oof" and a thud, and Mannig cried out in distress.

Setrak stepped in. "It sounds like a battleground here. It's noisier than the boom-boom was down the block."

Mannig helped Mardiros up and, seeing he was not broken or wounded by shards of glass, brought in a broom to sweep away the mess. She picked up the first photograph and glanced at the calligraphy script in the bottom margin, "*King Faisal I of Iraq, 1922.*"

Moved, she brushed a finger across the date—the year she and Mardiros were married. More than the coincidental significance of a coronation and her own wedding date, Mannig's thoughts fixed on Mardiros' proposal of marriage at the orphanage in Basra.

The ship Shuja, docked within view of the military tents that housed the survivors of the massacre, had prepared to transfer 900 orphans early next morning. Like all the children, Mannig and her sister Adriné were ecstatic about the forthcoming transfer from Basra to Jerusalem. Finally, they would receive proper schooling at a "real" orphanage for Armenians who endured the Ottoman atrocities during World War I.

Mannig remembered how she and Adriné were whisked to the quarters of the Captain of the Shuja, who officiated the wedding ceremony marrying her to Mardiros and Adriné to his friend Sebouh. The smells and sights of the scrumptious dinner served in the Captain's quarters following the rituals flitted in and out of her consciousness.

Mardiros had fallen in love with Mannig during his philanthropic efforts to save the survivors of the Armenian genocide. He couldn't bear seeing her disappear from his life and go on to enchant some other Armenian in Jerusalem.

On the eve of the ship's departure, he summoned Mannig to a meeting and proposed marriage. Even though Mannig secretly admired Mardiros, she was surprised at the way—contrary to Armenian customs—he confessed his love to her. "I would be honored to marry you," she had said, "but I cannot be separated from my one and only surviving sister."

As it turned out, Mannig's sister was not a major obstacle to their happiness. Mardiros was aware how Adriné had captivated Sebouh Papazian, another philanthropist from Baghdad. In no time Mardiros had arranged a double wedding aboard the ship Shuja, prior to its sailing.

Mannig's lips curled upward at the thought of the ceremony aboard the *Shuja*. It had gone so quickly she barely grasped its impact. Then the captain, having heard the exchange of vows between Mardiros and Mannig and again between Sebouh and Adriné, shook Mannig's hand and said, "May God bless your life, Mrs. Kouyoumdjian." She associated her new title, "Missus," with matrons mothering their children and felt demoralized. In a moment, her dreams of becoming a teacher and called "Miss" had evaporated. She was only fifteen years old!

Yes, the year 1922 was significant in Mannig's life. How did she actually fare when whisked out of the orphanage and launched into Baghdadi society?

Mardiros picked up the second photograph. "Aha!" he said, giving it to Mannig. "That was some occasion. No Kouyoumdjian will ever forget the day His Majesty stopped by for tea."

Chapter 4

Tea for the King

Mannig never learned how the friendly association between the Kouyoumdjians and the Royal Family of Iraq began. From conversations in the drawing rooms she assumed that the two brothers, Kerop Agha Kouyoumdjian and Hagop Agha Kouyoumdjian—the father-in-law she never met—earned their reputations from their philanthropy toward the Ottoman Empire. The Agha brothers retained their aristocratic status by contributing to the welfare of their ancestral land even after it formed a country all its own—Iraq.

Mannig's curiosity was piqued when the family received the courier from the royal palace bearing the king's regrets that he could not attend the forthcoming reception for the wedding of Mardiros and Mannig. She never doubted the existence of the relationship between the royal family and the Kouyoumdjians. Some family members recalled joining the royal hunt for mountain lions; others bragged about riding race horses on royal grounds. Any doubts she might have had were removed by the visits paid by King Faisal and his brother, Ali at the *qasr* in Felloujeh.

As was their custom to escape the summer heat, the Kouyoumdjians had moved to their Felloujeh *qasr* on the west bank of the Euphrates River, forty-five miles west of Baghdad. Like their permanent home, this one was designed to house the families of the five brothers in separate compartments. They would gather together at suppertime and chat afterward on the balcony, often past midnight. The taupe ceramic-tiled balcony jutted out of the drawing room and cantilevered over the riverbank. They relished the cool breeze off the river's bend along their peninsular property.

The balcony was Mannig's favorite location, not only because it was the perfect setting for a cool evening but because she, as the most recent bride, was no longer the focus of the family's attention. Everyone had so much to talk about. Their summer place offered a lot of space and many opportunities during the days for the fourteen children to expend their excess energy. The adults seemed to relive their youths when their offspring spoke of swinging from trees, riding horses or donkeys, swimming in the river and playing the sort of games children invent for themselves. Their juvenile dramatizations of how the cook slaughtered a lamb for dinner or strangled chickens for Sunday's supper were far more entertaining than finding a turkey egg in the chicken coop. Armen liked to brag about how he almost trapped a jackal. "We chased that wowie to the edge of the farm," Haig would add, completing his cousin's story. Mannig, only sixteen then seventeen years old, loved listening to tales of the children's shenanigans, wishing she could be with her nieces and nephews rather than her in-laws.

All this, however, did not stop the children from suffering the occasional reproofs from their parents, especially if Managuile Hanum shouted from her room, "Send for Mardiros to deal with these delinquents." The children feared him, but Mannig could not imagine her husband even stepping on a cockroach.

Knowing her place, Mannig refrained from entertaining ideas of childish adventures. She hoped to familiarize herself with the caprices and idiosyncrasies of the adults of her family.

One day, the supper bell—an empty three-inch cannon shell—was gonged several hours before the actual meal. The adults dashed out of their compartments and headed downstairs, Mannig in tow.

Once inside the drawing room, they found that instead of the eldest brother Khosrof, Mardiros had issued the unusual summons. He motioned to Mannig to sit on the divan closest to him while he remained standing in front of a silk *Sajadah*—Persian carpet—hanging on the wall.

"We have been given several days' notice that the King is about to visit," he began with no preliminaries.

Soprano and baritone oohs and ahs echoed about the room, which was as exuberant as the adults allowed themselves to get.

"King Faisal, His Royal Highness," Mardiros said with self-assurance, "is returning to Baghdad from Damascus. He will need a short rest when he drives through Felloujeh."

Managuile Hanum called attention to herself by clicking her prayer beads. Speaking in Turkish, she said, "I assume you've arranged for him to rest in the *qasr*."

"Of course," they responded unanimously, making Mannig question her own understanding of her in-laws' position. She had assumed the departure from Baghdad society and the decorum required there would give her respite

From Left to Right: His Majesty King Faisal I, Margot (Dikran's daughter), Rose (Karnig's widow), Siranousch (Dikran's wife), Vartanousch (sister of Siranousch), Vartohi (Hagop Agha's daughter)

from learning the rules. Suddenly Felloujeh was becoming the site of a royal visit.

"Furthermore," Mardiros said, waiting for them to quiet down, "His Majesty's brother, Prince Ali, will come from Baghdad to meet the King here."

Prince Ali, still with no kingdom of his own to rule, was anxious to learn from Faisal about his own future duties. Faisal, crowned king of Iraq since 1922, had been meeting in Damascus, Syria and Amman, Transjordan—now Jordan—with the British and the French emissaries to determine which territories ought to be ruled by whom. He and his two brothers from Saudi Arabia had assisted the Allies against the Axis during WWI, and each claimed the right to rule the territories lost by the Ottoman Empire. Ali had traveled to Baghdad, counting on Faisal's influence with the European leaders.

Mardiros raised his arm for attention. "Most major arrangements are done, but there is one problem. The Governor of Felloujeh feels offended that the King should take his rest at the *qasr* of "those Armenians," as he called us, instead of the Government House. So I invited him to pay us a visit to see for himself if his Government House could offer better accommodations for his Royal Highness."

"Good diplomacy," the men in the room affirmed Mardiros' handling of a sensitive situation.

"But when is he coming?" The women needed to know if they had enough time to prepare for an outsider.

"Considering the lateness of the day, we agreed he should come sometime tomorrow."

"There's much to be done." Khosrof stood and grabbed his redingote from the coat tree. "This is a *first*. We have entertained many dignitaries, but never two kings at once—even if I'm stretching the truth about Ali. I'm sure his kingdom will be Transjordan."

The family scattered and plunged into a thousand and one tasks and arrangements. The gentlemen of the *qasr* saw to it that every detail of protocol was taken care of. They assigned Siranoush, Dikran's wife who hailed from Moscow and a girls' finishing school, to practice how and where on the King's route to the drawing room they should curtsy.

"Felloujeh cannot offer proper cakes," Diggin Hermine said. She was Toros' wife and revered for her culinary expertise. "I'll order the cakes and the gateaux from Baghdad." She saw to it that Mahmoud the chauffeur would deliver them on the exact day so they would be as fresh as if made locally.

The biggest problem was that none of the servants in the *qasr* was of sufficient standing to serve the coffee and the tea which, according to local custom, were served already poured in the cups and set in saucers on a large round tray.

"How about Farid Abbosh?" Diggin Sara, Khosrof's wife suggested. Farid, an acquaintance living in Felloujeh, had spoken of previous experiences serving dignitaries.

Farid consented to do the honors and the Kouyoumdjian ladies began training him the proper way. He was told that under no circumstances should he turn his back on the King and that, after serving the coffee, he should withdraw backwards. Farid, being a man of considerable girth, found it difficult to get his bearings when walking backward. Even Mannig couldn't control her mirth at his "test runs."

When the Governor visited the *qasr*, he saw the extent and quality of the preparations and realized that in no way could he have matched them.

"It will be my honor," he confided to Mardiros, "to direct His Royal Highness to your *qasr*."

On the day of the visit everybody woke up early. The ruckus the children made while being washed and then dressed in their Sunday best filled the courtyard.

"You better stay clean," Mannig heard one mother after another warn her child, "or else Uncle Mardiros will see that you never sit on your buttocks without pain."

Mannig gave her husband a puzzled look, but not for long. "I've become …." Mardiros explained, brushing the velvet collar of his redingote. "No, they've *made* me the disciplinarian of these children. Ever since I spanked one of my nephews, the reputation stuck with the rest, making the mothers quite content to associate my name freely with the threat of the rod."

"I noticed Diggin Hermine pressing Toros' morning suit," Mannig said. "Should I do the same to yours?"

"It's not necessary," Mardiros said. "But perhaps you ought to attend to your own clothing."

"Oh, I will," Mannig said, showing him her yellow silk dress, dotted with pearls. Maggie, Khosrof's seventeen-year-old daughter from his late wife, had chosen it for her at Orozdi Bek, the Swiss department store in Baghdad.

"That's a perfect outfit for tea," he said, face brightening and eyes shining.

"Maggie said this was the most fashionable style these days," Mannig said.

"Maggie has good taste," Mardiros said. Then, walking out of their compartment, he leaned on the banister and called the men-servants, who dashed to the courtyard, looking up. "Collect all the Persian carpets in the *qasr*," he instructed. "Dust each one and examine their condition. Then lay them end-to-end from the roadway all the way to the drawing room. Do you understand? His Majesty's feet should not touch the bare ground."

Clad in his redingote, Dikran's twin brother Toros stepped out of his compartment and said, "Hermine and I decided one of our bedrooms should be reserved for the King, in case he needs an afternoon repose."

"Perhaps Mannig should give Hermine a hand," Mardiros said. He gestured toward her, and Mannig's heart leapt with gratitude at his confidence. She squeezed the tip of his forefinger and gave him a smile so broad it split her face in two.

"May I help?" she asked Diggin Hermine, who hugged the sheets, folded in a unique geometrical style.

"I wouldn't have to do this," Diggin Hermine said, "if all the help were not already overextended." She handed Mannig the two corners of the top layer of the white satin sheet and held the corners at the bottom end. The two ladies smacked the sheet in the air and across the mattress.

Mannig's fingers brushed across the opening of the pillow case. She studied the elaborate monogramed T & H in satin-stitched embroidery. "This is beautiful. The seamstress must have been a talented artist—Toros and Hermine?"

Diggin Hermine lowered her eyes. "These sheets were part of my trousseaux. But this is the first time they will be used. All this and after four sons and nearly twenty years of marriage."

Mannig gave her a surprised look.

"I was endowed with several trunks filled with bed sheets and linens," Diggin Hermine said. "Somehow, I saved this set for a very special occasion."

No one could argue that the special occasion was at hand.

By the time of the King's arrival, everything was ready except for the cakes, due from Baghdad. The ladies shook their heads nervously. "You can't depend on servants these days."

Prince Ali arrived before noon and was received with the courtesy due to Royalty. He was taken to the drawing room where he was introduced to the members of the family and had a photograph taken with them. A lunch of roasted chicken, aromatic ambar rice and tomato-stewed okra were served to him and to the four Kouyoumdjian brothers.

Soon after lunch, bringing an end to Diggin Hermine's anxiety, Mahmoud arrived from Baghdad, carrying the sponge cake and cardamom pastries. Immediately, she placed them on separate sterling platters and gave Farid Abbosh serving instructions for when the King arrived.

A red limousine drove up to the front gate of the *qasr* and King Faisal stepped out. He was greeted by the Kouyoumdjian gentlemen and Nuri el-Said, the Prime Minister who had arrived from Baghdad with other ministers. Like Ali, Nuri el-Said, being the first prime minister for Iraq, was also anxious to learn about the decisions made with the European leaders.

The King was taken to the drawing room, where the ladies curtsied and were introduced by their husbands. Mardiros, being the youngest brother, was the last to introduce his wife. "May I present my new bride, Your Royal Highness. Meet Diggin Mannig."

Mannig curtsied, eyes bolted to her beige satin heels that concealed half of a calligraphic red poppy on the Persian carpet.

"*Mabrook, Sayid* Mardiros," the King congratulated Mardiros for his marriage. Likewise he had either said, "I'm honored," or "Greetings," to the other ladies.

When all were seated, Farid Abbosh served the coffee—with no mishap.

After relishing the strong and sweetened coffee, the King stood up. Everyone scurried to their feet.

"You must excuse me, please," the King said. "I wish to rest for a while."

"Farid will show you the room prepared for Your Royal Highness," Mardiros said, trailing the King into the courtyard.

The King leaned toward Farid and seemed to whisper, whereupon Farid's path was diverted toward the family bathhouse.

The ladies and the gentlemen were stunned. No one had foreseen that a King was also a human being with urgent needs, especially while traveling.

The ladies wanted to slap their heads with "*Amahn-Amahn!*" of embarrassment for not preparing the toilet for a king; the gentlemen crushed their cigarettes with their shoes and the children who had lined up in the courtyard would have giggled had not Mardiros raised a hand to clamp their throats.

"Farid can manage from now on," Khosrof said and urged all to withdraw into the drawing room, lest they embarrass the King upon exiting the WC.

Within an hour or so, the King left Toros' bedroom and returned to the drawing room for tea—and of course the cakes from Baghdad. Within the next half hour, appreciation was expressed and thanks conveyed. Moments after the two kings had been chauffeured to Baghdad, pandemonium ensued at the Kouyoumdjians.

After all these years, Mannig still felt a surge of elation when she remembered sipping tea with the King and the King-to-be.

Once again she brushed her fingers across the photograph—the memento must be protected not just for itself, but to prevent harm to her family, should the rebels make a connection between the now obsolete and hated royalty and her family.

"Desert Transport." Eldorado Photo.
Mardiros wrote on the back, "This is the last pontoon bridge on the River Euphrates in Felloujeh that linked the Ottoman Empire with Mesopotamia and was burnt to ashes by the retreating British army in April, 1917, under the happy eyes of Mardiros Kouyoumdjian, standing on the balcony of our house, which was burnt to the group by RAF in 1941."

Felloujeh Bridge, where Aida used to rollerskate. This green metal bridge replaced the Pontoon Bridge. Eldorado Photo.

Chapter 5

The Jews are Leaving—Again

Mannig wrapped the royal memento in a towel and slipped it inside the piano. The felt-padded hammers whimpered ever so slightly, and she worried about possible damage from the weight of the photograph—well, actually, the three framed photographs—so far. *This ... is ... so ...* she thought, as her gaze glided to Setrak, who was coaxing Mardiros to see something for himself.

"See what?" she asked, lowering the top lid of the piano ever so carefully.

"There's a lorry at Albert's house," Setrak said.

Sure enough a lorry, usually used to transfer furniture, was parked across the street in front of their Jewish neighbors. Darkness had set in, and their porch light was not turned on. The silhouettes of all three family members wafted in and out the house, loading bundles wrapped in sheets.

Albert, the thirty-year-old bachelor who was head of that household, worked for the Department of Education and had supported his widowed mother and aunt for several years. He was fluent in English and the intellectual of the neighborhood. He often gave Aida books in English and, knowing her devotion to the Brontë sisters, sent a gift of an embossed set of their complete works for her graduation. Every summer Mannig and the neighbors treasured his invitations to watch American movies from his roof. The huge screen of the Open Air Cinema in their residential district was visible, if not audible, from the back end. He placed lounge chairs cinema-style and offered his guests ice-cold Coca Cola, the new craze of the Baghdadi youth. *Alice Faye and Betty Grable!*

Mannig recalled the two dancing and apparently singing too, in *Tin Pan Alley*.

Albert's mother and aunt kept a strict Sabbath but otherwise they mingled with all the neighbors over a cup of tea and shared observations gathered at the *souq*. To pre-cook their Saturday meals, they grilled and fried, baked and stewed all day long on Fridays, permeating the street with the fragrance of simmering sesame oil. Mannig took her neighborly turn to ignite their kitchen stove on Saturdays in case they needed to reheat their meals, as it was forbidden by their orthodox belief for them do it themselves on the Sabbath.

"Setrak," Mannig directed him. "Go see if you can carry some of their stuff and … be sure to find out what's going on."

Tongue-tied with adults, Setrak objected. "Why doesn't Baba go?"

"Your father is old," she said, gulping on her blunt choice of words. "What I mean is, Baba's heart is weak, and he shouldn't be lifting things. Now go. Find out why they are packing."

Leaning on her husband, she peered out the living room window. Seeing how Setrak's offer was refused, she felt a stab of pain. *Ahkh! Poor Setrak … not trusted … not even by Albert.* She sighed in frustration but her head pounded with curiosity.

Upon his return, Setrak said, "They're just going away."

"That's not a good answer," Mardiros said, stomping outside.

Mannig watched him cross the street. Albert shook his head, just as he had done with Setrak. But, there was a difference in Albert's demeanor—he cocked his head and whispered. Mardiros leaned in and pretended to shift a bundle while Albert rearranged their belongings for a better fit. The two seemed to carry on a conversation without once making eye-to-eye contact; meanwhile Albert stacked enveloped wraps, topped them with bundles and staggered bags and luggage.

Even their sewing machine, Mannig thought, seeing Albert snuggling it between two rolls of carpets.

Mardiros retrieved a cooking pot from Albert's mother and a couple of pans from the aunt, who were attempting to reduce the noise of the clanging as they carried their loads from the house to the lorry. Albert slithered shiny items between the bundles. Finally, he threw a blanket across the pile, tucking its corners deep into the flat bottom of the lorry. Within the hour, he struggled to padlock the yard gate—from the inside. *To keep from arousing suspicion about an empty home?*

Mannig watched as he climbed into the driver's seat and drove the three of them away from Bustan al-Khass. Not once did Albert poke his head out his window for another view of their home.

Mardiros restrained from waving goodbye. Instead, he padlocked the gate of his yard. "I hope they make it to Israel," he whispered to Mannig.

There were not many Jewish families living in Baghdad in 1958. Most of them had left for Israel ten years earlier, when the United Nations declared

Mardiros wrote: "Picture taken at my desk in Basrah where I had gone on specific job and where I remained about 48 days, Dec-January, 1958."

Israel a sovereign state in the Middle East. The main Jewish exodus had occurred in 1948 and 1949—not just from Iraq, but from all other surrounding Arab countries, after they had been granted a diplomatic departure.

Shortly after that, a handful of Jewish families resurfaced in Baghdad. They had chosen to remain in the lands of their ancestral births. Like Albert they held important positions with the government. A few had amassed wealth and achieved prominence. They had decided to remain and continue with their lives as their forefathers had done for centuries—until now.

Mannig could never forget that day in 1949, when Aida came home from school, her head hanging—atypical, considering her normal youthful energy. Her older daughter was a good storyteller, and after an arduous day as a housewife, she relished their chit-chat in the afternoons.

She had already prepared the Turkish coffee for the daily ritual she enjoyed with her daughters. As soon as Aida and Maro came home from school, they lounged on the side patio beside the small grape arbor and sipped coffee. Mannig clung to the stories about the girls' day in an academic setting. Never having attended a traditional school, she lived their experiences vicariously. The coffee break usually concluded with flipping the coffee cups upside down on their saucers. In minutes Mannig would scrutinize the trails the grounds made inside the cups, telling her daughters' daily fortunes. Knowing them inside out, it was not hard to make up stories they wanted to hear. Neither remembered the predictions by the next day, anyway.

Her daughters attended the American Missionary School for Girls—within walking distance. Most neighborhood girls also went there, by choice or convenience—it was hard to tell which, even though Baghdad Society was enamored with Americanization. Mannig wanted the best possible education for her children, and at an American institution like the one her mother had attended. *In Adapazar ... before the deportation.*

"Half of the students were not in school today," Aida had said on that afternoon in 1949. "Even Evelyn was absent." Aida slurped the last drop of the coffee but dispensed with flipping the cup upside down on the saucer. "I must go tell her about our homework. Maybe she is sick. But I don't know why she didn't phone yesterday to tell me."

Mannig was surprised to see Aida bike back home within five minutes. Evelyn Shasha, who lived a block away, and Aida had been top students in their ninth grade class, and close friends for the last four years. The two studied together for the weekly tests or crammed together for the end of the year baccalaureate exams. They biked together, listened to records, and played cards. However, they were not inseparable; Evelyn socialized with the Jewish youth group, and Aida, with friends at the Armenian Club.

"No one was home," Aida whispered as if intimidated by her discovery. "I couldn't knock on their front door either …. There was a chain and a lock on their yard gate. I called and called but no one came out. Mom! Their house looked strange. No sound … all the curtains closed shut. I called Evelyn many times … but nothing. I don't know where they've gone and … and the padlock was latched from the inside."

A few days later Mardiros came home from work and declared, "I knew this would happen. I knew it. But I didn't say anything. I actually did suspect all the Jews would immigrate to Israel immediately, and that's what they've done. They didn't tell anyone about their plans but they planned it thoroughly among themselves. They literally escaped their birthplace and sneaked out of Iraq in the middle of the night, so they wouldn't be detected. They left in cars. No one bought travel tickets, no one used Nairn buses or airplanes. They just took their jewelry and crammed everything into private cars and drove out of Baghdad. They crossed the Euphrates River in Felloujeh at midnight, without rousing anyone or creating suspicions. Apparently they headed straight into Transjordan and then into Israel. Over 200,000 people managed to disappear from the city in one night without anyone knowing anything. Amazing strategy."

"Amazing people," Mannig said.

She wanted to say the same about Albert's departure, but the words didn't come out. His clandestine move was triggering images of a forced deportation—half a century ago—riding atop a pile of bundles stacked not in a lorry but in a wagon drawn by two donkeys ... her mother's sewing machine rubbing against her hip along the muddy path out of Adapazar. *And I ... seven years old.*

The telephone began to ring.

Instead of all three dashing to answer it—picking up the receiver had always been a joyous habit—Mardiros and Setrak stood still, gazing at the black telephone on the wall.

Chapter 6

Adriné's Visit

"It's Die-dye," Setrak said, pointing the receiver at his father, as if relieved from the delegated responsibility of answering the phone. "He wants to talk to you."

Mardiros relaxed and looked heavenward, while Mannig fretted beside him.

Why would Sebouh, her brother-in-law, call? Something must have happened to her sister. "Is Adriné in trouble?" she mouthed.

No, Mardiros shook his head and kept his ear against the phone. "Of course!" he was saying. "Of course … as soon as you can. It won't be any trouble. It's a very good idea." Then his tone turned harsh. "No. No! You shouldn't drive your Ford. Keep it hidden in your garage. You will risk parking it on our street and label our home 'pro-west.' My Jeep is in the garage, and it will stay out of sight for I don't know how long. I won't be using it," he mumbled sadly. "Perhaps never! Yes, yes …. Take an *arabana*."

"What? What?" Mannig stared at her husband.

"They're coming here," he said. "Sami sent him a sealed message with a courier cautioning him to be wary about the mood in their neighborhood."

Sebouh and Adriné lived in an apartment complex downtown with Anita, fourteen, their youngest child. Heranoush, their oldest daughter, was named after the mother of Adriné and Mannig—a victim of the Ottoman purge of the Armenians. Heranoush had married a German petroleum engineer and was living in Tripoli, Libya. Hratch, their son, having received his PhD in pharmaceuticals from Columbus University in Ohio, had accepted a faculty position with the American University in Beirut. Their other daughter Sirarpi—named after the youngest Dobajian sibling who suffocated in the overcrowded cattle car aboard the deportation trek—was a graduate of

Colorado University. She had secured a top position with the Bank of Industry, located on the western bank of the Tigris River. After marrying Sami, an Arab engineer, she lived with him and their two sons in a suburb close to the bank where most of the residents were Muslim.

Sami must know something. Mannig's eyes flashed with more speculation than curiosity before she plunged into rearranging her home to accommodate her sister's family.

In general Baghdadis rarely hosted overnight guests. A few years back, Adrine's children and hers had spent weekends together. Otherwise, friends or relatives were entertained only at tea parties, holidays and name-day celebrations. *So unlike the Felloujeh qasr.*

Mannig would have rather reminisced about the glorious years of her early married life, now flitting by in a haze. Yesteryears boasted about her life from rags to riches—how Mardiros plucked her from the orphanage and planted her on a pedestal amid a family struggling to take its final aristocratic breaths. Had she failed more than succeeded in her attempts to adapt to the Kouyoumdjian lifestyle? The exciting times they entertained royalty and government dignitaries often flashed in and out of her thoughts.

Not now. I don't have the luxury for nostalgia.

"They can use the girls' bedrooms," she said in a flurry, plunging herself into planning, executing and adjusting to yet another unexpected situation. Ever since their day-maid Jasmiyeh had resigned, claiming her family didn't want her to work for non-Muslims anymore, Mannig had assumed all the housekeeping chores herself. Mardiros too had to adjust to the turn of events and consented to the daily trek to the *souq*. "Besides," she said, handing Mardiros three sets of sheets and pillow cases, "everyone will sleep on the roof."

He hugged the neatly folded stack of bedding and, with the support of one elbow against the wall, balanced his ascent to the niche by the door to their roof and plopped them beside the stored summer beddings. Then he sat on a step and huffed.

In hindsight, Mannig regretted delegating that chore to her husband. In the spiraling shifts of routines and expeditious decisions, she forgot his heart condition and arthritic knees. It was too late to stop him. She hoped his college athleticism would somewhat offset the pain in his joints.

Mannig prepared her two daughters' bedrooms with apprehension, sensing nothing would ever go back to normal. Would Aida or Maro ever return to Baghdad? They'd left for the United States nearly four years earlier without news about a date for homecoming. Now, with the revolution in Iraq, she was glad that they were far away, but suspected she might not see them anytime in the near future. Well, at least she didn't have to worry about the

Mannig and her sister Adriné in Baghdad, 1963

girls. The two of them assumed responsibility for themselves as soon as they stepped out of the country. Worrying about Setrak's future with the onslaught of governmental changes had suddenly taken precedence. Somehow she was glad for the added concern for her sister and her family.

Again she wondered if she might ever enjoy Adriné's hospitality. The apartment where her sister's family lived boasted two balconies overlooking Al-Rashid Street. These provided the perfect view of special processions along Baghdad's main thoroughfare. From the balcony, Mannig had been privy to the regent and the prime minister parade on the opening day of parliament. Since the ascension of King Faisal II to his throne in 1953, the aura of royalty waving to the public overwhelmed her. Unlike those standing along the sidewalk below, she was induced by the view from the balcony to assume honorific status. The glitter from the gilded chariots on the king's inauguration day still flashed in her memory. Now that the ill-fated king was assassinated, she'd always remember him waving his innocent twenty-three-year old arm to her.

The butchers! What next?

Mannig never missed visiting her sister when she needed to shop at the popular and perhaps world-renown Baghdad *Souq*, a few blocks from her apartment. The five-story building faced the plaza, which branched to classy stores and car dealerships as well as the Quai'lani Mosque and its mosaic minaret.

Must be their proximity to everything imminent in political upheavals that caused Sami's cautionary message to Sebouh.

"They're here, Mom," Setrak thumped into the kitchen, announcing the arrival of the *arabana*.

"Go help them bring in the bags," Mannig yelled back and pulled her hand out of the crock. She set the garlic-pickled cucumbers in a dish, wiped her hands on her apron and faced Adriné, who was already in the hallway.

"I can't stay here. I must go back home. I'm confused ...." Adriné ranted.

Knowing Adriné's repulsion to hugging of any kind—be it for consolation, affection or simple greeting—Mannig raised her head to make eye-to-eye contact. Seeing Adriné's dazed expression, she waved her arm. "No problem," she said. "We'll all go back soon. But first, let's eat lunch. I fixed something you like." She directed Adriné to the dining room, called everyone for lunch, and then served the bulghur-lentil pilaf steamed with sautéed onions and tomatoes.

The clicking of forks against the plates replaced the silence of pensive diners. Except for Adriné's. She held the fork in her hand, and that's where it remained.

No one spoke. No one looked at one another. The only movement was of forks from plates to mouths. Everyone seemed to adjust to this unexpected family reunion by not saying anything.

Eventually, Sebouh spoke. "This is delicious," he said, expressing his appreciation as he nudged Adriné. "Mannig must have been very generous with the ghee. We should fix our meals this way, too."

After a moment's silence, Mardiros spoke. "Mannig is a good cook. This is very delicious," he said with a full mouth, all the while pointing across the table near Anita.

Setrak, knowing his dad's habit of gesturing toward any item on the table without mentioning it, passed the platter of romaine leaves and green onions, a regular item on most Armenian menus.

Anita reached for the salt and passed it on to Mardiros, who declined it. "My doctor won't allow me to add salt to my greens. I must eat like a cow!" He crunched the stalk of romaine.

"Take a bite, Adriné *Jahn*," Mannig urged her sister. "You can use salt and so can I. It's important to eat. A full stomach will give you a better outlook on all the changes that are happening."

"What changes?" Adriné screeched, standing up.

"Your visit to our house," Mannig said, standing along with her sister. "This time it's your turn to stay with us. Remember ten years ago? We had to remain in your apartment. Now, you are with us. So let me see .... Remember how I helped you with housekeeping then? Well, now I need your help. Come help me fix your bedding."

Instead of following Mannig, Adriné veered to the bathroom. Without closing the door, she began to wash her hands under a fully cranked open faucet. She washed her hands, not once, but several times. She lathered them over and over again, rinsed the suds, and lathered them again. Mannig knew that, if left on her own, her sister would not stop cleansing her hands. At the rate of Adriné's chronic hand-washing, Mannig suspected her beautiful Ivory Soap that Mardiros had brought as a gift from his American contacts at his office would not last the day.

I must replace it with a local saboon.

Mannig had envied her sister's position in her childhood family. Four years older than she, Adriné had gone to school in Adapazar, was smart, beautiful and adulated by her parents. In all instances, Mannig had wished to have been the "older" one. But seeing Adriné obsessed with cleanliness as a result of being raped by the gendarme on the deportation trek, Mannig counted her blessings. Only lately had she realized being shooed away in famine-stricken Mosul as "small, ugly and useless" had been a blessing. *That's why no one raped me.*

"That's enough," Mannig said, turning off the faucet. She handed her sister a carefully folded towel, assuring her that it hadn't been used by anyone yet. "I'm glad you'll be staying with us. I am looking forward to sitting with you and catching up. It's been a long, long time since you and I have had such an opportunity ... just the two of us. The men confide in each other often, and the youngsters know how to entertain themselves. So now, it's our turn to sit and talk ...." She wanted to talk about *Adapazar* and *the orphanage days at the vorpanots*, but didn't, lest Adriné react negatively. Instead, she said, "We can talk about anything, even gossip." She giggled, hoping for a similar fun expression from her sister.

Instead of taking the towel, Adriné wrung her hands, clasped them and wrung them again and again. Vigorously. Nonstop ... until the hush-hush murmuring in the hallway captured even her attention.

"Yes, from the street ...." Sebouh was speaking. "I saw markings on your brick fence."

"What? Where? Show me!" Mardiros insisted.

The two men stepped outside the gate, only to rush back in and lock it. "I'll take care of it when it gets dark."

Mannig thought bedtime would never come. By nightfall, she was exhausted, not just physically but emotionally. She dreaded aggravating her sister's disposition unwittingly. It would be a tough adjustment to relax in someone else's home for reasons no one fully understood, anyway, but especially for Adriné, whose fearful memories seemed to haunt her more each day.

Near midnight, everyone climbed up to the roof.

"Where are the mosquito nets?" Sebouh asked, being the first to climb the stairs.

"We're lucky not to need any in this neighborhood," Mardiros said, setting the clay water jug and a copper cup on the brick fence of the roof. "This is a recently developed area, you know. Besides, we're not close enough to the river for mosquitoes to settle on their victims."

"We enjoy God's nocturnal creation," Mannig added, "and get a splendid night's rest under a plethora of stars."

"How about your privacy?" Sebouh asked.

"We have that, too," Mardiros chuckled. "There's only one house with a higher roof than ours. I've never seen anyone peeping at us."

Sometime during the night, Mannig noticed that Mardiros was not in bed. She didn't see movement anywhere near the WC enclave. She tiptoed downstairs and caught him locking the yard fence gate. "What is it?"

"Oh, it's n-n-nothing," he stuttered. "Sebouh urged me to do it when no one could see me. Someone marked our fence in red. I cleaned everything. Let's go back to bed."

Only after she prodded did he divulge the details. "I scrubbed the marked bricks. There was something that looked like a print of a bleeding palm. I'm sure it was a mistake. Sebouh said he'd heard that Jewish homes were marked similarly. All's fine. Let's go back up. I cleaned it. If needs be, I'll clean it tomorrow again."

They went back to the roof without another word and crept into bed without a sound or silhouette.

Mannig's thoughts whirred and whirled about what else needed to be taken care of. *So lucky Sebouh came over.* Otherwise, their home would have remained a marked residence. Eventually, she must have fallen asleep—only to be hissed awake at the brink of sunrise by Adriné, a couple of beds away from hers. "Mannig. I'm afraid to get out of bed. There are some faces ... boy faces ... scanning your roof from theirs, and things in their hands sticking out of the fence."

"What things?" Mannig said, on the verge of jumping out of bed.

"Don't get out of bed," Adriné cautioned. "Don't move. Don't disturb the status quo. Just look."

"Mardiros," Mannig nudged him. "Wake up. Look at Mansour's roof. What are their boys pointing at us?"

Mardiros glanced and then laid his head back on the pillow. "I told them that we would be having guests sleeping with us on the roof. They're probably checking up on my word."

"But what are they pointing this way?" she asked again.

He raised his head again. "Machine guns."

Chapter 7

Family Ties

Only upon reflection did Mardiros and Mannig suddenly worry about their son.

As a boy of nineteen—out of school, unemployed and without a skill of any sort—Setrak's fate was predictable. Since the neighbors' boys were recruited into the militia, what would prevent Setrak's induction?

"I'll talk to Zuwaydeh about a deferral or something." Mardiros adjusted his necktie inside the third button of his khaki shirt. "He is not political. He's probably still heading the Irrigation Department." Zuwaydeh had been Mardiros's boss for more than twenty years until the higher-up directors appointed Mardiros as a consultant to the American Engineering firm. The two men had maintained their professional relationship especially when Mardiros was the liaison between the Iraqi and American directors, sitting in on many board meetings.

"Take the bus," Mannig urged him. "It's a long walk in this summer heat."

"I'll go with him," her brother-in-law Sebouh said, leading the way out the door. "Adriné wants some of her clothes from our house and I want to hear the talk of the *souq* myself."

As normal life dictated, as soon as the two men left, Mannig plunged into her daily chores. "Let's make *yalanchi dolma*," she said to Adriné. "If the iceman doesn't come again, we can eat the dolma anyway. It doesn't need refrigeration."

Seeing how Anita and Setrak were huddled in the living room, she felt grateful to own a radio and a record player. Since the teenagers were restricted from roaming downtown or cooling off by the riverside, this modern technology saved the day. Nevertheless, she interrupted them. "I need grape leaves," she said, after getting their attention. "Let's see which one of you can collect the shiniest, most tender mid-sized leaves."

Anita jumped up to oblige.

But not Setrak.

Mannig repeated her request with considerable emphasis. "Setrak, up! I'm not sending you to the *souq*—just to the back yard. The music will have to wait until you do something in the house."

"That's a woman's job," he grumbled.

But Mannig didn't let him continue. "As Haji-doo, my grandmother, used to say, 'If a man must eat, he must also submit.' " She waited until the pair dragged their feet out.

She meditated over what she had just said about Haji-doo, but mostly about the saying. Had her grandmother actually said that, or had Mannig invented it to fit the situation? Either way, she chuckled.

Fifteen minutes later, the kids handed Mannig a stack of fresh, pale mid-sized leaves, and then dashed back to the parlor and the radio.

"At least the bread man is still keeping his old routine," Mannig said to Adriné as she urged her sister to chop a few green onions and two large round ones to stuff grape leaves for the *yalanchi dolma*. "The garbage collectors haven't picked up the bins at the end of our street in two weeks, even though I understand they've begun to do it in downtown Baghdad. Heaven knows how we'll tolerate the stink, especially in this heat. I do hope the iceman resumes delivering. Otherwise, it's back to primitivism, like the orphanage days."

Adriné stopped chopping the onions and perked up her ears. "Those were my happiest days."

"Mine, too," Mannig said.

"We didn't worry about anything," Adriné said. "We laughed all the time, even though we had so little."

"We lived without parents, but our tent-mates cared for us; we passed the time without expecting much and we relished whatever we got."

"I liked teaching the little orphans," Adriné whispered.

"I liked learning geography from Barone Eghishe." Mannig stopped reminiscing and turned the faucet on to rinse the grape leaves in preparation for stuffing them with a mixture of raw rice with sautéed chopped onions, parsley and spices. "With all the changes coming to us in Baghdad, I hope the flow of our water remains the same."

"I liked running to the river in the mornings to wash my face," Adriné said, the knife still in her hand, even though the chopped onions were in the pan sautéing. "I liked teaching the little orphans."

Mannig kept quiet. She suspected further reminiscing might put Adriné into a trance and perhaps tilt her into the nightmare of her rape. "That's enough kitchen work for now," she said. "Let's sit with the children and listen

Aida, Setrak, Maro, 1952.

to music—American songs." The girls couldn't find room in their suitcases for their records, so now Setrak had all the freedom to play them himself.

Mannig carefully retrieved the knife from Adriné and lifted her apron to wipe her hands. They sauntered through the hall and took their seats in the parlor.

"Who's singing?" Mannig asked.

"Dick Haymes," Setrak said, shushing with his finger.

Mannig cocked her ears toward the street windows, suspecting some activity outside the yard gate. "Setrak, go see if someone is at the door."

"Do I have to do everything?" He raised his voice, and grudgingly stood up. He tiptoed to the gate and then dashed back to his seat by the record-player. "It's Baba."

Mardiros back home already?

Mannig feared his heart problem had prompted him to return home to escape the noon heat of the asphalt paved streets downtown. After a careful look, she realized something was wrong. His troubled gaze radiated calamity. This man, her husband of thirty-six years, must have encountered adversity—a first in his life. The golden spoon had not left his mouth since his birth—unlike Mannig, who had been accustomed to all kinds of hardship ever since she was seven years old. She was, let's say, used to distress. As a consequence, she could be rational in the face of any disaster. Not Mardiros. Whatever he had discovered at the Irrigation Department that morning must have knocked his sensibilities out of kilter. She took his tie off and helped him settle on the divan at the far end of the parlor. She told the kids to turn the music off and go do something else.

"Did you see Zuwaydeh?" she asked after serving him a glass of *tahn*, the plain yoghurt diluted with water and usually served on ice cubes and a sprig of mint. The mint was in it but not the ice—the iceman had not come. Nevertheless, the *tahn* must have refreshed Mardiros because he gulped it down and let out a polite belch.

"He was there," Mardiros mumbled. "He was also the bearer of bad news."

He handed Mannig the empty glass and relived his day with her. Zuwaydeh had been retained by the revolutionary regime to head the Irrigation Department. The man, although unable to help him, was generous with dispensing advice. He urged Mardiros to find a way, any way, to slip his son out of the country—otherwise, Setrak would be conscripted. He gestured with crossed wrists symbolizing his powerlessness; he could not rehire Mardiros back into his former engineering position. Mardiros reflected upon his own predicament. With the American company expelled from Iraq and the Irrigation Department head unable to rehire him back, it appeared that he, at his age, wasn't going to be actively employed with a regular income. Maybe now was the time to claim his retirement privileges guaranteed by the government. He could have begun drawing on that income a few years ago, but had delayed his rights due to his assigned transfer to the American firm, with higher wages.

"Maybe I should apply for my *taka-ood*," Mardiros had asked Zuwaydeh. "I've put in thirty years serving our country. Perhaps I should retire and spend time with my son before he leaves home."

Zuwaydeh replied in a hush-hush voice, "There's nothing in the till. It's empty. The new rulers confiscated all the financial assets of employees of the former monarchical government. They ravaged the Treasury Department and no one knows how they're organizing their ministries. Not even I have a *fils* in my name in the former government's administration. Frankly, I am grateful they let me maintain my position. Perhaps they have no one who wants to occupy this office—a job at the bottom of their priorities, you know."

Mardiros was taken aback. What kind of leaders would steal its people's future? He wanted to assume his hearing was impaired, but Zuwaydah's tone, staccato speech and the tenor of the man's complexion projected a dismal end to Mardiros' dreams of retirement.

The two commiserated over their fates in silence as the male gender does.

Not for long.

Mardiros took his leave.

Zuwaydeh walked him to the door. "If you have any savings," he advised, "go to the bank and take it out."

Savings?

"*Shukran! Jezeelan!*" Mardiros thanked him earnestly, for he would have not thought about money. Even though he had agreed to meet Sebouh at their favorite café in the *souq*, he found himself hurrying to the bank.

Instead of the customary two soldiers guarding the Rafidain Bank that occupied one third of a block on Al-Rashid Street, iron grids were mounted onto the tall mahogany double doors. Hefty chains and locks glistened in the noonday sun, just below a commercial sign with black paint that read, "Closed forever."

The bastards! They confiscated everything.

His savings wouldn't be grand loot to the revolutionaries, but the lack of it meant his family would need to survive without cash. The annual 300 dinars he received from renting out the house adjacent to his residence had only recently been deposited into the bank. *That's gone, too.* He'd have to wait until next January for the rental money. He must hurry home and count how much he had stashed in his dresser.

That would not last long, he thought as he walked toward home. *I'd never ask my brothers for a handout.* He suspected that they too would find themselves in a similar predicament. Nevertheless, he ought to consult them. Perhaps the Kouyoumdjians would become dependent upon each other again, as they used to be in Felloujeh, soon after their father's death. Throughout the Great War things went smoothly and they maintained their wealth and status. But by 1930, cooperation among the brothers did not exist anymore. One by one, each brother collected his family and established himself independently in Baghdad. Why did Mardiros assume the current situation would bring them to cooperate now? He'd think about that later. Talk about it with Mannig. Wait for the city to return to normalcy. First things first. But where should anything begin?

Mardiros slid his hands into the pockets of his khaki pants. All he had was five dinars. *Take the bus*, he remembered Mannig urging him earlier that day. *Not on anyone's life.* He wasn't about to spend a single fils frivolously.

"Get your son out of Iraq," Zuwaydeh had advised.

But how?

Chapter 8

From Riches to Rags

THE IDEA OF APPROACHING HIS siblings for a loan occupied Mardiros' thoughts. So did Mannig's maternal instincts. To send their son anywhere beyond the Iraqi borders required cash, and not just for traveling expenses. To acquire a passport, they had to guarantee Setrak's return to Iraq with a non-refundable deposit of $2,000—an exorbitant amount, considering Mardiros' monthly salary with the Irrigation Department of $150 per month, which was no longer coming in, anyway.

"I'll teach piano," Mannig suggested.

Mardiros gave her a look of wonder. Did his wife actually intend to support a Kouyoumdjian? Even so, it would take years to save every *fils*, and by then, it would definitely be too late for their son to avoid the call to the army.

"I'll sell my Jeep," Mardiros said reluctantly. Public advertising was in its infancy in Baghdad and even that was limited to the latest fads of cinema posters and the locally brewed Diana Beer. Obviously, it would be imprudent to announce the sale of an American product, except to acquaintances, who out of friendship might discreetly mention its availability for sale.

"But they are, probably, in a similar dilemma," Mannig cautioned. "You'll embarrass them if they can't help."

The ensuing silence was shakier than the midnight deliberations between the couple. Day and night, they proposed the names of possible purchasers, but always came up with one or more reasons the candidate was inappropriate.

"I really should make use of all the piano lessons I've taken," Mannig said again. "Remember, I taught Aida how to play before we signed her up with Professor Hertz—and he complimented me on my technique. I can teach piano to Princess, Maro's friend. Whenever she came over, she wanted to touch the keys. I think her folks are one of the few Jewish families who didn't immigrate to Israel. I'll see if she'll be my first pupil—well after Aida, that is. She would be my first paying pupil." She hesitated a moment, while Mardiros cast his eyes down, shaking his head. She continued, using the term of endearment, "Mardiros *Jahn*, now is the time to reap some benefit from the lessons I took. You must have paid exorbitant rates to Miss Hripsimeh when she came all the way to Felloujeh to teach me piano after we moved from Baghdad."

"Those were different times," Mardiros mumbled. "When you agreed to marry me, you wanted to become a musician, like your mother. I really wanted you, and I kept my promise. Didn't I?"

"Of course you did," Mannig said. "Now, it is my turn to validate your deed and emulate your determination."

"If only I hadn't loaned money to so and so," Mardiros pondered aloud. He seldom quoted the Bible—and if he did, sometimes erroneously—but these days he must have felt a need. "God commands not to lend money to your relatives. I should have listened."

Mannig knew he was talking about the monitory assistance he extended to Tourabian-*Effendi*, his sister's husband. "You did what is expected of family."

Taking advantage of the reputation of his in-laws, Tourabian had unabashedly invested east and west, and lost everything within a short time. To avoid a foreseeable disgrace to the Kouyoumdjians, Mardiros, unmarried at the time, had staked much of his share of his estate to prevent Tourabian's bankruptcy.

A few years after World War I had ended, facing considerable financial hardship, the Kouyoumdjian brothers had to abandon their cooperative farming enterprises in Felloujeh. Each brother assumed the responsibility to his own family. Mardiros appealed to Tourabian for repayment, but was dismissed without even a *fils* of gratitude. "That was a gift," Tourabian retorted. "Would a Kouyoumdjian require the return of a gift?"

Mardiros, the most tempestuous of the brothers, had disowned his sister. Furthermore, he forbade Mannig and his three children from associating with any Tourabians or even speaking about them in his presence. Should he be a guest at a friend's home and learn that a Tourabian was at the same party, he would leave the premises without so much as a word of explanation. Everyone knew how Mardiros carried a grudge.

Tourabian was not a landowner like the Kouyoumdjians or employed by the royal government. As a commodities merchant, he had escaped the confiscation of his property by the current revolutionary regime. Even so, Mannig dared not ask her husband to request assistance on their son's behalf.

"Well, if you find someone to buy the Jeep, then we might also find people who want to buy those crystal chandeliers," Mannig pointed to the two antique light fixtures hanging at each archway of their parlor. "But the one in the dining room, with black etchings on pink glass, might appeal to Baghdadis more." The two began, keeping their emotions under control, to list dispensable household items.

"My flute might interest Barone …." Mardiros began but was interrupted.

"We will *not* sell musical instruments." Mannig was adamant. "If I was able to defy death in the desert, the flute and the piano can rise above our pitiful state of affairs."

The next day, the two pushed and pulled the piano out of the closet and rolled it back to the parlor.

Soon after carefully placing the black ebony flute on its throne upon the white needlework runner atop the piano, Mannig heard Mardiros ushering Roupen Ter-Minassian into the parlor.

Roupen and his wife Hermine were close friends and frequent bridge partners.

Roupen occasionally stopped by after his day's work to chat with Mardiros. He was a chemical engineer at the German-owned research labs on the outskirts of Baghdad. The Kouyoumdjian residence was conveniently located between the lab and his home and he especially relished Mannig's home-made plum juice.

"I've been asking around if anyone wants to buy your Jeep," he said, swishing the ice in the glass before taking a swig. "Everyone at the Chem Labs promised to ask around. I'm sure a buyer will surface soon—at my office or in the *souq*."

"Once we save enough money for Setrak's passport and exit visa," Mardiros said, "we'll have to figure out where to send him."

"Unfortunately," Mannig said, "we can't consider England or America while the political hostility permeates our atmosphere. I must show you something." She dashed to the bedroom and back. "Look! You must see what they're doing at the post office." She brought out a letter from Aida, their oldest daughter, written from Seattle, Washington, where she was attending the University of Washington. "Look!" She pointed at the thick black lines across certain words, phrases and even a complete sentence. "See? They are concealing things the postal office doesn't want us to know about America. Aida says our letters to her are also censored like this."

"What do you think Aida wrote?" Roupen asked.

"Raving about America, of course," Mardiros said. "Almost all her letters describe the wonders of America."

"And the Iraqis," Mannig said, "don't want the outside world to know how awful our lives have become in Baghdad."

"So our letters to her, and to Maro, are very bland these days," Mardiros said. "We just write about our health and the weather. So you see, Setrak must go somewhere else. I don't want him to stay in the Middle East. All the neighboring countries of Iraq will, sooner or later, go through revolutions. Since the Iranian uprising of Mosaddegh in 1951, although unsuccessful, the fire for getting rid of British rule has been ignited within the belly of the Islamic nations."

"Let's not forget what happened in Egypt," Roupen said. "Remember how Col. Naguib kicked out the king."

"Ah, the king," Mannig said. "King Farouk. When the girls were here, we talked about the king all the time. As a child, he was so good looking. But by the time he was forced to abdicate his throne, he had become a fat slob."

Both Roupen and Mardiros gave Mannig a second look. She seldom criticized anyone in public, but apparently that moment inspired her to pour out her heart.

"Well," she said without changing her tone, "unlike our poor king, who was so cute and young and he had just announced his engagement …." She rose and grabbed one of the three black-and-white framed photographs that used to decorate the wall of their living room. "Here's His Royal Highness King Faisal the II, wearing his coronation suit, and here is his fiancée, the eighteen-year-old aristocrat from Turkey. The Iraqis butchered him, and Mardiros was privy to the sight of his youthful body being dragged down Al-Rashid Street. The Egyptians acted so much more civilized—even to their oversized king. They allowed him to exit honorably."

"Yes," said Mardiros, picking up on his last thought before Mannig had blurted out her heartache for royalty. "In my soul I know I'm right … especially after what has happened to us in Iraq. I want to see Setrak in a civilized country."

"I have an idea," Roupen said. "He should go to Germany. My Alma Mater is in Heidelberg, and I still have contacts … well, one contact. He now lives in Basel, Switzerland, just across the Neckar River from Heidelberg. I'll write to him tonight."

When Roupen departed, both Mannig and Mardiros breathed a sigh of hope.

Their son might have opportunities in life after all—not in their homeland, as they had, but in foreign territories.

From that day forward, Mannig taught piano and saved every *fils*. Mardiros sold his Jeep to a former colleague whose son had just returned to Iraq after getting his engineering degree at Santa Clara University in California. They had also saved the $300 from next year's rental of their neighboring house, which they owned.

Perhaps they had enough for the exit visa.

Would Setrak be accepted at the University of Heidelberg?

Chapter 9

The Swallow's Nest

Mannig often found herself playing "The Swallows Nest" on the piano. It was an ancient Armenian ballad in a minor key, suitable for a flute. When Mardiros was not at home or not in the mood to accompany her, she took the time to incorporate the melody into the piano part. Even without the lyrics, the melisma of the rhythm soothed her aching heart. She played in the mornings, and then again at night.

> Building her nest was the swallow
> Building and singing
> Singing and building.
> Twig after twig she attached to the nest
> Remembering her former nest.
> Fetching a twig, flew the swallow
> Fetching and singing
> Singing and fetching.
> By and by approached she the nest
> Discovering a ruined nest.
> Building afresh was the swallow
> Building and singing
> Singing and building.
> Twig after twig attached she to the nest
> Remembering her former nest.

She longed for the extraordinary style of living she had enjoyed with the Kouyoumdjians—long passed into history. Might those memories help her overcome the hardships looming ahead? So far she had overcome her longing for the female camaraderie of her two daughters who resided in the United States by plunging into the demanding chores of housekeeping. But lately, her appetite for such work seemed curbed as if she had developed a sudden revulsion to spicy foods. Whatever ailed her, she told herself, couldn't be worse than the ache of starvation.

She found solace in jotting down her thoughts and discovered a renewed outlook on life. She dismissed the divisive political atmosphere of Baghdad and ignored the aches and pains emanating from her stomach. All she wanted to do was to reminisce about her first days as a newlywed at the Baghdad *Qasr* with the Kouyoumdjians.

THE KOUYOUMDJIANS HAD KNOWN BOTH grand days and lowly times. Notwithstanding the tea for the king, as well as several other occasions hosting the Iraqi monarchy, they led a sophisticated life like the elite of Europe, first in Baghdad and later in Felloujeh.

The moment Mannig and Adriné had stepped off the train from Basra as the brides of two prominent bachelors from Baghdad, they were plunged into affluence, each within her husband's extended family.

Mannig could hardly catch her breath or confide in her husband during their first years of marriage in the Baghdad *Qasr* on the Tigris River. She often wished she could time-travel back to 1922 and witness firsthand her reactions at that first meeting with the classy and sophisticated families of her brothers-in-law.

The circumstances of the incident were anchored firmly in her psyche, but the images hovered in a fog of memory. Still in her orphanage blue uniform, she had been helped off the train at the Baghdad Station by Mardiros and introduced to his family—the families of his five brothers. From that point on she plunged into the refined life of the Kouyoumdjians.

"There they are," Mardiros had said, leaning toward Mannig and pointing at the gleeful people at the train station in Baghdad. "Every one of them must have come." He brushed a gentle kiss on her forehead. "They're anxious to welcome you. As of this moment that's your family."

Intimidated, Mannig recoiled—not at the sheer number of new relatives crowding the platform but their attire.

Mardiros had described his kinfolk by name and, with characteristic masculine brevity, tagged them to their professions and education rather than their looks. Any apprehension she harbored about living in his family home with thirteen adults and eighteen children waned when compared to the intimidation of confronting the regalia they had donned to receive her at the Baghdad train station.

Wedding Portrait: Mannig and Mardiros, 1922

Feathered chapeaux topped wide-rimmed lace hats. The ladies' heels, decorated with buckles and straps, complemented the above-the-ankle fitted skirts. Beyond the stylish aura of the Kouyoumdjian ladies blew spirals of smoke, puffed by the gentlemen. The men wore custom-tailored black suits, held cigarettes between their fingers, and carried ornamental canes. They conversed with reserved gestures and nodding silk hats.

Mannig's gaze followed a teenage Arab boy in striped *dizhdasheh*, carrying toasty *simit* pretzels in a basket. *Simit*? Her mouth watered as it had during those days of near-starvation, foraging in the alleys of Mosul. She used to savor its aroma and crave its crunchy texture and tangy taste. The boy displayed a *simit*, the sesame shining atop the puffed arc of the ring, and tried to cajole one gentleman after another into buying. To her surprise, unlike the people of Mosul, these gentlemen shooed the boy away with the wave of either a hand or a cane. Did they abhor *simit* or the Arab boy's proximity? Mannig wondered at the absurdity of observing social distinctions at a Baghdad train station.

The brakes screeched to a stop, its spewing steam stopping short of the congregated relatives. But a slight wind blew in dust from the neighboring wasteland and charcoal smoke from the engine, forcing the ladies to hold their hats while others turned their backs.

"I see a few dignitaries have also come to see us," Mardiros said, looking out the window. "The board members of AGBU"—he meant the Armenian General Benevolent Union, where he served as chairman in Baghdad—"must be really curious about you. I shouldn't be surprised at all. After all, you are an orphan whose survival depended on their efforts. Albeit, most of them have never seen an orphan .... Aha! Even the Archbishop is here. You do see him, don't you? He is tall for a clergyman but his miter dominates the hats. We must both kiss his hand."

If Mardiros was attempting to facilitate Mannig's entrance into his family, he was failing. She was confounded as to his family's stature. During the train ride his manners and relaxed demeanor had calmed her fears. He was a good storyteller, seeming to relish his audience of one—his new bride. She was enthralled by his unreserved enthusiasm. He had made her so comfortable that even in her speech, she addressed him in the singular form 'you' rather than the plural honorific 'you'—Armenian tradition when addressing anyone older.

He had described the characteristics of each family member with one or two adjectives. Toros, one of his older brothers, was smaller than his twin brother Dikran. Diggin Rose, his oldest brother's widow, was the snob. He neglected to describe their looks or habits.

He did elaborate when speaking of his mother. "She favors me, I think," he said nonchalantly. "Even though I'm her 'baby' child, I have to call her Hanim-*Effendi*. None of us call her 'Mother' or 'Mama.' Ever since the passing on of my father, no one calls her Managuile anymore, her given name. She doesn't speak Armenian—her family in Tallas was forbidden to use any other language but Turkish, an edict in force throughout the Ottoman territories. Since her marriage into our Baghdadi community, she has come to understand Armenian and Arabic but refrains from speaking either." He squeezed her hand with confidence. "Unlike her other daughters-in-law, you will win her heart with your Turkish."

Turkish? Not since entering the orphanage ... actually, not since rummaging the streets of Mosul had she resorted to speaking Turkish. In Mosul she spoke only street Arabic, and at the orphanage only Armenian. Not in her wildest dreams could she have fathomed using a survival language

Bagdhad, 1922 or 1923. Right to Left: Adriné, Mardiros, Mannig, Sebouh Papaizan (Adriné's husband) and Sebouh's two children.

when she married into Baghdadi society. She hoped she had not forgotten the language of deportation during the Ottoman purge of ethnic communities.

The imperturbable attitude nurtured by Mardiros during the four hour click-clacking of the train wheels vanished at the moment of facing his family. Assuming she would get along best with his mother, Mannig scanned the throng of relatives and asked, "Which one is the Hanum-*Effendi*?"

"She's too old to leave the *Qasr*," he said. Then he added, "You'll meet her at suppertime. Don't worry. She'll receive you with open arms."

Mannig was about to be merged with relatives whose physical appearance, education or experiences had no niche in her experience. She recalled her parents in Adapazar. Yes, they were educated, spoke French, if necessary, and donned continental clothing. But they were modest in comparison—nothing frilly, feathery or flaunty about them. These people on the platform, in their fine clothes, made her lose her bearings.

"I'm sure you notice the odd display my family puts on," Mardiros said pensively. "A journalist might question it with 'What is sophistication doing in a wasteland?' Don't dwell too much upon how jarring high society can be in the midst of peasantry. It just is."

Mannig glanced at her husband with amazement. How had he read her thoughts? His words, especially since their arrival in Baghdad, seemed to be exactly what she needed to hear. She held his forearm and gave him a gentle squeeze. But her eyes remained riveted to his kinfolk waiting on the platform.

They were all trying to get a glimpse of the newest bride in the Kouyoumdjian dynasty.

Only a few hours earlier, a ship full of Armenian orphans bid her goodbye off the dock in Basra. She and Adriné—her only surviving sibling from the massacres perpetrated by the Ottoman gendarmes—remained ashore with their grooms. The sisters from Adapazar had captured the hearts of two benefactors from Baghdad who wooed them into marriage just before the ship of orphans headed to Jerusalem for permanent residency. The captain had performed the official marital ceremony and the two newlywed couples disembarked the ship before it sailed away. Three years of cozy togetherness in several orphanages in Iraq had come to an end for Mannig and Adriné. Mannig's heart tore in two—the sadness of casting away orphanage camaraderie clamped onto her left side while the anxiety produced by the hazy prospect of adapting to marriage crowded into the right. She could neither agonize about separating from her cherished friends nor rejoice over joining her husband's family.

In the blink of an eye she had been transformed into *Mrs.* Kouyoumdjian. What would the strangers—her in-laws—on the platform call her?

And now, at the Baghdad train station her vow not to be separated from her sister was being broken. She had reconciled herself to being physically parted from Adriné, especially after Mardiros had assured her that they would visit each other as often as their hearts desired.

As Adriné and Sebouh approached the Papazian relatives at the station, Mannig faced the welcoming party of Kouyoumdjians.

She focused on a few young girls, whose gazes were fixing on one passenger cabin after another. *Ah, Mardiros's nieces.* Which one was Maggie? Or Lizinka? Mannig hoped at least one teenager would soften her entrance into the cultural elite of Baghdad.

"Don't let their appearances intimidate you," Mardiros declared, standing shoulder to shoulder with her while waiting for a knock on the cabin door that would permit them to get off the train. "You have more substance in your petite body than all of them put together." His voice, his comment, and his timing were the antidotes she needed. Any apprehension she harbored dissipated, and she felt reassured once again that her husband of less than twenty-four hours would be a life-long confidant par excellence.

She had no time to consult with him on what to say or even in what language. It wouldn't be Turkish since his Mother remained at home, but everyone looked continental—not Armenian. Knowing how Mardiros spoke several languages, she feared being addressed in English or French, neither of which she knew, beyond reciting the alphabet or singing "Mary had a little lamb" or "*Frère Jacques.*"

"You don't have to say anything," Mardiros whispered, barely moving his lips.

She loved him even more—if possible—at that moment for his empathy. But what would these fancy people on the platform call her?

"Remember who you are, Mannig," he continued. "You are now my wife—Diggin Mardiros Kouyoumdjian."

Mannig lost the glitter in her eyes. *Even he wants me to be called Diggin.*

Mardiros scanned his relatives. "Huh! Diggin Rose is here, too. Other than the bishop's, you must not kiss anyone else's hand—especially Diggin Rose's. She will insist you place your lips on her wrist, but be sure to ignore any of her gestures. Pretend you don't understand."

She nodded but felt her shoulders rising with uncertainty. Would anyone accept her for who she was? What about her clothes? Disheartened, she slid her hands into her pockets. While her fingers clasped into fists, she felt something metallic rubbing the knuckles of her left hand. She pulled the object out and was surprised to have forgotten about the wedding gift from the captain of the ship.

She brought out the brooch with the golden crest and pinned it to her collar. She dusted the hem of her coarse blue uniform, straightened her shoulders and once again stared at her family-to-be.

Chapter 10

Who's Who

While Mardiros held Mannig's hand and helped her off the train, she concentrated on her sandaled feet, lest she trip and, at first sight, be tagged as clumsy. She suspected her in-laws already considered her an *odaar*—outsider—among the Kouyoumdjians. She didn't wish to mar her first introduction to his family any further.

Secure in Mardiros' grip, Mannig felt her anxieties about being different evaporate. She clasped her fingers in his and felt they were greeting his family as a united front.

His expression calm and commanding, he faced his oldest brother's widow. "Diggin Rose, may I introduce my wife? Diggin Mannig."

This time Mannig didn't dislike being called a Mrs. The form of address sounded better when uttered by her husband. Having heard about the snobbery and prudishness of Diggin Rose on the train, she wondered about this lady's reaction to an orphan girl bearing a similar title. She was impressed at how Mardiros honored his oldest sister-in-law by letting her be the first to meet his bride. He was wise to appease a difficult personality yet he was jeopardizing his wife's smooth entry into the family. Mannig felt more affinity with some of his nieces who, even though older than she, were at least still young ladies in their teens. Exposing her to Diggin Rose could increase Mannig's inferiority complex.

"She wanted me dead," Mardiros had recalled on the train, preparing Mannig for her new life in Baghdad.

Diggin Rose was the widow of his oldest brother Karnig who died of typhus in 1917 at the age of forty-two in an Ottoman prison. He and Mardiros were arrested on suspicion of spying for the British/French Allies and not released until the defeat of the Axis in 1918. Karnig had died but Mardiros had escaped contracting the disease. This made Diggin Rose resent his survival. Upon his discharge from the prison at the end of the war, she told him, "You are a bachelor. You have no children. You have nothing to live for. *You* should have died instead. Now I have five children to raise without a husband."

She resented Mardiros for yet another loss in her life.

Her oldest son, Antranig—close to Mardiros's age with similar classic features and athletic physique—was overseeing their Felloujeh farms on horseback when he was shot to death. During the trial proceedings, it was revealed that the assassin had a quarrel against Mardiros, but had mistakenly murdered the wrong Kouyoumdjian.

"Diggin Rose constantly mourns the two men she adored," Mardiros told Mannig. "And in my presence? She grieves for them vociferously. I must be overly kind to her. I am telling you this, Mannig-*Jahn*, to prepare you. She may very well resent your existence as much as mine."

Now on the platform of the train station, Mardiros led Mannig directly to Karnig's widow. "Diggin Rose," he said. "You honor me and my bride by your presence."

"What would the Baghdadi society say," she sputtered, "if I hadn't shown my face here?"

Mannig's heart pounded when she touched the lace-gloved hand of her oldest sister-in-law. Diggin Rose lowered her gaze; flared her nostrils, deployed a petrified handshake. Hearing no comment, Mannig felt safe. Henceforth, she could overcome any hurdle.

"Your most eminent holiness," Mardiros addressed the Archbishop of the Armenian Apostolic Church of Baghdad, "I'm honored by your presence. This is my wife, Diggin Mannig." He waited until Mannig placed her lips on his extended hand. "She is a survivor of the massacre and an orphan rescued by all of your prayers and works."

He then moved toward the dignitaries of AGBU. As Mannig shook their hands, she saw that they seemed proud of themselves—after all, they were beginning to reap the fruits of their philanthropy toward the surviving Armenian children. "Well, gentlemen," Mardiros said, "Thank you for coming to greet us. Hanim-*Effendi*, Managuile hopes to see you at the *qasr* this evening."

Mardiros guided Mannig back to his family. "It's customary to have friends drop by in the evenings," he explained as he began to introduce her to his sisters-in law who were next in line: Diggin Sara, Diggin Hermine and Diggin Siranoush, followed by his brothers, Khosrof, Toros and Dikran. Smiles accompanied the brief introductions to his family and a plethora of meaningly pleasantries. He then swept his arm along the row of eighteen children grouped apart from the adults, their eyes following Mannig's every

Mannig and Mardiros in Baghdad, 1922.

move. He named them down the list as if he were playing a game of memory. He concluded with an announcement loud enough for everyone to hear. "They are the Kouyoumdjian imps ... a lucky bunch if, and only if, they behave."

"Oh, no, Uncle Mardiros!" The children sighed, and some even stamped their feet with disappointment.

Only later did Mannig learn that Mardiros was the disciplinarian in the family.

Mannig wondered if she'd be tested to remember names or faces or the place of each on the family tree. The best she could do was lump the ladies as glamorous, the gentlemen as curious, and the offspring as playful. She complied with Mardiros, who hurried through the formalities and then escorted her toward the Kouyoumdjian car, while others waved toward a convoy of *arabanas* for hire—the limousine service of Baghdad at the time. The horse drawn carriages with no canopies transported three adults, facing forward, and two children seated across from them, looking backward.

Holding the door of the family car for Mannig, Mardiros whispered. "There are thirty-one Kouyoumdjians in my family but I'm the only one who drives our car." He then dismissed Mahmoud, the chauffeur, who rushed to secure transportation for the others.

Mannig sat in the car, speechless, neither dazed nor alarmed. Like a twig, she had floated in the wake of all proceedings initiated by Mardiros so far, and even now, she maintained the same flow, getting into his shiny 1920 black British Austin.

"Uncle Mardiros," three of his nieces pleaded, poking their faces into the car. "Can we ride in the back?"

Maggie, Lizinka, and Meliné scooted in without waiting for a response.

"I can't believe we're having a bride in the *qasr*," Maggie chattered away. Maggie was Khosrof's only child from his deceased first wife. Seventeen years old and beautiful with glistening green eyes, she was often teased as Leggy Maggie for being 5'5" tall—way beyond the height of most Armenian girls. "I'm so excited."

"Such a young one, too," chimed in Lizinka, the slender eighteen-year-old brunette, dubbed the Stern Cousin for smiling only in the company of girls her own age. She was Diggin Rose's second daughter.

"You look more like a pal than a Diggin," chuckled Meliné, the sixteen-year-old and Diggin Rose's youngest daughter. She had light brown hair, hazel eyes and was considered the pleasingly plump and beautiful one. "Can we play together?"

All three teenagers erupted into a torrent of giggles.

"What are you going to wear for supper, tonight?" Maggie asked, sticking her head between Mardiros and Mannig.

People change clothes for meals? Mannig wiped her sweaty hands on her blue orphanage uniform and raised her shoulders. She thought of wearing the other of her two uniforms, but wondered about its appropriateness since it was made of a thicker cloth, suitable for the winter.

"Uncle Mardiros," Meliné asked, "what are we supposed to call your bride?"

"Oh, yes," Lizinka interrupted. "She is not even as old as we are, yet she is a married woman."

"I wish I were a bride," Meliné said.

"I doubt if I'll ever get married," Lizinka chimed in.

"We'll all get married as soon as handsome and aristocratic men propose," Maggie said, resting her chin on the back of the front seat.

"So do we call her *Diggin Mannig*?" Lizinka returned to the original question. "How about *the bride*?"

"Maybe Auntie Mannig?"

"Let's just call her Mannig," Maggie put an end to the chattering girls' guesses. "If that's fine with you, Uncle Mardiros."

"I really haven't thought of it yet," Mardiros said. He removed his hands from the steering wheel and pressed his fingers against his temples. "Let me think ...."

The car veered, brushing against the sidewalk curb.

"Oooooh!" screamed the girls in the back, recoiling deep into their seats.

Mardiros grabbed the steering wheel and braked. Everyone lurched forward and the engine went dead.

"Is everyone s-s-safe?" Mardiros stuttered. He took a deep breath, swallowed, and added, "You must stop all this jabbering. Can't you wait until we're at the *qasr*?" He coughed, spit in his handkerchief and opened his door. Then he picked up the engine crank and got out.

Mannig sat speechless. Neither dazed nor alarmed. Having no idea what to expect, she hadn't foreseen the thrill of traveling in a motorized vehicle—a luxury enjoyed by only a few wealthy citizens in Iraq. To her right, several men wearing long *dizhdashehs* and passing by on foot stopped to admire the motor car. Across the street children peered at them from balconies of a three-story apartment building. People were enjoying the show—a rare appearance of a car stalled at the onlookers' feet.

Seeing Mardiros bobbing up and down, cranking the engine in front of the hood, pained Mannig. She had been the cause of all this. She looked at the girls in the back and, in solidarity with her husband, shushed them by putting an index finger to her lips.

The engine started quickly, but Mardiros' forehead was slick with sweat. "Next time, when you ladies are passengers, I'll let Mahmud drive. He is, after all, the chauffeur, and would pay attention to his driving without being swayed by your chatter." He wiped his hands on his handkerchief, soiling the white satin monogram, *M.H.K.*

No one said a word after that. Not until Mardiros drove to the front of the *qasr*—the Arabic word for a medieval castle, used to describe any large private dwelling in Central Baghdad, none of which remotely resembled one. He pulled the hand brake.

The Kouyoumdjian home was perched on the western bank of the Tigris River, slightly off Kerradeh Street, the main thoroughfare. Meandering along with the waterway, the *qasr* soared like a rampart.

Facing a wooden gate set in a brick fence as tall as a camel, Mardiros honked.

Startled at the sudden blast, Mannig hoped no one noticed her naiveté about modern vehicles. *Everything is going to be novel, so why am I so jumpy?*

Within a minute, the gates were opened by two attendants from within the *qasr*. "*Ahlen, Matruloze-Effendi*," they said in greeting.

"Keep the gates open," he said. "The rest of the family is not far behind me."

"What did they call you?" Mannig couldn't contain her curiosity.

"They're being funny," he said. "Our farmers in Felloujeh call me that because they can't pronounce my name. These Baghdadis heard about it, and they've not stopped teasing me."

"Come, Uncle Mardiros," Lizinka chided him, "*Matruloze* is a machine gun …. I think they also know how you spew your words when you are angry … like a machine gun."

All three girls dissolved into laughter.

Mannig looked at her husband. Was he blushing? She had not seen this side of him during their three years of sporadic encounters at the orphanage. His self-confidence had manifested itself in everything he had done or said. Well, maybe he had hesitated once—at the time he proposed marriage to her. He had given her a painful glance when revealing the disparity in their ages. At thirty-two, he was twice her age. "Are you rejecting me because I'm so much older than you?" he had said when she hadn't accepted his proposal instantly.

"No," Mannig interrupted. "No, the age difference doesn't matter. It's because … because I hadn't thought of marriage yet. I wanted to graduate from school first. I always wanted to be educated like my parents."

"That won't be a problem in our future," he had assured her. "I will see that you receive a full education right in Baghdad—the city is known for its learning institutions."

Bumping wheels on the courtyard bricks brought Mannig back to the present—still in the car but now within the confines of the *qasr*. She was married and a Diggin. Her husband's nieces and nephews were older than she. Her sisters-in-law might be as old as Haji-doo, her grandmother in Adapazar when her Dobajian family lived happily together before the Great War. Mannig had survived on her own since she was nine years old—scavenging food in the streets, finding shelter in nooks and crannies, learning to stay alive by hook or by crook. She'd had no one who cared for her for nearly six years, and she cared for no one until she found her sister. Her sister Adriné …. How was Adriné faring with Sebouh, her husband, and the clan of his family? As soon as she settled in Mardiros' *qasr*, she'd insist on visiting her sister. She had promised Adriné she would come to see her very soon. Mannig couldn't bask in her Cinderella luck until she was sure that Adriné was comfortably situated. Memories of schools, classrooms, teachers, desks and books receded back into the recesses of her thoughts.

Mardiros parked in front of the third compartment in the courtyard of the *qasr*. He released the clutch and locked the secondary brake. "All right girls," he said. "Off you go. We'll see you at suppertime."

The girls flared their skirts and then dashed, giggling all the way to the stairs leading to their compartments.

"Each of my brothers and his family reside in a separate quarter," Mardiros said, helping Mannig out of the car. "These stairs lead us to ours."

Dazzled, Mannig scanned a riot of colorful potted flowers along the balcony surrounding the courtyard.

A cool whiff of air brushed her face. *Where did that come from?*

"We're privileged to live by the river," Mardiros set his valise down and smelled the breeze. "Our summers get very hot—often above one hundred degrees Fahrenheit. Below the archway at the far end of the courtyard, the Tigris Rivers flows and the cool breeze sneaks in through it." He reached for her hand and added, "We're home. How do you like it?

Chapter 11

The *Qasr* at a Glance

Mardiros knew that life in the *qasr* would take some getting used to now. No one else in Baghdad lived like the Kouyoumdjians. They enjoyed an aristocratic lifestyle not unlike the rich and famous of London, Paris or the plantation owners of antebellum America. While in the European capitals many such families lived this grand manner, in Baghdad there existed less than a handful that the locals referred to as "The Landlords." While the city womenfolk remained generally illiterate, baked their bread and cooked their meals, the ladies of the *qasr* played musical instruments, discussed the latest fashions of Coco Chanel and Jean Patou and talked about Clara Bow, Douglas Fairbanks and Mary Pickford in their most recent Hollywood films. Their luxurious compound was like an oasis in this vast city of Baghdad, the capital of the recently established kingdom of Iraq.

Mardiros wondered about the effects of philanthropy upon his attitude and hoped he'd not be as crass as his extended family, with their ridiculous vanity and self-aggrandizement. Even though Mardiros had spent three years away from the affluence of his kinfolk, he felt his heritage and status. His concern was for Mannig. How would his bride adapt to this lifestyle? He knew where he stood but had his doubts about the rest of his family.

Even at the train station, while introducing his bride to his kin, he had wondered how much influence he could exert as a married gentleman with a very young wife, albeit from an orphanage. He determined to make Mannig's adjustment his priority.

"My suite ... I mean, *our* suite is on the second floor," he said. After helping her out of the car, he escorted his bride upstairs. Stepping into the parlor, he saw the expression of delight on Mannig's face. He opened the French doors to their balcony. "Ah!" he exclaimed, leading her onto the reddish-brown ceramic-tiled walkway—the balcony along the horseshoe shaped courtyard. He leaned on the cast-iron railings and pointed toward the source of the voices wafting from the area at the far end of the lower level. "That is the kitchen. The cook must be preparing a special supper in your honor. If I knew which of my sisters-in-law was in charge of the menu this week, I would describe tonight's cuisine to you. You see," he put his arm on her shoulders, "Hanim-*Effendi* wants each of her daughters-in-law to plan and pattern meals for a whole week. One week Diggin Siranoush will do the honors, the next Diggin Rose. Everyone looks forward to when Diggin Hermine is in charge. She has a flare for recipes from Lebanon, her birthplace. But I wouldn't be surprised," he chuckled, "if all four ladies of the *qasr* volunteered a menu item to impress you with their culinary expertise."

Mannig looked worried.

"It will be delicious food," he assured her and then added, "very much like the captain's table on the Shuja."

Mannig glanced at him, her eyebrows still raised. "Not that … do you mean the Hanim-*Effendi* will ask me to cook? I don't know how …. I don't even know anything about the different ingredients."

Mardiros gulped. Of course, Mannig wouldn't know how to cook. He recalled the reports by the Middle East Relief how the Armenians barely sustained themselves during their deportation trek, which Mannig had endured. She had told him how the Bedouin rescued her after the Ottoman gendarmes had tortured and killed six members of her family. Then at the end of WWI, she had fended for herself, foraging the streets of Mosul for edibles. The meager daily soup and bread Mannig relished at the orphanage for three years was the only real food she had known for the past six years. How would she know anything about menus or recipes? Besides, she was just fifteen years old.

"She won't ask that of you," he assured her. "Hanim-*Effendi* is thoughtful about everyone. She can be demanding sometimes, but has been considerate toward the wives of her sons." After a moment's reflection, he added, "She has always insisted that the new brides entering into her domain assume some responsibilities. Obviously, she understands the need for order when so many people are housed in one location. But more so, I think, she wants to involve different members of the family in a common activity."

Mannig remained expressionless.

"As I remember," he added, "none of the brides, except Diggin Hermine, knew how to cook when they first arrived at the *qasr*. Coming from families who hired cooks and butlers, they didn't even know how to boil water for tea."

"I hope," Mannig whispered to herself, "it won't be Diggin Rose who must teach me to cook." But hearing about the common ground between her

Mannig in 1922.

sisters-in-law and her—a strange similarity between the very rich and the very poor—Mannig took a deep breath. "I know how to make tea," she asserted herself. "I watched the supervisor at the orphanage fill a caldron with water, set it on burning wood until the water bubbled. Then she threw a handful of tea into it. When she said, '*Voilà!*' we knew the tea was ready."

"That's good," Mardiros said, suppressing a snicker. "You will learn my mother's way of brewing tea, too."

He then noticed the thoughtful way she was looking at Sami, the kitchen assistant, lugging a couple of pails of water inside the arched path to and from the river. "The *qasr* has its own running water for cooking and drinking," he tried to explain. "But the Hanim-*Effendi* insists on drawing water and taking advantage of what is naturally available at the base of our *qasr*—the streaming water of the Tigris."

"Oh," Mannig whispered. "My sister used to carry water for her mistress in Mosul …. I wished that someone would hire me, too, but no one wanted me."

Mardiros gulped again and immediately tried to comfort her. "Neither you nor Adriné will ever have to lug water. Your sister is, even as we speak, a lady in Sebouh's home, just as you are here."

A brief silence alerted him to the absence of the usual chatter of the *qasr* children. He surmised they were resting after an eventful afternoon at the station. He felt tired, too. "It's been a long day. Maybe we ought to rest ourselves before suppertime."

He left the balcony doors open for ventilation. Once again he held Mannig's hand and led her through a second set of lace-curtained French doors.

Inside the bedroom, Mannig hesitated.

He searched her face. Might the sight of the two four-poster brass beds set side-by-side be disconcerting?

But Mannig was mesmerized, looking at the dark mahogany wardrobe.

Before he could say anything about it, she opened its doors and frantically fingered through the hanging suits. Distraught, she pushed aside slacks and redingotes, over and over again—trousers, jackets, topcoats.

"What is the matter?" he finally ventured to ask.

"My yellow dress," she choked on her words. Dropping her hands to her sides, she closed her eyes. Tears streaked her face. "My mother used to keep my yellow dress in a similar place. For a moment, I thought I was back in Adapazar."

Mardiros barely controlled his emotions, but managed to hug her. "I will buy a yellow dress for you … tomorrow I'll send for a couturier from Orozdi Bek to fit you with not just a yellow dress, but any kind of clothes your heart desires."

"I loved my yellow dress," Mannig whispered, "but I've loved its memory more." She reminisced about how she danced in their Adapazar parlor, twirling in her organdy dress with ruffles at its hem to melodies her mother played on the violin. "I cried like I had never cried before when the bundle containing my dress slipped off the cart and into the rapids. We were crossing the river out of Adapazar."

"That's sad," he said.

"That happened on our first day of deportation. But the memory of dancing in my mother's parlor sustained me throughout our trek. After my family perished, remembering my dress kept me from becoming sad or lonely. Imagining twirling and dancing in my yellow dress cheered me up and made my pain disappear."

He noticed Mannig's eye scanning the room, again. "Did your family also have something like this?" He pointed to the marble-top vanity with a bowl and pitcher.

Mannig raised her shoulders, "Maybe … but I don't remember."

"Well," he exclaimed, going over to one of the two beds and brushing his fingers across the white satin pillowcase. His fingers traced the periwinkle embroidered initials of MHK. Looking across the second bed, he said, "How do you like your initials?" He pointed to the second bed, MDK gleaming in Armenian letters on its pillow. "It looks like they've chosen this bed for me and that one for you."

He wondered who had redecorated his suite. He had given only a few hours of notice about his nuptials, yet his bachelor's quarters had been transformed to suit a newly wedded couple. How did anyone manage to embroider the initials so quickly?

This being summer, seldom did anyone sleep indoors. If he needed to relax during the day, read a book or listen to his gramophone records, he'd stretch his legs on a sofa in his living room. Otherwise, like the rest of the Baghdadi residents during the seven hot summer months, he climbed the stairs to the roof for a good night's sleep. His cast-iron bed was lined up across the flat roof of the *qasr* along the brick fence with the rest of the Kouyoumdjians' beds.

Soon after sunset, in preparation for the night, one or two maids would climb to the roof and spread open the rolled up mattresses, tuck in the sheets and tie the mosquito nets to the poles. Each family had its own cluster of beds placed on the roof right above their own suites. At night no one mingled with the others. If anyone climbed upstairs, he or she meant to sleep. No talking or giggling. Absolutely forbidden. At sunrise, however, when the Muslim *mu'edhin* chanted his first prayers of the day, someone on their roof would stir at daybreak with a not so gracious yell, "It's time to wake up."

"I don't think they've prepared beds for us on the roof," he said, brushing a kiss across Mannig's forehead. "They're probably thinking that as newlyweds we ought to have our privacy." He patted the bedspread. "Right now, I agree with them."

He sat on the edge and drew her toward him.

Chapter 12

Hanim-*Effendi*

MARDIROS BRUSHED HIS HAND ACROSS the green velvet armchair and looked at Mannig. "Most things here reflect the Hanim-*Effendi*'s influence."

With one look at his face, Mannig knew he would be the coach for their marriage—this unusual partnership of an unequally matched couple. His mellow voice and earnestness lessened her feelings of inferiority in this luxurious environment. Standing in his, no *their* parlor, he'd become the catalyst for a smooth entry into his family but also her mentor in adjusting to his lifestyle. And what about her? She had been a good student at the orphanage—adaptive and creative—could she adjust to such lavish surroundings? Having forgotten her early years of luxury, she didn't know how to behave. She didn't know what a married woman was supposed to do.

"But this," Mardiros pointed to the ceiling-to-floor mahogany bookcase, "this is my favorite place. I know it will be yours, too." He pushed a second chair next to his. "I know the location of each book, by heart." He reached to the eye-level shelf containing Armenian translations. "This set is by Alexander Hugo; next to it you see the writings of Dumas and Flaubert and other European authors." Then he pointed to the top shelf. "Those are my college texts and books in English and French. Soon you too will have your favorites. Unfortunately, I haven't spent much time here, lately. It will be different from now on."

So, a married person reads books.

"I enjoy reading while listening to my Caruso records," he went on, lifting the lid of his upright gramophone.

"I remember that at the orphanage." Mannig stepped close to him and put her hand on his.

His eyes twinkled. "Do you know why I transported it there?"

"To teach us about modern things?"

"Well, yes ... and European dances." He faced her. "But, the real reason was to .... I wanted to hold you close. The only time I dared wrap my arm around your waist was while I showed you how to dance ... like this." He pulled her to him. "You were a natural. You didn't need any lessons. I had to invent a good excuse every evening."

"I think I knew that ...." Mannig whispered into his ear. "We all looked forward to the evenings when you came to visit the orphanage. Will you play it here?"

"Of course! Any time you want. You yourself can play it. I'll show you how. After supper ... tonight." He relaxed his shoulders. "Yes, tonight. We'll listen to all these records, and to as many as we like. I won't be wasting my evenings downtown with the Baghdadi bachelors anymore. We will enjoy music every night, if you'd like."

Mannig thought Mardiros was reading her mind again—he was describing what she hoped marriage would be like. They'd be sitting side-by-side, reading books, listening to music and staying home. The echo of the word "home" rang pleasantly in her memory. This might not be her home in Adapazar, but likewise, it would be musical. In Adapazar, her mother produced the melodies; in Baghdad, a nineteenth-century contraption would. Mannig's heart fluttered. *Being married meant being surrounded by songs and melodies.*

"I think the Hanim-*Effendi* is expecting us in her suite," Mardiros said, drawing the chain of his watch from his vest. "She'll appreciate a private meeting before supper." He led the way and Mannig tiptoed behind him along the balcony toward the river where the water quietly lapped against the shore.

"Her suite faces the Tigris," he said. "Next to hers, on the left, is Khosrof's suite and to her right is Diggin Rose's. Toros lives in the one next to ours, while Dikran, his twin, resides directly across from us. Dikran's door stands out from the others because of that shiny brass doorknob. His wife, Diggin Siranoush, brought it from Moscow as part of her trousseaux."

Mannig felt like a peasant. She knew nothing about Moscow or a trousseau. But she squelched her curiosity; she didn't want to dampen Mardiros' enthusiasm for playing tour guide.

He stopped in front of the carved walnut door and knocked.

"I should speak Turkish, right?" Mannig wanted to confirm her mother-in-law's lack of fluency in Armenian and so calm her worries about her ignorance concerning etiquette among the gentry.

Mardiros nodded. "Talking with you privately will give her a jump on the others. Furthermore, I'm sure Hanim-*Effendi* will enjoy talking with her new daughter-in-law before supper."

Grandmother Managuile, Hanim-*Effendi*, the year of Aida's birth, 1928.

He knocked on the tall door again and, without waiting for a response, opened it into the foyer.

Mannig felt she was entering a carpet store like the one in Mosul, where she'd been shooed away as a starveling. Persian rugs were everywhere—on the floors and walls, on the foyer stand, the divan, the lounging cushions and the tables—large or small—throughout the huge parlor.

A regal lady sat in a Victorian high-back chair beside doors opening to a balcony that cantilevered over the river. The brown hues of her silhouette melded into the dark and light shades of the setting sun beyond the Tigris River.

Mannig's attention was drawn to a string of turquoise gems of prayer beads, clinking between her fingers.

"*Salaam*, my Hanim-*Effendi*," Mardiros said, and, leaving Mannig behind, hurried to his mother and kissed her hand. "I brought my bride so the two of you might get acquainted before the rest of the family hovers all over her."

As Mannig advanced toward the lady, she noticed the way her eyes darted about—like hazel olives swimming in oil. Was it curiosity about the most recent bride in her family? Alas! Unlike as with the other four daughters-in-law, she'd had no say in choosing the wife of her youngest son, Mardiros—according to him, her favorite child. Or perhaps she was relieved that Mardiros, at thirty-two, had finally settled down. *Would she favor me as much as she singled him out?* Not knowing how to cope with such favoritism, she hoped for an inconspicuous status. The *qasr* and the orphanage were dichotomous entities. Until recently, Mannig had one familial concern—for Adriné, her sister. Now that she would be part of a host of high society relatives, what would be expected of her?

"*Gozleri guzel*," Hanim-*Effendi* uttered in Turkish. "Beautiful eyes. *Gel buraya*—come here, Mannig *Jahn*."

The sound of the endearment *jahn* relaxed Mannig. Then again, the Hanim-*Effendi*'s chair took prominence—it resembled her father's green velvet recliner in Adapazar. Before their deportation, her family used to gather for musical evenings in their parlor. Mannig and Setrak, her massacred brother, used to snuggle in their father's chair, squeezing hip to hip to make their childish six- and eight-year-old bodies fit. *Ah, the velvet texture … until Baba came in and they had to jump off. Oh, but that was such a long time ago.*

"Here is my bride," Mardiros was saying, holding Mannig's elbow and leading her to his mother. "Mannig's family was from Adapazar."

"I've heard that town has a lovely setting," Hanim-*Effendi* said, gesturing to the couple to sit across from her. "I have not traveled there myself, but before the war, people who visited it on their way to Constantinople described the beautiful stucco homes with a healthy *boghcha*—such orchards demand much labor."

Surprised that the Hanim knew something about her town, Mannig gasped in Armenian, "We had fruit trees!" Sensing the echo of her words, she quickly switched to Turkish. "A man came and worked in our orchard."

"Ah! Your bride speaks Turkish," Hanim-*Effendi* broke into a generous smile.

Mannig wanted to kiss the lady, and then sit by her feet, hear stories about her birthplace, her home, and about her own family. She craved details about the day-to-day goings on before the Big War, when life was normal. As it was, her heart writhed with sights of deaths during the trek—images of suffering imprinted in her memory.

Reaching for his wife's hand, Mardiros said. "Mannig was a Dobajian. Has anyone mentioned anything to you about the Dobajians of Adapazar?"

Mannig held her breath with pleading eyes. When his mother shook her head, Mannig discreetly released a disappointed sigh. She had yet to meet anyone who knew her family.

"I investigated them, myself," Mardiros said. "The Dobajians were a noble family, and successful business people, at that. My precious Mannig survived the Ottoman atrocities with only a sister—the rest of them suffered under the brutal whips of the gendarmes."

"Come to me, my child," Hanim-*Effendi* said. "I see how your eyes have seen un-godly sights—the ocean of pain of a hundred years seems to be burning in them." She hugged Mannig and placed several kisses on her cheeks. "Sit on my lap. You are still a child—so thin, so uncomplicated."

Mannig tensed. She hadn't sat on anyone's lap for what seemed like a century. The hem of her navy blue uniform crumpled up to her thighs and her bare legs brushed against the matriarch's light brown satin skirt. The luxurious texture of the fabric was not familiar, but sitting in a lap certainly was—her father and his trousers; her mother and her linen skirt; her grandmother in a woolen gown, and finally Miss Romella, her kindergarten teacher, on the deportation trek, wearing the coarse burlap tunic. No fond memories were triggered by the feel of the satin. Yet sitting in a lap evoked the warmth of belonging to family. She knew, right there and then, that she would love this gentle lady for the rest of her life. Might she be like Mama? No—her mother was in her thirties when she died of starvation in Deir Zor. Like Haji-doo? Her paternal grandmother was not fifty years old when the gendarmes shot her to death for being a straggler and slowing down the foot caravan of deportees. Hanim-*Effendi* was in her early seventies, and Mannig didn't know anyone who had lived as many years as her mother-in-law.

"I must confess," Hanim-*Effendi* sighed, "I have suffered just as much. Oh, don't judge by my demeanor or my clothes. My heart drowns in tears; my thoughts suffocate in pain; I pretend to be fine during my days, but at night, I pray to find peace of mind for the remainder of my life."

The silence in her suite embraced all three. Mannig's hope for a simple acquaintance halted at the precipice of a startling and unexpected route.

"One of my daughters was massacred, too," her mother-in-law continued. "My dearest Takouhi. The jewel of my eye. She perished along with her husband and three children."

Takouhi, twin sister of Vartouhi, had married a gentleman from outside the Armenian community of Baghdad and settled with her new family in Diar-Bekir, located in central Turkey. When the Ottoman onslaught against the Armenians began, the citizens of most towns, including Diar-Bekir, were either deported or rounded up and locked inside their local church. The building was set fire and they were burned to ashes. The Kouyoumdjians had heard nothing of their fates beyond the reports of catastrophic events of World War One.

Tears swelled in Hanim-*Effendi*'s eyes. She kissed Mannig again and gestured for her to return to the seat beside her husband. She reached inside her skirt pocket and brought out a starched white handkerchief, monogrammed in olive green satin appliqué—MBK for Managuile Baghdassarian Kouyoumdjian. She dabbed the edges of her nose and wiped away her tears. "God spared you, Mannig-*Jahn*, so you would preserve your Dobajian memory and the Almighty spared my Mardiros in prison so he, too, could fulfill His will."

Privy to how Mardiros escaped death while Karnig contracted typhus and died, Mannig said. "I met Diggin Rose at the train station."

"Don't let her bother you," Hanim-*Effendi* winked. "She has her whims but she is solid … she mothered my first grandchildren." After a few moments, she broke the silence. "Would you like to tell me about your mother?"

"Yes, please do," Mardiros urged. "We haven't heard family stories yet. What a perfect time and place to begin. Mannig, what do you remember most about your mother?"

Mannig choked. She was dumbfounded. Her mother existed now only in her dreams. Neither orphans nor patrons ever asked about her. Could she articulate her vision of Mama's real-life personality to this lady? She loved her mother and Mama had loved her until her demise. How did one describe such adoration, especially when even its memory might be a figment of her imagination? Mannig lowered her eyes and stayed mum.

"She was a musician, right?" Mardiros encouraged her.

Mannig hesitated, giving him a nod of affirmation. As with the rest of her past life, she held back her tears and replaced her sadness with happy memories. "She played the violin … and we danced to her melodies." Suddenly Mannig felt compelled to tell them everything she knew. "Miss Romella told me a few things. She was my kindergarten teacher, and after Mama died, she became our friend, my sister and me. Once when we were walking in the desert, she told us that Mama was an outstanding musician. She was good long before she became my Mama. One day when my Baba was walking down the street with a friend, he heard someone playing the violin on the second floor. The two friends leaned against the wall and listened until the conclusion of the piece. Then my Baba promised his friend that if the musician were a lady, he would make her his wife …." Mannig suddenly stopped speaking, worried that she had said too much. She wasn't used to dominating the conversation.

"And obviously, he kept his promise," Mardiros filled the silence. "I have a sense that Mannig will enlighten us with many more such wonderful vignettes about her family."

"Really," Mannig said. "All I know is she played for us every evening and we danced to her music—the children, all four of us. My Baba sat in a chair like yours, Hanim-*Effendi*. He watched, he twirled his mustache, he listened to Mama's music."

"That is a lovely family, Mannig-*Jahn*," Hanim-*Effendi* said. "The Kouyoumdjians cannot claim a musician among us."

"Come, Mother!" Mardiros jeered. "Maggie, Margot, Meliné ... all my nieces play the piano."

"Hah! You call that *play*?" She sneered. "They take lessons, yes, but I'd like to hear some good music sometime." She stood up, went over to a bookcase with drawers in its lower half, and pulled one open. "Come here, Mannig-*Jahn*," she said, unfolding a satin shawl with a paisley-swirl design in hues of azure and sapphire. She draped it around Mannig's bony shoulders. "This is just a little token—not a gift. The gifts and heirlooms will come later. I'm giving this shawl to you because you paid me a visit and ... interrupted my loneliness. You put joy into my day. Remember! This is not a gift. It is yours and has been in your possession for a long time. You will wear it at suppertime tonight. Tomorrow, Mardiros will see that your wardrobe is stocked properly. You will receive heirlooms and gifts soon. This shawl is for visiting me on your first day at the *qasr*."

Mannig cupped her palms on its silky fringes. A sudden unease jarred her. It felt strange, just as the orphanage uniform had felt that first time when its tent material had rubbed against her bodice. She dropped her hands to her sides, lest the roughened hangnails snag a thread of the fine fabric. The shawl clung securely on her left shoulder but apparently there was less roughness on the right sleeve to keep it in place. It slid to her back, draping only one shoulder and arm.

"Let me tie the ends for you." Mardiros came to her rescue.

"No!" Hanim-*Effendi* stopped him. "The way it is sitting now looks original. Creative. A novel style for a new member of the family. The decision is for Mannig. Come with me." She led them to her lavish bedroom and opened the door of an ornate black walnut wardrobe. "Look in the mirror," she suggested. "Do you like it draping on one side?"

Like? Mannig had not thought of likes or dislikes; preferring one thing more than another had no logic in an orphan's life. How should she respond to this lady of wealth?

The glint in her mother-in-law's eyes provided an answer. "It looks different," she whispered.

"Charming," Mardiros said. "You're a natural fashion setter." He scrutinized her face and, as he tidied her uniform collar, noticed the golden pin the captain of the ship had given her. "Aha!" he said. "Let me reposition this memento of our wedding ceremony ... here, onto your shoulder. *Voilà*! Now the shawl is fastened securely to your dress."

Mannig was beginning to enjoy being pampered when a sudden clanging from the courtyard transported her thoughts back to the orphanage. She jerked, intending to dash to what she thought must be the dinner call.

Mardiros calmed her down. "No need to rush. That's the cook. He enjoys striking the gong. Well, it is not a real gong. It's his contraption—an empty three-inch cannon shell that he salvaged from his days of fighting the Ottomans."

"I'm glad you're hungry, Mannig-*Jahn*," Hanim-*Effendi* said. "Your thin body needs a lot of nourishment." With a twinkle in her eyes, she added, "And you will make me very happy when you give me a healthy and a beautiful grandchild."

A baby? Only minutes ago, she sat me on her lap and called me *'child,'* she thought.

Chapter 13

Supper on the Veranda

MARDIROS STRAIGHTENED THE FRINGES OF the azure-paisley shawl on Mannig's left arm and said, "Let's go downstairs. I want to get there before the rest of the family arrives." He escorted both his bride and his mother to the courtyard level. Instead of entering the dining room, Hanim-*Effendi* veered toward the veranda, overhanging the Tigris River. Beyond the tall mahogany doors, flung wide open, were two long tables set for supper.

Stepping onto the veranda, Mannig heard the river lapping beneath her feet. She looked straight out—through the railing and beyond. There was nothing but water—roiling downstream in a hurry. She hesitated. Stepped back. Held her breath. Wrapped her fingers around her arm.

"What's the matter?" Mardiros looked at her as she took another step backward.

She shook her head and turned around to face the courtyard. "The water … the river …." She closed her eyes and wrapped herself with both arms. She shuddered while telling him how she had fallen off a *guffa*—the round fishing boat. Had an Arab not splashed toward her from the shore and grabbed her, she would have drowned, for sure. "I can never forget his grip." She squeezed her upper left arm. "Right here. That Arab saved my life."

"No one will fall off the veranda," Mardiros assured her. "It's very secure. We've had many guests here for parties, as well as family suppers for special occasions, such as this. Come, we shouldn't spoil my mother's plan to honor you."

Still holding her stance, Mannig glowered at the courtyard tiles. *I shouldn't disappoint. I must oblige!* She clasped Mardiros' hand and warily stepped on the sturdy planks. She stopped at the end of the first table, closest to the doors that spanned as high as the second level of the *qasr*.

"Mannig-*Jahn*," Hanim-*Effendi* pointed to the head of the table abutting the railings. "Tonight, you'll be sitting to my right—beside me."

Mardiros glanced at his white knuckles between Mannig's tensed fingers. "It will be all right," he whispered, kissing her hand. "Let me speak to the Hanim." He hurried over to his mother and while he was still whispering, Hanim-*Effendi* said, "Call Fareed, then. Ask him to switch my seat to the other end."

Relaxing somewhat, Mannig peered at the table settings. If she had ever experienced a similar occasion, she would have thought this arrangement elegant. As it was, she imagined the gathering of a family. Would being with the Kouyoumdjians alleviate past sufferings? If a child called on his or her mother, might that revive her agony anew? *I ought to channel the past away.* She clung to the present. She needed self-confidence, but didn't know how to acquire it; she wanted self-assertiveness, but dared not; she wanted attention, but how? Being in the *qasr* was even more intimidating because she loved Mardiros and didn't want to embarrass him. *I like him too much.*

Clicking heels prompted Mannig to turn around. Diggin Rose stepped onto the veranda, her three daughters and two sons, ages twenty-four to sixteen, in tow. Recognizing the youngest daughter Meliné by name, Mannig smiled, hoping that she'd approach her, if for no reason other than their age compatibility. Instead, Meliné fanned her pink skirt and, glancing at Mannig, pulled out a chair at the second table. Her siblings joined her, followed by the other children who filled the rest of the fourteen seats. They were all dressed in summer colors. In contrast, the adults wore 'elderly' colors—browns and grays. Mannig squirmed as if her coarse navy-blue uniform scratched her skin. Comforted by the feel of the pretty blue shawl, she fiddled with its fringe. Admiring the cowl neckline of Maggie's floral georgette dress, Mannig flipped her shawl's loose end across her other shoulder. *So much softer on my neck, too.*

"Diggin Rose," Hanim-*Effendi* said. "I have a favor to ask you for this evening. Do you mind relinquishing your seat? It will only be for tonight. I'd like the 'new bride' to sit beside me."

Diggin Rose flared her nostrils and cast a "Why not him?" glance at the seat to the Hanim's left, reserved for Khosrof, the eldest surviving son. Receiving no response, Rose resignedly pulled the third chair down from the head of the table.

"That's very kind of you," Mardiros said, hurrying to her side and taking hold of the chair. "Let me help. After tonight, Mannig and I will sit somewhere else. I mean, we will relinquish these seats back to you. You know, Diggin Rose, no matter where you are seated, you will always remain Hanim-*Effendi*'s first and foremost daughter-in-law."

At the Felloujeh *qasr*, 1926. Mardiros is on the far right, bottom row. Mannig is just above him.

"And you," Diggin Rose hissed, "you will always remain her youngest and favorite son." Her face remained placid but not her hands. She set her goblet slightly to the right and tilted up her long nose. Her slender fingers, flashing with diamond rings, circled the table then descended to rearrange the sterling silverware; her beady brown eyes searched under the china plate; her fingertips brushed against the embroidered satin fleur-de-lis designs of the white linen table cloth. She then stared at the glittering silver vases that lined the center of the long dining table.

Mannig, too, studied the ornate images of deer and gazelles hammered on the glistening surfaces of the vases, until the small bouquets of short-stemmed daisies in each vase redirected her focus. Was the yellow similar to that of a little girl's dress in Adapazar? They certainly resembled the flowers of the desert, one of the rare touches of beauty observed during the deportation. She couldn't remember her reaction to them at the time, but the memory linked her past to the present.

Mardiros drew up a chair between Rose and Mannig while the rest of the family trickled in. They took their seats at the Hanim's table, chronologically—tall Khosrof, being the oldest son sat immediately to the Hanim's left while his wife, blonde Sara slid into the chair next to him. Handsome Dikran and refined Siranoush, his wife, occupied the next two seats. The last couple, skinny Toros and Hermine with her plump-buttocks completed the adults' table.

"The supper will be similar to that of the captain's table," Mardiros, discreetly whispered to his wife. "There won't be surprises tonight. You adapted from the orphanage bench to the commander's chambers like a fish from a murky pond to a crystalline lake."

"All the food at the captain's table looked unfamiliar to me," Mannig confided in him. At the dinner party following their wedding ceremony on the ship, he had tactfully coached her how to use the various utensils. He never made her feel a lesser person. Even so, she was unable to swallow much of anything. Her stomach remained empty as it had been for most of her recent past. "I have never seen so much food and so much variety, not even in Adapazar." She cringed at how she had fumbled while attempting to pile grains of rice onto her fork. *Thank God, that nightmare is over.* She glanced at him and raised her left hand. "I should hold the fork always with this hand."

He smiled at the memory.

Toros, the younger of the twins, snuffed out his cigarette cleared his throat. Holding down the flapping corners of the table-cloth, he said, "God gave us this cool breeze to spare this special occasion from the onslaught of mosquitoes. Hanim-*Effendi*, you were wise to arrange our supper by the river."

Everyone nodded without further comment about the weather as they began to salivate, watching Fareed serve the roasted chicken, tomato-basted grilled zucchini and rice.

Not rice again!

Mannig was surprised at her own thoughts. Only a week earlier, at the Basra orphanage, she and her tent mates had longed for a meal of fluffy rice. *Is this what abundance does? Makes people choosy*? She wasn't being selective. She didn't want to fail in her attempt to use table manners her husband had thought important enough to teach her. She feared that using the silverware improperly would embarrass him. Noticing how Diggin Rose waved her hand at Hamid, declining rice, she decided to emulate her.

When Fareed came around to serve her, Mannig swung her hand so hard that the bowl, rice and serving spoon came crashing down onto the plank floor.

Simultaneously, words of consolation flew in from every which way, whipping into her head. "That's all right!" "There's a lot more!" "It happens all the time."

No amount of forgiveness placated Mannig. She felt fire darting from her cheeks, saliva drying in her throat, and noise cackling in her ears. She wanted to vanish into Aladdin's lamp like a jinni.

Fareed cleaned up the mess and, as if his duties had not been interrupted, continued to serve the supper while everyone else kept eating or conversing as they had before Mannig's fiasco.

Khosrof was waving his finger at some item at the far end of the table.

"What is it?" and "What do you want?" came the responses.

Khosrof kept his silence, still pointing.

"He wants the bread!" Vahram, Toros's oldest son, said from the children's table. "The bread. Pass the basket of bread to Uncle Khosrof."

Mardiros leaned toward Mannig. "Vahram is the only one who can read his mind."

Handsome Dikran, forty-two, the elder of the twins, took a bite of chicken breast. "God forbid!" he exclaimed with closed eyes. "I'm dying and going to heaven! Who is the villain? Not you, again, Diggin Hermine?"

Everyone looked at Hermine, whose smile accentuated the roundness of her face, but she did not speak. Her husband, skinny Toros, nodded. "Come, come, Dikran," he said. "We know you. You love chicken, anyway."

"I love chicken, yes!" Dikran agreed, taking a bite of a drumstick. "But you, you looooove to eat …. It's lucky that your wife is a fantastic cook."

"What's your secret?" elegant Siranoush, Dikran's wife, asked. "I can't identify the spices."

"No, secret," Hermine said. "I told chef Hamid to baste the bird with allspice-flavored butter, stuff the cavity with rosemary and roast it in the *toneer.*"

Toneer? Mannig's ears perked up and she cast off her self-pity. She knew everything one needed to know about a toneer. After all, she helped the Bedouin women of the desert bake the daily bread in a toneer which they called *tennoor*, the oven made of clay and placed tightly against the sides of a dugout. She knew how to stick a flat disc of dough on the sides of the hot toneer. When bubbles appeared on the bread's surface, she would kneel down to grab the top edge and pull it out. *How did Diggin Hermine stick in a whole chicken?* She squelched her curiosity, fearing these relatives considered the Bedouin, the desert people, to be the lowliest on earth. If she admitted her acquaintance with the Bedouin, these refined people might regard her as even lowlier than they already did. She'd ask Mardiros later, when they were alone. As it was, she already felt awkward to be seated among people with whom she had little in common. Furthermore, she knew nothing about their conversation, which concerned royalty and the politics of this new country of Iraq.

"Faisal will make a great king," Khosrof said. "It's better to have a king leading the affairs of our lands than those Ottoman thieves."

"I hope this new government will be different," Toros said. "I hope they won't require bribery for the public works they are planning."

"Ha! As if they'll complete the ones already in progress," Dikran said.

"You are ever the pessimist," Toros berated his twin. "Don't you realize our monarchy is supported by the British?"

"British, French or Russian," Mardiros said, "foreign powers are foreign powers—alien, outsiders, outliers. Iraqis will always need to cater to their whims. There's no guarantee of any continuous support to the Arab people, to the Kurds, to the Assyrians—or to us, the Armenians. These days the oil wells in Kirkuk and Mosul are lubricating their pockets. One day they will dry up. Do you think those foreign empires will pay attention to our king then? To the plights of any of us?"

Dikran gave Mardiros a disgusted look. "Your outlook on the future is worse than anyone's I've heard in all of Baghdad."

Mardiros kept his silence—after all, the speaker was an older sibling.

Then Khosrof held up his finger up again.

Everyone waited for Vahram to identify his need.

Soon enough, Vahram said, "Uncle Khosrof wants everyone's attention."

Khosrof lowered his hand, glanced across the dining table, and addressed Mardiros. "I suppose you know something about petrol because you're an engineer."

"Oh, yes, Uncle Mardiros," Vahram, bound for Robert College in Istanbul—Mardiros' alma mater—said from across the children's table. "Do you think there may be petrol in our lands in Felloujeh?"

They all hushed each other and gazed at Mardiros, waiting for his answer.

Mardiros shook his head. "I'm not that kind of engineer," he said and sipped some water. "But who is to say that all of Iraq is not an island floating on oil?"

Mannig, who up till now had been listening to the chatter unconcerned, suddenly craned her neck to look at her husband. Only a romantic would describe Iraq as *a country floating on oil*. Mr. Antelias, the journalist who was one of the witnesses at their marriage ceremony in the Captain's chambers, had called him a romantic. Her husband was a romantic not only for marrying an orphan but also for his vision of Iraq's future.

"I do see a bright spot in Iraq's future," Mardiros continued. "That future is in the hands of the prime minister, Nuri el-Said."

"He's a British stooge," Khosrof snorted. "He'll be kicked out as soon as his usefulness ends."

Mannig was confused, not because the discussion had no relevance to her, but because she was surprised to hear one brother belittling the stance of another. Weren't the Kouyoumdjians grateful to have their family intact and together? She had one surviving sibling and would go to the ends of the earth for her. Was it because there were so many Kouyoumdjians? Or was it because they hadn't experienced the pain and suffering of losing their family to atrocities as she had? She felt content to be excluded from the discussion.

While everyone began to enjoy second helpings, she had hardly taken a bite. Again, her stomach remained as empty as during the deportation.

Hanim-*Effendi* called everyone to attention. "Enough politics for this evening, boys. Before the watermelon is served, let's plan the celebration. We must put on a party for the new bride."

"Party?" "Party?" "Party?" Echoed back and forth between the children's and the parents' tables.

"We must introduce our newest Kouyoumdjian to our Baghdadi society," Hanim-*Effendi* said. Sighing, she added, "Well, whoever is still a *who's who* in Baghdad. That awful Big War reduced our body of friends to a mere skeleton."

Mannig squirmed in her seat. She would be expected to become the focus of Baghdadi society? She had felt like a mouse at the captain's table. How could she feel any lowlier? What was lowlier than a mouse, a rat? But a rat had guts. She had nothing.

"I want a new dress!" "I want a different hairstyle!" "I want to invite so-and-so …." Similar comments wafted in and out of Mannig's hearing range, complicating her feelings beyond her inferiority complex. Those people talked about *wants* as if their survival depended upon a coiffure or a new dress. She had fallen into an alien reality and she didn't know how to rise to the occasion. Was her sister Adriné facing similar predicaments? *Adriné knows how to cope with everything. She is smart. She is older. She has resolve. What am I going to do?*

"Mardiros," Hanim-*Effendi* called on him, waiting for eye contact. "Tomorrow, you must contact Orozdi Bek to send new clothes for Mannig. Have them send a lady-fitter, too."

Meliné dashed over to Mannig's chair. "May I come to your suite to watch?"

"Me, too?" Maggie, Lizinka and Margot chimed in, almost in harmony. "I want to see the latest styles." "I've been waiting for such an occasion." And "I can't wait until tomorrow!"

Mannig smiled and nodded. *I must cooperate. Not for my sake but for Mardiros'.*

"All right, girls." Hanim-*Effendi* gestured for her granddaughters to return to their seats. "We have more important matters to discuss." She then leaned forward to get Diggin Hermine's attention. "I've already asked chef Hamid to secure a couple of good cooks to help with the cuisine. Of course, the ultimate decision will be yours." She addressed her other three daughters-in-law. "I expect that each of you will also contribute your own specialty. I want to make this to be a signature event for the Kouyoumdjians."

Amid nods of agreement, Fareed approached Mardiros and whispered, "Your friends are in the parlor."

Mardiros jumped up. "They are? But why?"

"They said they knew they weren't expected," Fareed explained, hiding a smile. "They've heard you married a very beautiful lady and couldn't wait to meet her."

Before Mardiros got up to attend to his friends, his mother said, "Invite them to the soirée. There they will enjoy the privilege of meeting your bride."

Chapter 14

The Soirée

OVER THE NEXT TWO DAYS, Mannig formed the eye of a hurricane. Her in-laws, nieces and nephews, all older than she, swirled around her, for her and about her, saying, "For Diggin Mannig," "About Diggin Mannig," or "To please Diggin Mannig." Mannig could no longer distinguish between what was real or surreal.

She was not only engulfed in completing her journey from orphanage to opulence, but she was also swept up into the providential coincidence of celebrating her marriage while Iraq was inaugurating its first king. In 1921, the country was proclaimed a monarchy by the League of Nations and Prince Faisal from Saudi Arabia, its first king. While the new Iraqi government prepared for a national and international celebration of Iraq's monarchy in the spring of 1922, the Kouyoumdjians were getting ready to announce and rejoice in the marriage of their youngest son.

The four brothers reported the country's preparations on a regular basis—how Baghdadi streets were being swept clean of horse manure and hosed down. Likewise, the servants at the *qasr* washed and scrubbed the courtyard tiles, swept and dusted the carpets and set the dining room with china and crystal.

"They've wrapped palm branches around the pillars along Al-Rashid Street," Dikran said, "and displayed flags of all colors at the store fronts."

"Fareed," Hanim-*Effendi* instructed the valet, "let's place plants in pots throughout the courtyard, in addition to baskets of flowers hanging from the balcony eaves." Upon further reflection, she continued, "You must also hang Chinese lanterns along the veranda."

"There will be marching bands preceding the Royal entourage," Toros said. "Everybody is looking forward to the parade down Al-Rashid Street."

"Our *qasr* too, will reverberate with music," Hanim-*Effendi* said and, addressing Diggin Siranoush, added, "Would you ask Margot's piano teacher to play for us? I believe she knows pieces besides etudes and Russian folk songs." Then she addressed Mardiros, "See that you bring your Master's Voice downstairs. Make sure to designate someone other than you to change the records. We must have a lot of dancing. And you must take the lead."

"It's so entertaining to stroll down Al-Rashid Street these days," Khosrof said. "The whole city is clad in newness—as if it had not existed for centuries."

"Mardiros," Hanim-*Effendi* said, "see that the saleslady from Orozdi-Bek is here the first thing in the morning."

The dress fitter from the department store came to fit Mannig, but spent more time satisfying the Kouyoumdjian single ladies who invaded Mannig's privacy. Maggie, Lizinka, Meliné, Iskouhi and Margo suggested this or that for Mannig, who focused on a sheer beaded overdress that reminded her of what Mamma had worn in Adapazar. She would wear it at the soirée. It was a quick decision for her. Meanwhile her nieces selected four to five outfits each for themselves—straight-lined, low-waisted chemises similar to the latest fashions they'd seen in French and English magazines.

"The Prince of Wales would like this," Iskouhi said to Meliné, touching a pale blue georgette camisole. "When he comes to propose to you, you ought to wear this one."

"Since the Prince of Wales is for Meliné," Lizinka said, "Who's for me, then?"

"The Prince of Romania, of course."

"I thought he was meant for you," Lizinka said.

"I don't think so," Iskouhi said resignedly. "I will marry an Armenian. I don't have grandiose aspirations as you do."

Mannig didn't know how much of this conversation was in jest and how much was in earnest. She learned later on that Meliné was smitten by the Prince of Wales and encouraged in her aspirations by Diggin Rose. Meliné treasured every magazine with his pictures and memorized comments about his activities, whether in London or in the other European capitals. At seventeen, Meliné was beautiful indeed—the most talked-about maiden in Baghdad society. Her complexion was fine-pored and pale, eyes greenish and locks silky. Anytime she walked down Al-Rashid Street, wearing a Chanel cloche and silk heels, people stopped to admire her. She was aware of her aura and, *à la* Kouyoumdjians, seldom flaunted it. Everyone at the *qasr* liked her—despite her mother Diggin Rose, who relentlessly reminded her of the power of her beauty. Mannig came to believe in Meliné's self-delusion of marrying royalty, and her sisters would become the ladies-in-waiting.

"Vye! Vye! Vye!" the girls exclaimed when they saw the milliner walk in

The five Kouyoumdjian brothers, photographed in Baghdad in 1913. Seated, from left: Karnig (the eldest); Khosrof (five years younger). Standing from left: Toros; Mardiros (center); Dikran. Toros and Dikran were twins, ten years older than Mardiros. Mardiros was the youngest in the family.

with boxes and boxes of hats. The five girls modeled this hat and that, back and forth. Not one of them helped Mannig, their reason for gathering in the sitting room. "This is lovely on you," "No. That one is for an older woman," and "This one is the style." Mannig became more and more confused.

After her nieces left with their selections, Mannig chose a simple white satin hat banded with a chinchilla tail. That, too, reminded her of Mamma. She could almost see her mother walking ahead to the train station the day the gendarmes deported them from Adapazar—a long, long time ago. Mannig could not forget how they were hustled and pushed onto a train car, her family of eight barely making it on board. The train chugged on, leaving behind Mamma's sewing machine—too cumbersome to be loaded quickly onto the train—next to the tracks, her pretty hat perched atop it. Mannig wiped away a tear, just as her mother had done so many years earlier.

Mannig admired herself in the mirror, wearing her new chinchilla. *Mamma would approve.*

On the day before the reception, the *qasr* was transformed into a bathhouse-like mood—for the females, that is. All the men and their sons spent the day at the public bathhouse in downtown Baghdad. The ladies, on the other hand, queued up at the door of the *quasr's* one and only washroom.

"The bride will be first," they said, and handed Mannig a burnoose, her initials embroidered in pink on one sleeve. *Just like Mamma's.* Even though the bathroom was no more than an ordinary room with a water tank heated from the outside by a charcoal brazier, it brought back memories of being with Mamma, who once a month used to take her three daughters and Hajidoo to the public bathhouse in Adapazar. *Such a long time ago.* On that last visit, the Turkish proprietress had shooed them out for contaminating her establishment with 'Armeny filth.' A few days later they were deported with the other Armenians from her town.

Inside the *qasr's* private tiny bathroom, Mannig sat on the wooden stool. *Mamma used to adjust the temperature of the water.* She mixed the hot and cold water in a metal basin. *Mamma rinsed my hair.* She dunked the tin tass and splashed water over her body. She grabbed the cube of soap and rubbed it against her head, enjoying its pine fragrance. It didn't remind her of the coarse bars Mamma used in Adapazar; its suds didn't sting her eyes, either. She enjoyed lounging, pouring water over her and feeling refreshed but missed being a child, running naked with her kindergarten friends on the slippery floors of the public bathhouse. She poured more water to douse her nostalgia.

Between splashes she heard whispering against the door. "She deserves to lounge as long as she wants." Followed by, "Maybe on other days, but today there are ten women waiting."

Mannig wrapped herself in the burnoose and opened the door. Diggin Rose faced her, her arms folded across her burnoose. Without a word, nod, or glance, she walked in and banged the door shut behind her.

Early in the morning of the soirée, there seemed to be more workers in the *qasr* than residents. They were setting tables, moving sofas, watering the hanging baskets, all to the accompaniment of clanging pots and pans in the kitchen. Mannig could hear the voices of three chefs arguing about sprinkling curry powder on the *shabboot*—fresh water salmon of the Tigris—or sumac on the roasted chicken. All conflict was quelled by the gentling presence of Diggin Hermine, who had found a chair to sit on in the kitchen and create harmony between the cackling cooks.

At around noon, deliveries from downtown arrived—freshly baked bread, Greek black olives, sliced *basturma*, baskets of grapes and a gunnysack of watermelons. Later on, the horse-drawn *arabana* delivered several blocks of ice.

A few hours before the arrival of the guests, there was a knock on the door of Mannig's suite. Thinking one of the girls needed something, she opened the door, and was surprised to see a stranger facing her.

"I am the bartender," he said. "May I speak with Mardiros-*Effendi*?"

Mardiros tucked his starched white shirt inside his white suit pants and said, "What is the problem, Garbiz?"

"How many waiters should I hire?" he asked.

"Three or four," Mardiros said. "As many as you need to make everything go smoothly."

"Are you sure, *Effendi*?" The bartender's voice dropped to a hush-hush. "These men want assurance of getting paid."

"Of course they will get paid," Mardiros sounded irritated.

"Are you sure, *Effendi*?" Garbiz insisted. "Two of them haven't received any pay since the last time they came over to serve."

"Why n-not?" Mardiros said, stammering slightly.

"I understand there has been some problems with cash flow," he whispered.

"Impossible!" Mardiros said. "That can never be the case."

"The men claim to have been warned by friends at church. Some of their buddies who worked at the *qasr* on various occasions haven't been paid yet."

Mardiros stood, pale as a ghost, cheeks flushed and tongue tied. "I'm sure there's been a m-m-mistake," he stuttered.

He looked extremely agitated, making Mannig wonder about the imminence of a disaster.

"Garbiz-*Jahn*," Mardiros said and looked beyond the man, searching for the proverb at the tip of his tongue. "My dear man—'*haye hayov, hayoon hamar.*' As one Armenian to another, let's work together for our own good. I assure you there's some m-m-misunderstanding. I ask you t-t-to relax. Now that I'm home, everything will be like old times. Go! Finish p-p-preparing for this evening. Today is my day to celebrate."

Chapter 15

La fille aux cheveux de lin

WALTZES WAFTED FROM THE GRAMOPHONE on the veranda above the chitchat of glamorously gowned ladies flitting around the gentlemen in evening attire. Matrons, lounging in clusters, thrust forward their bejeweled necklines when someone approached them in particular. The children, also decked out in finery, banded together at the other end of the courtyard, teasing each other. Mannig weaved and shadowed in Mardiros' wake.

Mannig was whisked here and there, her groom's hand clasped firmly in hers. She smiled and acknowledged every compliment, but the most exciting moment was when her sister Adriné entered in the arms of Sebouh Papazian, her groom.

The sisters had not seen each other since the train station in Baghdad. Each had joined her new family in marriage, and each had promised to see the other often. A whole week had gone by since then, and Mannig was delighted to see her sister. Adriné was beautifully dressed in a lemon-green jersey that hugged her svelte bodice and flared at the ankle-length hem. She flew to her and the two hugged. Neither wished to be parted and or to join in the festivities, yet they did their best to mingle with the guests, often winding their paths to touch hands. "Your dress is beautiful," Mannig managed to whisper to her once.

"There were so many to choose from," Adriné said. "It comes from Sebouh's store." At their next encounter, Adriné said, "Don't you hate the flattening brassieres?"

"What a silly fashion," Mannig agreed, and then whispered, "Are you happy?"

"I don't know yet. Are you?"

"I think I should be …. Yes, I am," Mannig hesitated. "Well, I think I am

… but, I really don't know what that means, yet. Everyone is very nice to me, and every activity in the *qasr* seems to be for me and about me. If Mamma saw me, she'd know."

"Wish she were here."

The two sisters tearfully gazed at each other.

"Aha!" Mardiros said, getting Mannig's attention. "Enough private talk. Come and meet my rascal friends."

Mannig shook hands with Mihran Bezdjian, the local tennis champion, Levon Donatossian, the daring businessman, Vahé Sevian, the prominent engineer at the the government irrigation department, and lastly, Yeprem Damlayan, the newcomer from Lebanon, who wouldn't let go of her hand. He led her to the veranda and the two stepped into a foxtrot that was being played on the gramophone. Before the final step, Mannig was pulled away by Levon, who swung her into a Viennese waltz. Still dizzy but not breathless, Mannig expected Mihran to take his turn, but Yeprem was at her heels, tapping on Levon's shoulder.

"You? Again?" Mannig asked.

"Forever!" He chuckled. "Until that lucky Mardiros stops me …."

Mardiros interrupted the couple's dance with, "Come, Mannig. Barone Antelias has arrived," and he led her away to greet his guests.

Barone Antelias? Oh! The newspaperman friend who witnessed their marriage on the ship Shuja in Basra. She delighted in greeting an "old" friend from her pre-marriage life, even though she had seen him only once and even then, fleetingly. Exhilarated, she extended her arms for a hug, only to feel Mardiros's hand gently lowering her left hand to her side. *Is he hinting that I should not*? Discreetly, she extended her right hand for a firm shake. "I'm so happy to see you."

"What a transformation!" Antelias said, placing a kiss on her hand. He handed Mardiros a narrow velvet box. "This is a gift for the *Cinderella of Mesopotamia*."

Mannig couldn't wait to see her gift as Mardiros flipped the lid open. "How beautiful!"

Mannig felt her skin tingle when Mardiros clasped the delicate choker necklace at her neck. "Now my bride looks more beautiful than Cinderella."

"Here, here!" Antelias echoed.

When he noticed other guests at the entrance, Antelias stepped aside. Mardiros put Mannig's hand on his arm and excused himself. "We'll talk later on the veranda," he said.

"This is for you, Diggin Kouyoumdjian," the arriving guests said, handing over a pair of bracelets made of pearls strung in a gold setting. "We've been saving these for your bride, Mardiros."

"These will fit her beautifully," the next guest said, handing over a gold-filigreed bracelet, designed for the upper arm.

The next gift of a sapphire pendant sparkled in Mannig's hand before Mardiros pinned it near her collar bone. Each guest showered her with jewelry, studded with dazzling precious stones. Glittering ornaments covered her simple shear over-dress. She no longer felt demure or like herself. She felt ridiculous. The jewelry interfered with her lightheartedness. It hindered her free spirit. Above all, it hampered her dancing.

"Mardiros," she whispered into his ear. "Do you think it would be all right if I don't wear this necklace?"

"Of course," he said, scrutinizing it, "but why?"

"It's too heavy," she said and removed it.

He slipped it into his pocket.

"And this?" She handed him another glittering strand. "That one, too." Pretty soon, the pockets of his white linen jacket bulged with heirloom jewelry. The only necklace she didn't remove was the delicate choker Barone Antelias had given her.

Garbiz, the valet/chauffeur and the overseer of the party, tapped Mardiros on the shoulder. "Hanim-*Effendi* wishes to see you on the veranda—with your bride."

Mannig noticed that the music had stopped and the guests were shuffling their chairs. Even the children had stopped stuffing their faces with delectable *dolma* or luscious *kubbeh* and were flocking around.

"Come here, my newest bride," Hanim-*Effendi* gestured to Mannig, the turquoise prayer beads dangling from her left hand. "You are like sweetened air. I feel so much joy when I watch you. I hope you can feel the excitement you are infusing into our family. Your youthful zest invigorates us all. Watching you makes even me feel young." She then reached into the side pocket of her satin gown and brought out a diamond necklace. "Frankly, you don't need ornaments because God has endowed you with his best gifts. I can only pass on to you a token given to me by my mother-in-law—may she rest in peace." She laced the dazzling necklace around Mannig's neck and closed the clasp. Diamond pendants were strung on each side of a large pear-shaped diamond, which dangled to where Mannig's cleavage began, had it been exposed. As it was, Hanim-*Effendi* reached inside the neck of her dress and arranged the pear-shape diamond to lie between Mannig's breasts.

Mannig could not see herself, but the oohs and ahs were testament enough to the necklace's beauty. Instinctively she kissed her mother-in-law's hand.

"No, no! Not necessary," Hanim-*Effendi* said. "I look forward to placing my lips upon the grandson. I pray the Lord will bless us all."

A loud applause deafened Mannig. She didn't know whether to smile, curtsy, hide or ignore it all. Her face flushed, her breathing became more rapid and her throat went dry. She wanted to melt out of sight in her embarrassment even as Mardiros was speaking.

"Hanim-*Effendi*," he said, holding his bride's hand. "We thank you for your generosity, and we shall honor your wishes with our lives, our habits and our heritage."

Excusing himself, he led Mannig into the center of the veranda. "Garbiz!" he said. "You may resume playing the gramophone. Start with a slow waltz for us."

The couple danced, moving as one. Mannig loved the feel of his arms around her waist. Still more, she adored his breath against her ear. Her palm felt warm and secure in his, and she let herself be drawn into the waltz, knowing she could trust his lead. She followed his every step as if by instinct. With each twirl, she swung closer to him.

Everyone watched in silence, breaking into spontaneous applause when the waltz ended.

Garbiz changed the record, and the men approached their partners of choice until they were all swept up in the music. The only ladies who remained seated were Hanim-*Effendi* and Diggin Rose. Mannig considered sitting beside them, but then she heard a solo piano piece wafting in from the parlor. She sauntered in, joining her nieces on the sofa.

Mesmerized, she listened.

Chin resting in one hand, she felt her eyelids drooping when the lady played the lower notes. Then the pianist's fingers wandered to the higher notes. Mannig's thoughts reached heights she never knew existed. Her emotions were spiraled into swaying forests and trickling brooks—all the while, the pianist's fingers moved across the black and white keys. In a trance, Mannig forgot where she was, who surrounded her and why she was so lost in heavenly wonder. Was she hearing Mama's music in Adapazar? Not quite, but like her mother's, this music was produced by human fingers.

She opened her eyes, disoriented by the ensuing silence.

The pianist had ended the piece and was flipping to the next sheet of music.

Mannig approached her. "That was very beautiful," she said. "Does it have a name?"

"Oh, thank you," the lady smiled. "That's "*La fille aux cheveux de lin*," by Debussy"—"The Girl with the Flaxen Hair."

"Oh, there you are," Mardiros said, poking his head inside the parlor. "I've been looking for you. Come. We need to bid the guests *adieu*."

It was near dawn when Mardiros escorted his bride to their suite. "Did you enjoy the celebration?" he asked.

"Oh, yes!"

"What was the best part?" he asked her later, as he put on his pajamas.

"The music."

"I *do* have a fine selection of records," he nodded.

"I liked the piano music best," Mannig said.

As they crawled into bed, she murmured to him. "Do you remember your promise when you asked me to marry you?"

"I remember every moment of that day," he said, kissing her.

"You promised me music lessons."

"Yes, yes. I remember."

"I want to learn to play the piano," Mannig said. "I want to play '*La fille aux cheveux de lin*,' by Debussy, just like the pianist."

Chapter 16

The Haircut

MADAM MELBA, THE PIANO TEACHER, was amazed at how easily Mannig learned the fingering of the scales. She had been yearning to teach a budding talent, and as her student progressed, she convinced her to urge Mardiros to purchase a better instrument. The new Baldwin was hoisted upstairs to Mannig's compartment and, much to Hanim-*Effendi*'s dismay, the old one remained in the parlor so that the mediocre practicing of her granddaughters continued within earshot.

At first, Mannig felt honored by the special attention Madam Melba gave her. Gradually, she found herself locked into boring exercises when all she wanted to do was be left alone to experiment with the melodies that popped into her head. She relished the privacy of her parlor and rejoiced in a newly discovered freedom to practice without being heard by the Kouyoumdjians.

Grateful that their compartment was at the far end of the *qasr*, Mannig kept the doors shut and the curtains drawn tightly, lest she bother her in-laws. She loved her piano and was enthralled by how her fingers were able to produce music. She'd like nothing better than to practice throughout the day and all night long—if Mardiros were absent, that is. What bothered her most were all the interruptions by her nieces or nephews.

"Will you help me with my history lesson?" Hagop, her fourteen-year-old nephew, asked. "My mother says you've learned more about King Dirtad of Armenia at the orphanage than we'll ever read in this textbook."

I, a teacher? she thought. *Even though I've never been a pupil in a regular school?*

The first glance at the cover of the book gave her the confidence she needed—it depicted Mount Ararat, which Armenians claimed to be the heart of their origin. "This is Armenia," she said, uncurling the corners of the mistreated text. "Did you know that Noah of the World's Greatest Flood, mentioned in the Bible, landed here?"

"You mean on Mount Ararat?" Hagop's brown eyes grew rounder.

"And that Noah instantly became an Armenian?" she teased. "Furthermore, his first crop was grapes."

"So what?" Hagop let out a peep of a question.

"Well, that's why our bishop sips grape-juice during mass," Mannig said.

"My friends say he sips *wine*," Hagop interrupted.

"Wine … grape juice … only he would know the difference," Mannig said, flipping the book cover. She brushed her palm across the title page, relishing the feel of paper. She reverently turned the pages. "We didn't have books at the orphanage. Our teacher held a textbook like this one in his left hand and, with a piece of chalk stored in his pocket, wrote the whole paragraph on the slate. We, the orphans, sat on *mindares*. Do you know what a *mindare* is?"

He nodded. "A floor-cushion to sit on?"

"Yes. That's all we owned. My knees were my desk. I copied the text on the one sheet of paper I owned and later on, in my tent, I memorized it before I erased the whole page so I'd have a blank one for the next day's lesson."

"Why didn't you write the lesson in a notebook?" Hagop gave her a pensive look.

"We only had one piece of paper." She stared out the window, nostalgic for the days before the deportation. "I had a notebook in kindergarten. At the orphanage, I always dreamt of sitting on a bench with a desk like the ones in my kindergarten in Adapazar. How I loved that class. I worshipped my teacher—Miss Romella. I loved my friends—Hasmig and I played *tag* in the school courtyard. I even remember a rhyme we memorized together. The whole class recited it in unison. I still recall it." Mannig cleared her throat and closed her eyes. She pictured herself standing up to recite and imitated her own childish voice:

> To go to school is such delight,
> To play and sing, to read and write.
> I am still small, but always will
> Have the desire to learn and drill.
> Like my mother, she advises,
> Disciplines and admonishes.
> Like my mother, I will love her.
> Her lessons will last forever.

She cleared her throat again and resumed speaking in her normal tone. "You see, the gendarmes plucked us out of our normal lives and stranded us

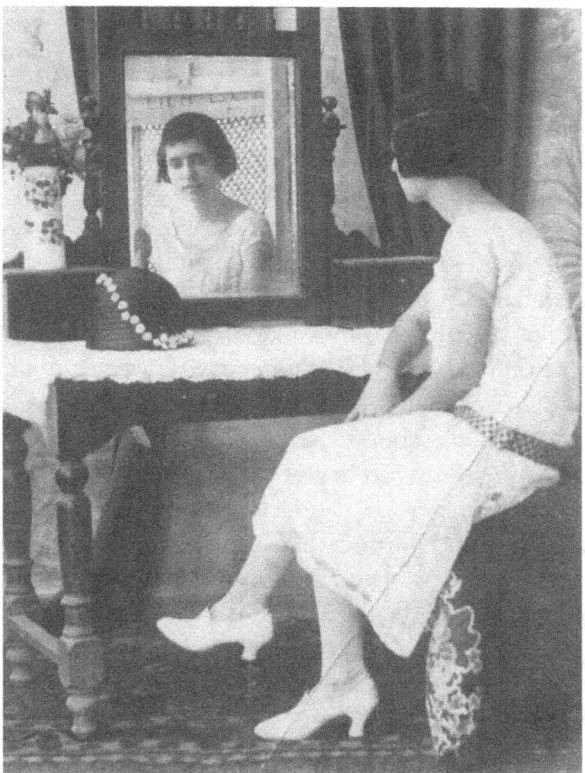

Mannig, 1922.

across the Mesopotamian desert." Her nephew had come to her for help with ancient history; instead he devoured Mannig's stories about her life before marrying Mardiros.

While she appreciated her popularity in the *qasr*, she craved solitude. *Will I ever be on my own?* She wanted the freedom to practice her piano lessons and the privacy to indulge in music.

Her nieces, too, demanded her time.

"I need a new dress for Evelyn's party," Meliné insisted, confronting Mannig at the door. "You have a great sense of style." Mannig felt flattered but unhappy about missing another day to practice the scores she wanted to memorize.

Her five nieces filled the car and Mahmoud drove them to Orozdi Bek. The girls tried on every dress the saleslady brought. Mannig was dazzled by the array of clothing. *Choices. Choices.* The girls' concentration on fabrics, flair and fit amazed her. There seemed no end to their continuous analysis of color, design or panache. She couldn't understand why one chiffon dress would be more suitable than another.

"This one hugs your body," Lizinka said to Meliné and then when Margot tried it on, she said, "That's not your color."

Isn't a dress just a cover? Its color, incidental?

The girls urged Mannig to try on a few outfits herself. She, too, could have selected as many gowns as her heart desired. But "wants" did not exist in her vocabulary. As an orphan, she only knew about needs. Still unused to listening to her heart, she decided that what she already owned was all she needed. Bemused, she watched her nieces experiment with this or that while they chattered on about their likes and dislikes as to style and color. She couldn't help but remark upon the jarring differences between the language of her nieces and that of her orphan friends. Only a few weeks earlier, if she worried at all about clothing it was about whether to wash the summer uniform and stay in her tent while it hung to dry or wear it one more day with its stains. Such thoughts were immaterial when it came to her winter uniform—it didn't get washed until spring. Not once had she wished for more clothing. Her nieces, on the other hand, wanted an unlimited number of new gowns.

A waste of a whole day! she thought. But she remained silent, wishing she were fingering the keys of her piano instead.

Another time, Maggie came knocking on her door. "Let's cut our hair," she suggested, walking in with a pair of sewing scissors in her hand. "Look at these pictures." She flipped the pages of a *Vogue Magazine*. Using her best French accent, she added, "I want to look *moderne* like this *modelle* on the runway."

Each of them scrutinized the photographs, then the models, before turning around to eye her own image in the mirror.

Maggie removed her tortoise-shell hairclip and shook out her brownish auburn tresses. "Do it!" she insisted, handing Mannig the scissors. "Cut here! Close to my ear."

Timidly, Mannig clasped the scissors, admired the sheen of the metal, opened and closed its blades. "I don't know how." The sound of the scratchy blades cut through her feelings of inferiority, taking her back to the time her mother had clipped off the hair of every member of her family to prevent the lice from nesting. She had actually saved their lives. They had pitched their makeshift tent in Katma on the deportation route and found themselves in the center of a typhus epidemic that was rampant in the Tent City of the Armenian refugees.

"The disease is spread by lice," her father had said, prompting her mother to resort to stealing a pair of scissors—more like a pair of garden shears. In the quiet of night, she hacked off everyone's hair. Mannig would never forget the shock on their faces the following day when all the children gazed at the bald heads of their siblings. Her father, too. But Mama had torn off a piece of her hem and wrapped it around her head. Months later, her mother's words haunted Mannig. When most of her family had perished under the whips of the gendarme, she had muttered, "I wish we could thwart off the deadly gendarmes as we did the lice in Katma."

Maggie was pulling on Mannig's sleeve. "What are you waiting for?" She held a strand away from her face. "I want you to clip right down to here. See my earlobe? I want my hair that short."

After a moment's hesitation, Mannig convinced herself. *If my mother could do it, I can, too.*

It took the whole morning to shape Maggie's hairdo. When both finally nodded their approval, Maggie said, "It looks like it does in the movies! It's wonderful. I love it. You ought to do it, too. I'm sure you'll look even more like those flapper-girls. Come, Mannig. It's your turn."

"What would Mardiros say?" Mannig asked, setting the scissors aside. Mardiros had gone to Felloujeh to settle some disputes among their farm workers. He was accompanied by his brother Dikran and nephew Badrig—Rose's twenty-year-old son, the jewel of her eye and resembling the late Karnig, the oldest male of the family. They wouldn't be back for several days.

"Uncle Mardiros is a great sport," Maggie asserted, picking up the scissors. "He is courageous himself. He married you, didn't he?"

"Isn't this too radical a thing to do without his consent?" Mannig whispered. After all, he had been her confidant and advisor in all matters since their marriage.

"He will probably not even notice the difference," Maggie said, removing the ivory hair clip from Mannig's bun. "The men are too intense about the farmlands these days. Besides, yours isn't even as long as mine used to be."

Within the hour, the two teenagers stared at their images and giggled. Both were proud of their *moderne* look—their description of their angular hairdos.

The supper gong chimed and the two gazed at each other. Neither said a word.

After the second chime, Maggie whispered as if afraid of being overheard. "Let's wait …. Let the others flock into the dining room before we do."

"Should we cover our heads?" Mannig asked.

"That will call everyone's attention to us," Maggie said. "Normally, they'd be chattering amongst themselves and not even notice us."

Maggie couldn't have been more wrong, but Mannig couldn't tell whether the eerie atmosphere in the dining room was real or due to her anxiety. Even so, she scooted into her seat at the adult table following Maggie, who slithered into hers at the children's table.

The one-second-long silence before the storm ended with a litany of criticism from the far end of the table.

"I will not tolerate a hussy at my dinner table," Khosrof shouted, banging the table top with his hand. "You're disgracing the Lord's table with that head of yours."

While Sara, his wife was startled by the shaking of the goblets, the others stared toward the object of his wrath—Mannig.

"*Amahn! Amahn!*" Exclamations came from every direction.

Mannig stole a quick glance at Maggie, who instantly cast her eyes down at her plate. Discreetly, Mannig, too, dropped her chin, staring at her lap. *What have we done?*

"Is this what they teach you at the orphanage?" Khosrof rattled on, "to look like a prostitute? To have no respect for decency? To foul tradition? How foolish of me to have wasted my money on those orphans—Kouyoumdjian money, no less."

Mannig wanted to defend herself and her orphanage. She wished she could explain that she never, ever had heard of European fashions until she joined their family; and that it was not her idea—that the real instigator was Maggie, Khosrof's own daughter.

If only Mardiros were here.

"Are you taking advantage of Mardiros' absence?" Khosrof continued. "You think you're a free mouse when the cat's away?"

His gaze pricked her. She shuddered.

"Did Mardiros realize he was marrying a trollop?" he continued.

Why hadn't Mardiros warned her about his oldest brother? Not that she could have done anything. Mardiros had only cautioned her about Rose. If she had anticipated any criticism, it should have come from her oldest sister-in-law. With those thoughts, Mannig sensed penetrating looks from Rose. She stayed unaware of how the rest of the in-laws were reacting to the venom being spewed from Khosrof's mouth.

Mannig kept mum as she felt her face flush. She knew she couldn't betray Maggie's friendship.

"I'm going to wait and see," Khosrof controlled his disgusted tone, "how Mardiros will discipline his wayward wife."

"I like that new haircut," interrupted Siranoush, Dikran's wife.

"Are you speaking up because your husband is in Felloujeh with Mardiros?" Khosrof disliked being challenged.

"Maggie's done it, too!" A voice from the children's table rang in Mannig's ear.

Along with the rest of her in-laws, she stared at Maggie as if looking at her accomplice for the first time. Not really … she stared at the culprit.

Now all eyes were on Khosrof. What would he say now that Maggie, his own daughter, had short hair, too?

"Oh! Ah!" rang throughout the dining room. "That's so pretty!" "It's clever!" "Magazine-like." "I want short hair, too!"

"The Americans call it *groovy*," Maggie said, shaking her short hair.

"Margot would look cute in that style, too," Siranoush exclaimed, nodding at her daughter.

"Shame on you, Diggin Siranoush," Khosrof wagged his finger at her. "You are also defending her because Dikran isn't here. Now *he* would have behaved like a real man." Looking at Toros, he continued, "You're Dikran's twin. What do you think he'd do?"

Toros shrugged his shoulders. So did Hermine, his wife. They didn't need to consider such issues, since they had given birth to four sons.

Siranoush defended her stance. "I know Dikran's thoughts. He'd agree that Margot would look very attractive in a modern haircut ... I mean, *groovy* haircut."

"If any of my daughters are tempted to copy *her*," Rose said, sticking her nose toward Mannig, "my Antranig would stand firm. I'm sure you'll hear his disapproval when he returns from Felloujeh. My son has character."

Suddenly, Lizinka pushed her chair back and stood up to face Rose, her mother. "We should all be cutting our hair. We copy every other European style. We hope to marry Romanian princes and English Dukes. I don't see why we shouldn't look like them as well." She grabbed a magazine she was hiding under her seat and, turning a few pages, displayed Madam Chanel's models parading down the hallway of a hotel in Monte Carlo. "See? They all have short hair."

"This is a conspiracy!" Khosrof said, clearing his throat. "A female plot. I don't know where you've learned such despicable manners." He cleared his throat again. "Must be the influence of the Chicago gangsters. Are they publishing a *how-to* magazine for women's indiscretions?"

Some giggled; others chuckled; all let out short bursts of relief. The mood changed. It was no longer about Mannig or haircuts. The pressure eased. Yet her throat was still dry, her breathing labored, her thoughts frozen in place. *What would Mardiros say? Really?*

A ruckus at the front door grabbed everyone's attention.

Mardiros, disheveled, rushed in. A disoriented Dikran followed.

Rose shoved her chair aside and rushed across the courtyard, yelling, "What happened? Where is Antranig?"

Chapter 17

Mistaken Identity

Frustrated at having failed to settle anything with the farmers in Felloujeh, Mardiros decided to return to Baghdad. He kicked off his knee-high boots and dusted off his khakis—an outfit similar to the military uniform he had worn in WWI that had intimidated so many, especially the farmers of the Kouyoumdjian lands. He swung his leg over his Arabian. "I don't know where those *fellaheen* are learning such insubordination," he said to his brother Dikran and Rose's son Badrig who had accompanied him on these parleys.

"What did you expect?" Dikran said. "Your temper puts off everyone." He, too, climbed upon his horse.

"Yelling is the only way to make Mustafa understand," Mardiros said in justification of his behavior. "I tried to control my real self. You must have noticed my shouts came from tightly sealed lips."

"That Mustafa got really angry," Badrig said. "Every time you yelled, his eyes flared, and he muttered through his mustache. He even spit after you turned your back to him. The two of you *eat each other's flesh.*"

"He'll recover. Like my radio, after a couple of slaps to its side." Mardiros tried to underplay the breakdown in settling Mustafa's demands. Ignoring the lateness of the hour, he added, "Let's get going." It would take three to four hours to cover the desert stretch of forty miles between Felloujeh and Baghdad. "We will have a bite in Abu Ghraib," he said, clicking his tongue and reining his horse eastward. "Sheikh Dhari will welcome us."

"I realize he was Hagop Agha's friend," Badrig said, "but does the Sheikh's son remember him as my grandfather?"

"He is a Bedou, isn't he?" Mardiros referred to the long memories of the Bedouin and their traditional welcome to all visitors.

The setting sun behind them quickly gave way to a moonless night—not much light to guide their path. They might have relied on the North Star, but instead kept to the asphalt road built by the British from Baghdad to Felloujeh (and beyond to Ramadi, to Rutba and finally to Amman, Jordan), which glistened beneath the plethora of awakening stars.

After an hour of riding, Mardiros' thighs ached. If, at thirty-two, bodily discomforts occupied his mind, how much worse was his brother, ten years his senior, feeling? "Dikran," he said, "we could dismount if you need to stretch your legs. The horses need relief, too."

"I'm too old for this," Dikran grunted. "Next time, we either drive or you get Toros to deal with the *fellaheen*, even if he isn't the best negotiator."

"The women needed the car," Badrig said. "They were invited to tea at Diggin Sarah Tatossian's house."

"Since you brought your bride to the *qasr*," Dikran said to Mardiros, "there seems to be no end to those tea parties. With all the farming problems we're having, it's time to consider business before pleasure."

"I'll take care of ...." Mardiros began, but before his voice could float into the dank evening air, it was consumed by a gunshot. Startled, he slid off his saddle onto his stomach, grabbing the prancing legs of his horse. While patting the horse's hind leg with his left hand, he pulled out his revolver with his right, desert soil spraying onto his face.

He spit out the dirt as quietly as he could, but a bulky thump shook the ground under his belly.

"My ankle!" Dikran moaned.

"Did they hit you?" Enraged, Mardiros cocked his revolver and glued his ear to the desert sand. Encouraged by the diminishing sound of galloping horses, he hissed, "Badrig? Get your revolver and back me up."

"No, no," Dikran said. "The bullet missed me. I hurt myself dismounting.... I panicked."

"Badrig! Let's go get him, anyway," Mardiros insisted.

Whinnying disturbed the silence. Fuming snuffles filtered into the stillness in rhythm to the scraping of hoofs.

No sound came from Badrig.

Seeing the silhouette of a slumped figure, Mardiros dashed to the horse.

No breath or movement came from him. "He is hit! They've shot him!" Mardiros shouted so loudly he could have been heard within one hundred miles. Even as his voice dissipated in the desert air, the pain inflicted by the sight of warm blood dripping down the saddle stopped his breath and roiled his veins.

The pain increased as they escorted Badrig's body to Baghdad on a cart provided by Sheikh Dhari. How terrible to be the bearer of bad news to Rose,

Mannig, 1926, at the *qasr* in Felloujeh.

again! He had already played that role ten years earlier when he'd informed her of the death of Karnig, her husband—dead of typhus in a Turkish prison.

Especially penitent, Mardiros was doubly sorrowful. He refused to imagine what awaited him at the *qasr* when he announced Badrig's demise. Badrig was her only son and heir to the Kouyoumdjian side of her family. Aside from him, she had only three daughters. He was the jewel of her eye.

While the whole Kouyoumdjian family became consumed in preparations for the funeral, Mardiros struggled with his role. He empathized with Rose. Her pent-up agony might have been vented had the Kouyoumdjians taken part in the classical wailing and lamenting Middle Eastern tradition demanded. He wanted to hibernate in his own compartment, to be consoled by Mannig. Instead, he relied on his brothers to assign him to the duties funeral arrangements required. His manliness demanded that he control his emotions and tolerate the accusatory eyes of his sister-in-law. He stayed busy to avoid reliving his pain.

Everyone sympathized with Rose's double misfortune. She had already been clad in black for the past ten years to mourn her husband. The women dressed in black as well, albeit patterned and sewn by several seamstresses; each of them already had at least one black dress in her closet. For forty days they also covered their hair with black sashes in her presence or in public, while the men maintained a black satin band on their jacket sleeve. Dancing, music or amusements were forbidden, and they kept a constant eye on the children so they did not run around or laugh. Other than the regular mealtimes, the *qasr* was as quiet as a tomb.

After the formal funeral procession and the lowering of the casket into the Kouyoumdjian plot at the Armenian Apostolic Church of Baghdad, the mourners paid their respects at the *qasr*, sipping bitter coffee or cognac.

Rose sat at the far end of the parlor, surrounded by her three daughters—Iskouhi, Lizinka and Meliné. Veiled in black lace, she remained stoic and cast her eyes to the floor as the long line of Baghdad society expressed their condolences.

Mardiros stood watch at the front door to greet the guests. Acting as sentry served its purpose. He wished to experience his pain in his own way rather than camouflage it with civilities. Listening to eulogies would be torturous—be it in the parlor with the ladies or in the courtyard with the men, who smoked incessantly. Mannig's presence, standing behind him, was all the affection he needed.

During a lull in the stream of visitors, he delegated Fareed, the *qasr* valet, to stand in for him. He felt the need to approach Rose. He wanted to weep with her, for her and about the tragedy of losing his young nephew. "Come with me," he said to Mannig. "I don't know what to say, but with you beside me, I will think of something."

He surprised himself when he knelt before Rose and kissed her hand.

Unflinching, she remained passive.

Mardiros backed away and was about to sit nearby when Fareed approached and whispered into his ear. "The assassin's lawyer is at the door. He wishes to speak with you."

Mardiros took leave of Rose.

"What can I add? Hasn't our lawyer disclosed all the details to him?"

"I told him so, myself," Fareed said, "but the fellow insists upon speaking with you."

"We were ambushed within a mile or two of Abu Ghraib," Mardiros said to the lawyer. "We didn't see anyone or hear anything. His shot came out of nowhere, and the rider disappeared. Sheikh Dhari came to our aid."

"The judge dismissed the case," the lawyer explained to Mardiros. "He says that vendetta cases are beyond his jurisdiction."

"What vendetta?"

"Mustafa—the assassin …."

"M-m-mustafa?" Mardiros stuttered. "What Mustafa?"

"He says he fired the shot."

"Are you talking about Mustafa, our Felloujeh overseer?" Mardiros mumbled, not believing his ears.

The lawyer nodded. "Mustafa told the judge he shot the wrong person. He aimed to kill Matruloze-*Effendi*."

The Kouyoumdjians mourned the unprecedented murder of one of their own. Badrig had been gunned down en route to Baghdad from Felloujeh—by an assassin who had intended to kill Mardiros.

Chapter 18

Good News, Good News

"The fish stinks from the head," Mardiros confided in Mannig. He was using a Turkish idiom to describe the tense atmosphere of the *qasr* trickling down from Rose's seniority status. She remained inconsolable, even after the marriage proposal to her oldest daughter, Iskouhi. She chose not to be present when the Kouyoumdjians choreographed the engagement soirée, which was the responsibility of the bride's family, according to Armenian custom. She was uninterested in the bride's trousseau—normally the most pleasurable task of the wedding arrangements. She abstained from dictating or rejecting any details about her daughter's nuptials. No one could ascertain whether her gloom was due to grief over her son's death or to the fact that the wedding, traditionally arranged by the groom's family, would be conducted in Alexandria, Egypt.

Her mood changed, however, when the groom, Telemaque Tutunjian, asked her and her two other daughters to move in with his family. After all, Egypt had accommodated a large number of Rose's ancestors, the Gulbenkians, another proud dynasty in the Middle East. Her family had consented to Rose's betrothal to Karnig but resented her move to Baghdad.

"I'm not surprised," Mardiros continued, "she can't wait for the day she won't have to see my face anymore."

Hanim-*Effendi*'s plea to her to stay with the Kouyoumdjians was half-hearted. With Rose and her family gone, there would be fewer mouths to feed and one less residence at the *qasr* needing maintenance. Her family's concern, lately, was financial. The crops at the farms in Felloujeh had failed several years in a row. Her sons' grandiose schemes to reep profits similar to those of American plantations collapsed. The cotton crop failed the first year due to swarms of locusts. The next year weevils attacked. Instead of returning to the traditional wheat and barley crops on the third year, the brothers pursued their misguided ambitions for supremacy in cotton production. Drought dried every shrub the following year and the next season most of their acreage on the Felloujeh Peninsula was flooded by that meandering and unregulated river, the Euphrates.

Having to manage a ledger with more expenses than income placed Hanim-*Effendi* in a new role. In a country where few embraced the concept of savings in a bank, she resorted to selling heirloom sterling silverware for cash. Meanwhile the family maintained its façade of glamour and sociability, accepting and reciprocating dinner invitations, tea gatherings and philanthropic events.

Mannig enjoyed most of these social occasions as long as Mardiros was with her. The tea parties were a different story. She wanted to become one of the ladies of Baghdad society, but lacking upper class airs, she felt distinctly apart. It did not bother her because the ladies were sophisticated, educated, and sociable. They accepted and respected her without prejudice, but she couldn't help feeling inferior. She didn't know how to express her opinions—not that she had political views about the Iraqi royal family and the Prime Minister or could share her literary analysis of the works of Somerset Maugham or Gertrude Stein. Talk about celebrities or famous vacation spots in Northern Africa sounded like a foreign language to her. She was afraid to open her mouth lest she reveal her lowly history at the orphanage. It didn't occur to her that she might contribute to the understanding of these high class ladies about lives beyond their own. She feared being tagged "simple," and thus a regrettable choice for a bride in the Kouyoumdjian *qasr*. Being self-conscious, she could hardly swallow a bite of the scrumptious *ghoorabia* or luscious baklava. Her thoughts revolved around how to participate in the afternoon chat even when the conversation veered to complaints about the servants. She always returned home disgusted with herself for being so timid.

No matter how much she psyched herself up to be otherwise, at the end of the day, she went to bed wishing she had established some sort of a rapport with the ladies. She was reluctant to confess to Mardiros how awkward she felt at these female gatherings. She wanted to prove her worth. She even neglected to mention how queasy she sometimes felt. She was glad he hadn't noticed how she abstained from eating confections, and instead imbibed black and unsweetened tea.

"Hanim-*Effendi* has received a tea invitation from a Diggin Sara Zengeeneh," she informed Mardiros.

"Wonderful!" Mardiros said. "She is probably the richest lady in Baghdad. That's why they call her Zengeeneh … meaning 'rich' in Arabic."

The lady's title alone intimidated Mannig, not to mention the continuous reminder of how flattering it was to be the guest of honor. As the honoree, she consented to buy a new dress, Maggie as her consultant. As usual, she would have settled for the first outfit she tried on.

"That's too tight," Maggie dismissed her choice. "You must be getting fat!"

Eventually they agreed on a white wool-jersey suit with a brown velvet collar and cuffs, and a slight flare at the hem, which skimmed her ankles. Brown, ankle-high buttoned shoes completed her ensemble.

She felt comfortable in Diggin Zengeeneh's spacious parlor but squirmed and fidgeted, debating the most opportune moment to contribute to the ladies' chat. Moments came and moments went, and she failed to muster the courage to say anything. While the ladies were engrossed in tasting the pastries or sipping tea, her eyes scanned her surroundings. A beautiful white grand piano was tucked in the corner, behind an oriental screen. Plucking up her courage, she looked at the hostess and said, "I'm sure your beautiful piano produces beautiful music."

Acknowledging the compliment, Sara Zengeeneh told her older daughter to play for the guests. The pretty girl shook her head and bent down to smooth the ruffles of her georgette dress. The younger sister, too, lowered her gaze and declined. The hostess appeared embarrassed. She crushed her handkerchief in her fist when no one volunteered to entertain.

Mannig surprised herself. She approached the piano, carefully lifted the lid, and couldn't prevent herself from touching the keys. Lost in her passion, she slid onto the stool and played Schubert's "Serenade," one of her favorite pieces she had memorized. Before she concluded it, she switched keys and segued into Beethoven's "Moonlight Sonata." Immersed in her playing, she was about to begin another piece when she was startled by the applause of the ladies, who hovered around her, hurling a slew of questions.

"Where did you learn to play like that?"

"I didn't know orphanages trained master pianists."

"Are you sure you weren't enrolled at a conservatory?"

Mannig felt dizzy, but not from their accolades. She had experienced a similar disorientation earlier.

Hanim-*Effendi* was thumping the floor with her cane, halting the jabber and alerting Mannig again to her surroundings. "Mannig is a natural—a good student," she said, praising her daughter-in-law, which Armenians were wont to do. "She has been taking lessons for only a few months. She doesn't stop at the end of those lessons; she practices and plays all the time. Best of all, she concocts her own melodies. I wish her room were next to mine so I'd hear her all the time."

Mannig couldn't have imagined such raves coming from anyone, least of all her mother-in-law. How wrong she had been to have feared the practicing might disturb her! She hoped the compliments weren't because Mardiros was her favorite son.

Once again, she felt dizzy … especially as she returned to her seat with the ladies.

"Are you all right?"

"Her face is white …."

"What is the matter?"

Mannig collapsed.

One of Sara Zengeeneh's servants dashed to the Kouyoumdjians', several blocks away, to inform Mardiros, and another went to the clinic to fetch Dr. Kurdian, the Armenian physician in Baghdad.

By the time medical assistance arrived, Mannig had regained consciousness, unaware of the fuss she had caused. Hanim-*Effendi* was holding her hand while Sara Zengeeneh calmly stood by.

Dr. Kurdian greeted them and asked everyone but Hanim-*Effendi* to leave the room. He set his black bag beside Mannig and brought out the stethoscope.

Never having been checked by a physician, Mannig freed her hand from her mother-in-law's grip and recoiled. She folded her arms, closed her eyes and wished for the magical genie to save her.

Her wish materialized in a familiar voice. "It's all right."

She looked up and Mardiros was at her side. She wanted to jump out of her seat, hold his hand and vanish with him somewhere—anywhere but this parlor. The scene she had created embarrassed her beyond belief. *Those classy ladies wouldn't faint,* she thought, *not ever …. None would make a spectacle of herself. They're cultured … know how to behave … are trained to control mishaps. They'd never succumb under similar circumstances.*

The doctor removed the stethoscope from his ears, slid it into his physician's bag and locked its clasp. "It's all right," he declared, "your heart is fine. You'll be fine, too." He then turned to Mardiros. "May I speak with you?"

As in a dream, Mannig saw the two men walk toward the parlor door. Dr. Kurdian whispered something. The two men shook hands. The Doctor tipped his hat and left. Mardiros approached his mother and whispered to her. The two embraced each other.

Mannig felt his warm lips on her forehead.

She heard his joyous voice. "You are pregnant."

Chapter 19

Escape from the *Qasr*

THE COUPLE WAS BLESSED WITH a beautiful and healthy baby boy. Mardiros named him Hagop, after his father. Mannig would have preferred Bedros, her father's name, or Setrak, the name of the brother who had both been massacred by the Ottoman gendarmes. Her sister, Adriné, had named her two daughters Heranoush for their mother, and Sirarpi for their sister, who had also perished during the massacre of the Armenians.

The name Hagop sounded too old to Mannig, so she added the diminutive "*ig.*" Hagopig revived the past in ways Mannig could not have foreseen. While caring for her tiny son, she relived her own babyhood. His cries at bath time reminded her of her own tears—on wash-days in a round metal tub in Adapazar while her grandmother, Haji-doo, scrubbed her knees and elbows. *He must remember me.* She scrubbed his elbows and knees. His squeals of delight while taking his first steps prompted smiles of her own infant exuberance when she had escaped from her mother's grip. Not too long ago, really—barely fifteen years earlier. She was a child herself. Her parents must have had their own hopes and visions for their family, but alas, these were tragically interrupted at the onset of the War in 1914.

Mardiros imagined pursuits he had not thought of until he held his son in his arms. His life had taken on new meaning at thirty-two when he married Mannig, but Hagopig's birth made it richer still. The children of his friends became more interesting; he enjoyed exchanging stories. Anytime he hugged Hagopig, new aspirations for his son filled his thoughts. *His square jaw is certainly mine!* Hagopig's wide forehead was his, too. *He'll make a world-renowned judge.* Likewise, his son inherited Mannig's dark-brown almond eyes. *Might he love music as his wife did?*

For two years, Hagopig's presence guaranteed further assurance that the Kouyoumdjian family line would be perpetuated. The severity of their financial problems, however, could not be hidden. Year after year, the crops in Felloujeh failed—due to swarms of locust one year, flooding of the Euphrates the next. The following season a great drought hit the whole region of Diwaniyeh, including their farms. Upon Hanim-*Effendi*'s insistence, the four brothers applied themselves to saving their family's reputation even as they were losing their wealth. They agreed to relinquish their Baghdad *qasr* and move to Felloujeh, where the four brothers could devote their energy full-time to make farming profitable.

Neither Mardiros nor Mannig knew when Hagop Agha (the patriarch of the Kouyoumdjians who had died in 1913) acquired the prime property across the Euphrates in Felloujeh, sixty miles west of Baghdad. This "summer" *qasr* was the only house for miles on their vast property, in the peninsula jutting along the meandering river flowing from the north. Similar to their residence in Baghdad, this, too, was a *qasr*, "castle" in Arabic. No particular architectural style or shape, it consisted of a long building with a short wing at each end. Hanim-*Effendi*, her sons and their families settled into their private living quarters on the second floor. The ground floor comprised the kitchen, the bathroom, and an office. The rest of the space was used to store grains. The only projection that disturbed the otherwise flat façade of the building was a balcony that looked as if it had been stuck on the wall as an afterthought.

The family soon became settled into their *qasr* on the Euphrates, admittedly not as lavish a domain as the Baghdadi one. With a few minor changes, the Felloujeh *qasr* was easily remodeled to accommodate all five families in separate compartments. The smallest quarters again housed Mardiros and his small but growing family—Mannig being close to delivering her second child.

Their new flat was next to the huge cantilevered balcony that overhung the river. Mannig strolled along its wooden railing often to inhale the breeze chasing the current. She relished fresh air. She had sought open air ever since her near death experience on a train during the deportation of her family, when they were crammed in one cattle boxcar along with fifty to one hundred refugees. Near suffocation, Mannig had crawled, slithered and dragged herself through the feet of the crowd to reach a hole in the wall of the boxcar. She stuck her nose into it, for the breath of life. Her younger sister, Sirarpi, suffocated to death, as did several other deportee children. Mannig was convinced her survival was due to this one source of fresh air.

From the balcony, she faced the Felloujeh village on the river's meandering east bank. The green-painted, single-lane metal bridge edged their property on the east bank, which connected it to mainland Felloujeh, the link between Baghdad and Amman, Jordan. Their Felloujeh *qasr* was the only residence and

Early Family Portrait at the *qasr* in Felloujeh, 1929.
Left to right: Mannig, Aida, Hagopig, Mardiros.

the last trace of civilization for travelers between Iraq and the Mediterranean Sea for 2,000 miles.

Mannig was content with her husband and Hagopig, but it was her piano that made her happy. She took advantage of their location in the *qasr*. The far end overlooking the Euphrates allowed her to play whenever she felt like it. A day never passed that she didn't entertain Hagopig with music.

Mardiros, too, appreciated their location. After a day's horseback riding across the fields, yelling at the farmers or demonstrating modern technologies to primitive laborers, he'd return home without alerting his relatives. He could relax in their flat, listening to his records on the gramophone. Occasionally he'd pick up his flute and accompany Mannig with a lullaby at Hagopig's bedtime. The comfortable routine evolved into Mannig's desire to learn English—she wanted to read Alexander Dumas and Victor Hugo, the English translations on Mardiros' bookshelf. Mardiros enjoyed teaching her and she proved him to be an outstanding instructor by learning quickly. Within a few weeks, she mastered the beginner's text of *"Run mouse, run. If you do not run, the cat will catch you."* Mardiros rummaged around the bookshelves of his brothers for a suitable text. Finding none, he created lessons and drills of his own, until such time as he could drive to Baghdad and find a text book seller.

Mardiros spent some nights away from the *qasr*, sending word that he needed to parlay with the sheikh whose tribe worked on the wheat fields. He would set up his own tent and then send a messenger to notify his mother, including a note for Mannig—a love letter in English—telling her *to practice on her own.*

Unbeknownst to him, Mannig, too, aspired to advance her studies. During his absences, she'd read a page of *Les Miserables* aloud. Hearing her voice pronounce the foreign words in private increased the drama of the plight of Cosette—an orphan whose struggles paralleled hers. Next she picked *The Count of Monte Cristo.* She mouthed the words, from the first page to the last. It didn't matter if she understood only ten percent of the story. At the end of each chapter, she took pride in her accomplishment.

In the meantime, education became a problem for the eight school-age Kouyoumdjian children. Felloujeh had only one small Arab school for girls and another for boys—both located in the center of the village across the river.

"We can't send our children to the government public schools!" the mothers objected. "Isn't there a private school for the cream of Felloujeh society?"

"Of course not!" scoffed the fathers. "What's in the village couldn't meet our needs. Besides, every subject is taught in Arabic."

"They already speak Arabic," murmured a few voices. "Some, better than Armenian!"

They all agreed that Felloujeh could not meet the needs of their sophisticated style and that the children needed to learn Armenian. And English. And French.

The eight cousins' romping in the farms with Bedouin children, hunting rabbits and jackals, came to a halt. The adults organized homeschooling to keep them out of mischief. Siranoush, Dikran's wife—the most cultured among the women—took it upon herself to offer the sort of education befitting the "standing" of the family.

A room in the *qasr* was allocated for that purpose and completely equipped with desks, blackboard and all the other necessities. The cousins attended school during regular hours, six days a week. The adults instructed them in the three Rs in Armenian, taught them English as a second language and French as a third.

Mannig wished to sit at one of those desks with her nieces and nephews. Instead, she was flabbergasted when Siranoush appointed her to teach the history of ancient Armenia. She was barely a year older than the Kouyoumdjian children and had no training as a teacher. In fact, her education consisted entirely of the lowly schooling at the orphanage. These sophisticated ladies who scoffed at the Iraq public schools now trusted their children's formative brains to her. With Mardiros's urging, Mannig obliged. Within a few weeks, she gained enough self-confidence to enjoy divulging details about the great wars waged by the Romans and then by the Persians against the Armenian Kingdom. Within a couple of months, she stopped, due to her pregnancy. Giving birth to a child in the countryside could be risky.

"Mardiros," Dikran's wife Siranoush said, "perhaps you ought to drive her to Baghdad and stay at a hotel until it's time to go to the hospital."

"It might be better to drive the doctor here," Khosrof's spouse Sara suggested.

"And deliver a baby in the *qasr*?" several others joined in to express their disbelief.

Being responsible for planning the family meals, Toros' wife Hermine asked, "How long would a doctor need to stay with us?"

Amid general conjecturing, Khosrof's daughter Maggie raised her hand. "There's an Armenian doctor in the village."

All eyes were on her. "How do you know?"

"Selma, my friend, said so," she explained, having just spent a night at the Mayor's residence across the river.

"Mardiros," Hanim-*Effendi* pointed at him. "Your job is to find that doctor first thing in the morning."

So Mardiros put on his black morning suit and paid his respects to the *Quaimaquam*—the Mayor of Felloujeh—who, also dressed in a suit, was reading the Arabic version of *The Baghdad Weekly*. The two chatted for an hour about the crops, the weather, and the latest British plans for Iraq. They sipped Arabic coffee, strong and bitter, not Mardiros' favorite. He preferred Turkish coffee. He limited his intake to one. He offered the mayor one of his pre-rolled cigarettes, even though the man preferred to inhale his smoke from the bubbling *nargeeleh*.

Finally the name of the Armenian physician in the village was revealed.

"Dr. Kurkjian." The *Quaimaquam* seemed delighted to be of use to Mardiros. "He is a good man. Good stock. We are fortunate our honorable government appointed him. A very knowledgeable person."

The Mayor then yelled out for his deputy, who scurried in, flipping one edge of his black-and-white checkered *keffiyeh* atop his head.

"Show our venerable Mardiros-*Effendi* where the doctor lives," he said. "Stay with him until he is done."

Mardiros cranked up his Ford and, seeing the deputy's hesitation, said,

"Come on, get in. There's nothing to fear. It's just like riding a bus. Haven't you gone to Baghdad in a bus?"

"*Laa, Effendi.*" The deputy shook his head, rearranging the flaps of his *dizhdasheh* within the silver-carved buckle of his belt. "It's not that. It's a long way to drive. But it's a short way to walk."

"Well, then," Mardiros said, swinging the door shut. "*Imshee.* Let's walk."

He followed the guide through the canvas-roofed alley of coppersmiths pounding on outsized trays or miniature decorative wares then stepped into an infusion of aromas wafting from gunnysacks of spices checkering the mud-packed path of the bazaar.

"Your *souq* looks like the one in Baghdad," Mardiros said.

"All *souqs* are based on the original one," the deputy said, and then politely added, "The original one, you know, *Effendi*, was set up by us, outside the walls of Baghdad—more than a thousand years ago."

The chatter of haggling females cut their conversation short but flavored the colorful yardage section. The cacophony ended with their entrance into the village center. A minaret looming in the east and several brick buildings completed the circle.

They stopped in front of a two-story structure. "The honorable doctor lives on the second floor, but his clinic is on the street level."

Before Mardiros pushed open the half open door, he handed his guide a dinar, for which the man reached to kiss his hand. "*Laa, laa,*" Mardiros dismissed the man, "you did a good job."

He and Dr. Leon Kurkjian bonded quickly. At the end of their first meeting, Mardiros extended a dinner invitation to the *qasr*.

Dr. Kurkjian, his very pregnant wife, Fortinee, and their two sons, Hrandt and Ara, both under seven years, delighted the Kouyoumdjians with their acquaintance. The boys learned how to ride horses from the host's children, and the adults enjoyed the social interaction with people outside their usual circle.

Within a month the doctor was rushed to the *qasr*.

Mardiros isolated himself in his parlor, worried about the consequences of having his child delivered outside of a hospital setting. He played record after record, flipped through the yellowed pages of his books. He paced the parlor, staring at the pastoral paintings on the walls, at the paisley designs flirting with ochre flowerets of the carpets. He focused on plaster holes on the walls. It was a colossal test of his nerves; the proof was in the four packs of cigarettes he smoked—one pack a day was usually his limit. Verdi's opera, *Aida,* was blaring when Dr. Kurkjian emerged from the bedroom, carrying an infant draped in lacey blankets.

"Well, Mardiros-*Effendi*," he said. "You now have a balanced family. Hagopig has a sister."

Even before Mardiros hugged his daughter, he knew he'd name her Aida.

Mannig liked the opera, too, so she didn't object to his choice, even though she had hoped to have a say in naming their children. She often wondered what prompted her own parents in their choices. If and when she bore another child, she would assert her will and name it herself.

"I think," Mardiros announced to Mannig a few months later, "this flat is too small for us. I will build a house just for us. There's a lot of space on our peninsula—not only for one house, but for several. Wouldn't you like to have your own private home?"

She was sure whatever Mardiros said or did was right. She'd had no problem adjusting from the Basra orphanage to a palatial abode in Baghdad, and then again to a large household in Felloujeh. She had blended well with his family, but unlike them, she did not concern herself with their problems, big or small—most recently with their bickering about the unprofitability of the farms. She did not understand finances, and it never occurred to her to question the expense of building a new house.

Instead, she knew she would adapt to their new situation. "We'll be raising our children independently from the family, then," she said.

"Like the Americans," Mardiros reminded her.

Within a few days, Lorry-trucks delivered bricks and cement, hustling along the makeshift mud road behind the *qasr* to the tip of the peninsula on the Euphrates. Watching their future home rise, one layer of bricks upon another, kept the couple fully occupied. That is, until Hagopig's constant fussing reminded them of their priorities.

A sudden high fever transformed Hagopig into a screaming toddler, choking for breath. Mardiros and Mannig rushed him to Dr. Kurkjian's clinic. The general practitioner assumed the child's fever was due to his inflamed tonsils. When simple aspirin failed to normalize his temperature, the doctor recommended surgery. "Tonsillectomy is a common procedure," he explained. "The medical community has embraced it since the beginning of civilization. A month doesn't go by without a surgeon somewhere cutting out those infected glands. Take him to Baghdad."

Hagopig's ear-piercing cries wrenched his parents' hearts. They elected surgery on the little boy. Mardiros drove his sick son to the hospital in Baghdad.

"You can take him home tomorrow," the surgeon suggested after removing the child's tonsils.

The following morning, Mardiros drove back to Felloujeh before Hagopig had fully recovered from the anesthetic.

He burned in high fever. They bathed him in cool waters. His body remained as hot as fiery coal.

In a few days, more infection set in.

Neither Dr. Kurkjian nor anyone else could do more.

Hagopig died.

Mannig screamed, hugging him. "Wake up, Hagopig! I should not have sent you to Baghdad. Why didn't I keep you here? I could have made you well. Wake up …. Even now, I can make you well … Wake up …."

Mardiros was in shock. He felt completely empty, incapable of expressing his pain. His throat dried up and his mind went blank.

He grabbed Hagopig from Mannig; held the child's head up. It slumped.

He cuddled it up again, leaning his chin against the baby's forehead for support. It drooped again.

He smacked his lips on the child's mouth. He blew. He blew more air, again and again.

The child remained lifeless.

Mardiros laid his son in his crib and then dashed out, calling out to his brothers to come and refute the reality he feared.

Later he sat on the floor beside the crib, devastated. He pressed his head in his hands. *I should have taken him to Beirut …. No, no. I should have taken him to Vienna. The world's best physicians are in Vienna.*

His regrets melted into tears, just as his hopes and dreams for his son evaporated into long sighs. He lay doubled over, prostrated beside the crib … and grieved.

Something in him died, too.

A large part of Mannig also died. Her life had been turned upside down. Her optimism was replaced by apathy; her desire for sociability vanished; her striving to improve herself faded. Losing her child was a far more brutal blow than losing her mother—actually, losing all six members of her family put together. They had died in torturous conditions, of starvation and beatings—this was a terrible fate in itself. But losing a son in the midst of affluence defied her understanding.

Her only escape from reality became the piano. She found solace in music. Without a plan or purpose, she touched the keys and became consumed in pieces in minor keys. She often forgot herself at the keyboard. Tears ran down her cheeks, no matter what she played. The more she played, the more profusely she cried, and this made her want to play more. Playing became an obsession.

As soon as their private home was completed, the couple welcomed the move. Neither of them wanted to be reminded of Hagopig. Their private abode offered a new environment without memories of Hagopig—a place unmarred by history, unfettered with the past. They sought a new beginning, a chance for a normal life.

They eagerly gave away all the furniture they had acquired for Hagopig. Mardiros assigned Farid, their chauffeur, to deliver it all to the Armenian Church.

Mannig offered Hagopig's clothing and toys to the maid who came to clean their compartment. "What should I do with this?" the maid asked, holding up a postcard sized piece of glossy paper.

"Where did you find this?" Mannig shrieked, snatching the photograph.

Without waiting for an answer, she tore into the bathroom and locked the door. With a pained heart, she leaned against the door and fell to her knees, tears rolling down. She peeked at the black and white picture of Hagopig supporting his one-year-old body on tiny legs while he grabbed the ribs of his crib. With a big happy smile, he looked straight at her.

It wrenched her heart.

Mardiros should not see this.

Chapter 20

"The Word Is ...."

What should I do? Mannig agonized over the glossy picture of Hagopig. Absentmindedly she wandered through their newly built home. *Discard it?* Perhaps she ought to cut it up into tiny pieces or burn it in the gas flames of her kitchen stove. *Vye! I would be torturing Hagopig.*

She walked to the center of their parlor. *I ought to hide it.* She closed her eyes and twirled in place as if she were playing hide-and-go-seek with her friends at the orphanage. Not quite dizzy, she stopped. Arms extended, she shuffled ahead until her middle fingers touched something. Sensing it was a book, she pulled it out. She flipped open the hardcover volume and placed the picture somewhere in the middle. Before closing the book, she removed the photograph one last time and let her lips touched its glossy surface. She remained that way—still and breathless—for several moments. Then she quickly snapped the book shut, picture and all, and slid it back into place, leveling its spine with the neighboring books.

She stepped backward and hesitated a moment before winding into a spin again. When she opened her eyes the walls of their parlor kept on spinning. She blinked and squatted on the carpet. Her huffing prevented the tears from spilling but sparked the memory of a little girl twirling in her yellow dress in Adapazar. As had that little girl so long ago, she dropped down onto the carpet and dried her tears. She didn't know where she had hidden Hagopig's picture.

"The word from the *qasr* is not good," Mardiros said, but paused when he saw her squatted on the floor. "What are you doing?" he chuckled. "You're so beautiful. Your pose is worthy of a picture. Too bad—the lighting is not good enough for my Kodak."

His voice alleviated the crushing pain in her heart, especially when he crouched beside her, hugged her in his lap and finger-brushed her hair. They sat, side-by-side, as one, but their thoughts couldn't have been farther apart.

"Dikran is very sick," he said of his brother. "Despite the medicine, he is not getting well." He stood up and helped her to her feet. "Hanim-*Effendi* told me to drive him to Baghdad immediately. Will you manage while I'm away?"

Mannig nodded. She'd managed orphanhood in famine and war-torn countryside. Why wouldn't she do the same in their new house?

"Siranoush is supposed to go with me," he said as he put on his fedora. He held the door open. "She ought to be near her husband in case he needs her."

He returned home the following day, only to be summoned by Hanim-*Effendi* again. This time to drive Margot, their daughter, to join her parents at the hospital. "The word is," Mardiros explained to Mannig, "that Dikran needs surgery. Apparently a wish-bone got stuck at the top of his intestines. It must have happened while he was gobbling chicken breast—you know how much he loves chicken!"

"How long will you be gone?" she asked.

"If he has to stay there, I'll be home tonight," he said. "But that means I will have to go back to fetch him when he is released from the hospital."

"You're becoming a regular chauffeur for the Kouyoumdjians," Mannig joked.

"Everyone says we're saving the salary we paid Farid to drive the family here and there."

Mannig would rather have him at home; she needed his confidence in her. She needed approval as much as she needed air or water. A new house, not fully finished or furnished, required a man's hand. She was learning about housekeeping by doing, but lack of experience often paralyzed her. *To cook rice with or without water* was a big question. When milk boiled over on the stove, she convinced herself that raw milk had to be less hazardous than the filthy edibles she had consumed for survival.

Why bother to dust? The wind blew from the tip of the peninsula daily, making dusting as useless as painting a snake and adding legs to it.

Motherhood overwhelmed her. Having lost a son, she now struggled to keep Aida safe and cope with another pregnancy.

Mardiros returned from Baghdad late in the evening. He stood by the front door and moaned. "Dikran is gone," he said. "The bone was not only stuck, but had punctured the membrane." He plopped down on the sofa, unable to continue.

"How about some tea?" Mannig offered, knowing how to brew it *à la* Kouyoumdjian—black, strong, sweetened and served with milk—from the time she had spent mingling with Baghdadi society.

"What I need is cognac," he said, and remained silent until he downed

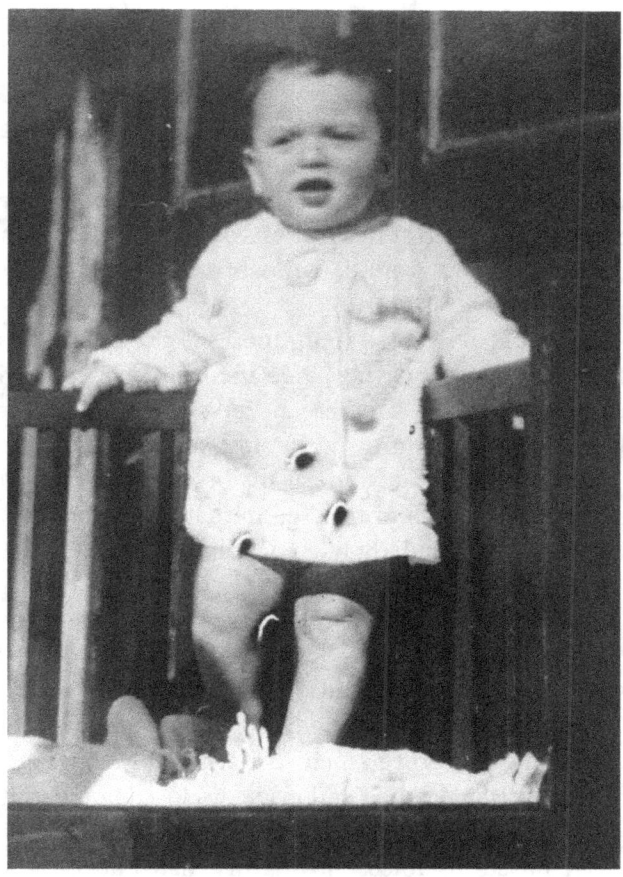

Hagopig at age 9 months, 1928.

two swigs, one after the other. "They say it was too late for him to benefit from surgery. The perforation had leaked into his abdomen. The poor man died of peritonitis … only forty-eight years old. Poor Margot, she is an orphan now."

Mannig couldn't understand how Margot would be an orphan when she still had a mother and lived with a bunch of aunts, uncles and cousins, not to mention that she was in her twenties. "What happened to Siranoush?"

"Sh-sh-she might as well be dead," Mardiros stammered. "She's locked herself in her room, won't eat anything, won't talk to anyone … won't even console her own daughter."

Articulate and compassionate, Siranoush was very likable. Mannig looked up to her—not only because of her classic beauty and elegant style but also because she was a role model. Mannig aspired to become as learned as her sister-in-law, even without the formal education that Siranoush had received at an elite school in Moscow.

Her hopes for camaraderie with her sister-in-law disappeared when word came that Siranoush was moving in with her sister's family in Baghdad.

The Kouyoumdjians in the *qasr* didn't like the idea.

They had resented Rose's departure to Egypt to live with her daughter's in-laws. Even more, they scoffed at her request to sell her Felloujeh share.

"She's adding salt to the wound," Khosrof said, pounding his fist on the dining table.

Now that Siranoush wanted out, too, the Kouyoumdjians hired a government-employed surveyor to divide the Felloujeh properties into five equal parcels—one for each brother and/or widow. Since Mardiros had already built a house for his growing family, that parcel of their property on the peninsula was deeded to him. If his brothers resented the privilege bestowed upon him by reason of residing in that prime location, they never told him. They hadn't particularly liked Mardiros' plan to live in a separate house, albeit a mere hundred yards away.

"It's not shameful," Hanim-*Effendi* had sighed. "I accept his wish for a separate life with his wife, as long as he retains his familial ties to the *qasr*."

Siranoush's move back to Baghdad seemed an affront to their elitist image. They had escaped the city to avoid an exposé of their dwindling fortune. Living together in one *qasr* proved their solidarity. Now, they could only hope Siranoush would be discreet when and if she disclosed family difficulties.

Khosrof blew a huge blob of phlegm into his handkerchief. "This is insufferable!" He raised his voice, shoving his chair out of the way to leave the dining room. "We're losing the long-standing reputation of our kinfolk." He took a few steps and faced his relatives, who, stunned, waited for his next outburst. "This is the last straw …. First, somebody moves to Alexandria; now this one goes to Baghdad. Are we going to proliferate across the whole universe? This is the end of our dynasty."

Chapter 21

The New Moon

Mardiros stopped at his front door, holding a *shabboot*—freshwater salmon of the Euphrates. Seeing his nephews and nieces poised at the entrance, he raised the fish in the air, proud of its three-foot length, and said, "This is a lucky day, eh?" He and the Mayor of Felloujeh had been surveying the extent of erosion along the bank of their peninsula. Rowing in calm waters, the two engineers had been startled when the fish had jumped into their boat, sending them into hysterical laughter.

"You brought luck," Mardiros told the Mayor, still shaking with amusement. "The *shabboot* jumped in for you."

"It's your boat," the Mayor chuckled. "The fish is yours."

"No, no, no!" Etiquette compelled Mardiros to object. "You are my guest. You are our esteemed Mayor. And this is God's gift to you."

"No, no, no!" the Quaimaquam argued, extending the quibble until Mardiros reached inside his khaki shorts for a coin to flip. Throughout the next hour they tittered about the suicidal salmon while gauging the depth and speed of the river. One controlled the plunger; the other attached the spindle to the depth rod. Mardiros reported the current speed and then the aquatic growth, while the Mayor recorded the details in his ledger. When they hit turbulent currents along the cliff-bank, they recorded their measurements without comment, the whirring winds of the September of 1930 filling the silence. Upon hitting excessive turbulence against the cliff banks, Mardiros promptly veered the boat along with the flow. "You're quite the irrigation expert," the Mayor repeated several times. "Our new government needs engineers like you. You shouldn't waste your luck on providential fishing."

The fish slapped its last throb at the bottom of the boat. The two guffawed, again.

"There are dams to be constructed." The Mayor, a civil engineer himself, clung to his idea. "Canals to be excavated, barrages to be built. I tell you, my friend, our whole country needs to be modernized. Did you tell me you studied in Istanbul?"

"I graduated from Robert College there," Mardiros said, nostalgic about his student life. "My nephew, Vahram, is finishing his last year there. His specialty is electrical engineering."

The Mayor glanced at Mardiros' khaki shirt, shorts and knee-high socks, reminiscent of the British military, and said, "I hope he'll work for our government."

"Oh, yes! The word is, he already has a job with the Iraqi Power Company."

"We need people with your skills, too," the mayor said.

"*Ee, wa'allah!*" Mardiros felt humbled. He removed his toppy, pulled a handkerchief from his shirt pocket and wiped away the sweat produced by the effort of rowing upstream. "I like to be of use. As the Armenians say, 'To be needed is the best way to be useful.'" After a pensive moment, they looked at each other and both opened their mouths to speak. Instead, they chuckled again. Mardiros gestured for the mayor to go first.

"The *Moudeer* of the Iraqi Irrigation Department is driving through tomorrow," he said, removing his *aqqal* and *keffiyeh* to also wipe his forehead—with the handkerchief pulled from his *dizhdasheh* robe. "Our King sent him on a mission to Jordan. I hear he is returning to Baghdad. He will stop at my office. I will speak with him about you. He and I are old friends, like kinfolk; we respect each other. Besides," he pointed with his index finger, "I'm older than he; he'd better listen to me!"

Mardiros liked the idea of his skills being put to use, and decided to reassure the Mayor of his qualifications. "As our honorable mayor, you know everything. You know my family's situation at the farms. We haven't been able to cover our expenses lately. This is our fourth year without profit. We've been selling parcels of land to get going. Our life has become like an onion—we peel and cry. I, myself, now own only this small peninsular area—and as you see, even that is eroding. I'm losing land to nature and yet the taxes don't go down. Everyone thinks we still own hectares and hectares."

"Now that I understand the situation," the Mayor said, swiping his keffiyeh across his neck, "my report will be different."

"Thank you, Mayor-*Effendi*. You do know I'm trying to become independent of my kin. I sketched the blueprint of my own house and built it so I could raise my family on my own. Two of my brothers have also left the *qasr*. I don't know how much longer Khosrof or Toros will hold onto their properties in Felloujeh. Of course, we have to consider the Hanim-*Effendi*. Even in her old age, her matriarchal authority is supreme with us."

"She'll go with Khosrof," the mayor suggested. "Isn't he the oldest among the Kouyoumdjians?"

"Yes, but the man has gone through a lot. His first wife died soon after Maggie was born. He has three children with his current wife. He loses his temper often. I can't see how he and my mother would get along. Well, these are some of the problems we face."

The men's conversation was minimal while they rowed downstream.

"I still think," Mardiros said upon mooring the boat, "this good luck fish belongs to you, *Quaimaquam-Effendi*."

"No, no, no," the Mayor objected again. "*You* are the one who needs good luck. After all, you will become the father of another child soon."

Mardiros dropped the fish on a stack of leftover bricks beside his new home and accompanied the Mayor to his car, where the chauffeur awaited him. "*Ma'a salaama, Quaimaquam-Effendi*," he bid the mayor goodbye and waited until the car drove on the dike behind the *qasr*, off their property and onto the green iron bridge that connected the Kouyoumdjian peninsula to the village of Felloujeh.

"I don't know how to gut this thing," he said to his young relatives from the *qasr* who hovered at his front door. "I think I need a knife. Any of you have something like that?"

They shook their heads.

"Why are you here, anyway?" he asked them. "Why aren't you swimming, huh? The horses need riders to stay fit."

Haig, the outspoken and most daring of his nephews said, "Hanim-*Effendi* promised a gold coin to the first one who gave her the news about the arrival of her newest grandson."

"I'm going to win the race," Armen boasted.

"Ho, ho, ho!" jeered Maggie. "Have you forgotten I run like a gazelle?"

"Wait. Wait!" Mardiros stopped the jabbering. "The baby isn't due for a month."

"But the doctor is here," they replied, almost in unison.

Mardiros dashed in to face his sisters-in-law, who were too busy to notice him. Sara was ironing diapers, and Hermine cooking soup.

Dr. Kurkjian met him in the hallway. "Congratulations, Mardiros-*Effendi*," he said. "You may go see Diggin Mannig—she's resting, and the baby is sleeping." He bid him goodbye and walked out, only to be swarmed by the children, who quickly released him with sounds of disgruntlement.

Mardiros hesitated in the hallway, filled with remorse. He shouldn't have left his wife alone. He felt guilty to have enjoyed the last days of summer while his wife was in labor.

"Don't let her get out of bed for two weeks," Hermine advised. "If she starts housework sooner than that, she will remain weak for a long time."

"We'll send Nazlu to do chores," added Sara. "We can spare her for an hour or so. Nothing in the *qasr* is urgent. Nazlu can wash the diapers and hang them to dry every day."

"Of course, she'll come," Hermine confirmed. "I'll send over some of your favorite foods, too."

"We'll see that you don't starve," his two sisters-in-law jested before walking back to the *qasr*.

Mardiros was glad to bid them adieu—until tomorrow. But now, he couldn't wait to see his wife. Even though he tiptoed into their bedroom, Mannig must have sensed his presence. She opened her eyes and whispered in a drowsy voice, "She is very beautiful. She has your light complexion and a round face."

"Truly?" Mardiros reached for her hand. He wanted to know the baby's eye color but remembered that could not be determined for a few months yet. "What about a name? Have you decided?"

"Maro," she mouthed the name, her eyelids too heavy to open.

"We have a second daughter?" He smiled.

"A *houri*," she said. "Beautiful as a swan, translucent like the moon." She gestured for him to hold the baby in his arms. "She looks like a daisy-marguerite. I think I ought to call her Marguerite, too. She looks to me as rare as those desert flowers that cheered me when I was lost during the deportation. They gave me hope in that arid and colorless wasteland between the two rivers."

"You can give her many names," Mardiros chuckled. "There's no law against such things."

"Good!" She took a deep breath and closed her eyes. "Maro-Marguerite."

"Will you allow me to give her a name, too?"

She nodded.

"How about Maral? Or Myda?"

"Of course," Mannig whispered. "There's no law against that."

She dozed on and off while the relatives from the *qasr* trickled in and out, not only to congratulate the birth of the youngest Kouyoumdjian, but to stock the kitchen pantry with confections, cakes and preserves. They all extended Hanim-*Effendi's* apologies, explaining that she was only absent because she was bedridden.

At dusk, Mardiros brought Aida to see her sister—younger by two years and nine months. "Our baby is tiny—the size of one of your dolls. But you mustn't play with it like a doll. You can hold it sometimes—when Mamma or I let you. The good news is that soon she will become your best friend. You won't want to be separated from each other. You will be like a big brother to her."

"Do you want to hold her?" Mannig asked.

Mardiros picked up the baby and, before letting Aida cuddle her, he asked Mannig, "What are we calling her?"

"Maro-Marguerite," she said, without noticing his disappointed look or Aida's hesitancy to hold the baby.

"It's all right," he said, attempting to put the tightly swaddled baby into Aida's arms, "it will love you."

"I'm afraid, Baba!" Aida whined. "She doesn't have arms."

In unison, her parents said, "She does!" Then Mannig explained, "Newborn babies need their arms and legs tightly bound against the body so they will grow with straight limbs."

Cautiously, Aida held the baby. Her eyes wandered out the window.

"Mamma has given it a name," Mardiros said. "As a matter of fact, not just one name. All of those sound like her name." He hoped Mannig would say something, but she kept her silence. "But you know, Aida? I think she should be called Maral. Or Myda, Maren and Melba."

"Stop it, Mardiros!" Mannig said. "You're confusing the poor child. Come to me. Let me kiss you. You don't have to remember all those names. You call her, Maro. That's it."

Mardiros retrieved the baby. "Hello, Maral," he said, winking at Mannig. Then he walked to the open window.

It was dusk. The cool breeze from the river fluttered the georgette curtains. The frogs croaked in their distance, seemingly pleased with their sound. The crescent moon was cradled in the azure sky like a newborn. Gradually, a plethora of stars bejeweled the distant canopy.

Mannig, too, raised her head up and gazed beyond the window, into the far side of the heavens. "Oh! I see the crescent moon."

Mardiros nodded. Today was lucky. A fish came willingly into his boat, the Mayor promised him employment, and now he had a new daughter to love. "Your Mamma calls you a *houri*," he said, touching the baby's puffy cheeks. "That makes you gazelle-like, a fairy princess, and one who might command the sun in the heavens. But I think you are already commanding the moon in our sky."

The moment filled him with elation.

"Come here, Aida," he said. "Do you see the first crescent moon? That's a good sign. Today has been a lucky day, indeed."

Chapter 22

Not Foreseen

AT TWENTY-SIX, EMBOLDENED BY HER position as mother of two daughters, Mannig advised her husband, "You must take the job."

"And become salaried?" He was tickled at the offer to become an irrigation engineer. "The son of a Pasha? *We* employed people? We paid *their* salaries. We've supported nearly half of the Baghdad and the Felloujeh populations for innumerable decades." He shook his head, "What will the Armenians say?"

What had secured this position? The influence of his aristocratic lineage? She wondered. Perhaps he thinks if the truth is not spoken, it will be forgotten.

"Work cannot be denigrating," she said. "You will be doing the country a service in your own way—like the Pasha and his father. The Iraqis aren't giving you a handout. You'll prove your value. You aren't even an orphan in a famine stricken city."

"What do you mean by that?"

"I was maybe not even ten years old," Mannig said to refresh his memory, "when I became an orphan in Mosul—before you took me into your orphanage. You probably don't really know how I survived until then."

"I have an idea," he said.

"I craved work. I never begged or stole food during those wretched years. I foraged the alleys for food. Oh, how I wanted to work as a maid like my sister! But people shooed me away for being small and useless. I wanted to be useful, but no one needed me. Imagine! The government needs you!"

"I've never worked for anyone," he said. "I don't even know what I'm supposed to do."

I didn't know how to be a wife, Mannig thought. *Or a mother … or a cook … or a homemaker.* "You'll fulfill your duties admirably," Mannig said, assuming her husband's education had secured him the job. She idolized schooling herself. Her wish to sit at a desk in a classroom one day occupied her thoughts continually—even while she was caring for her two daughters, now two and five years old.

"My office will be in Baghdad," he said, apologetically. "That means at least two hours of driving each day. What if the Kouyoumdjians need the car?"

Mannig wanted to say, "They'll do what everyone else in Felloujeh does," since only the Kouyoumdjians owned a car, anyway. But she kept her thoughts to herself. *Mardiros ought to resolve these issues himself.*

For one month the couple established a routine that eventually needed to be altered. He returned from Baghdad late, too tired and too engrossed in evaluating his own engineering skills. Checking his textbooks every evening became a habit not only to refresh his memory but to avoid failing those who trusted him at the Irrigation Department. One day he'd survey sites along the riverbanks for dikes; the next, he would assess the accessibility of a tributary to irrigate farmlands. However, his main responsibility was to evaluate bodies of water as future reservoirs. He always shared his findings with Mannig. Would the higher-ups in Government accept them?

"Isn't your assignment just to identify future possibilities?" she asked. "You can always change them. It will be more work for you, but, in the long run, those important people will appreciate your efforts."

At forty, Mardiros knew the demands of his work were taking their toll on his body. Although a great athlete in college—with first-place medals in hurdles and gymnastics, and the pole vault that qualified him for the 1912 Olympics in Sweden—he found that this job strained muscles long inactive in his head as well as in his body.

To cut his time spent on the road, the couple agreed to move to Baghdad. "We'll get the rent money from our Felloujeh house and pay rent on one in Baghdad," Mardiros said.

The idea was sound, but the reality was not.

No one wanted to rent their house. Although new and spacious, with a white brick facade, it sat alone at the tip of the peninsula—its only neighbor, the overseer of the *qasr*. By then, even Khosrof and his family had moved away.

Upon Mannig's insistence, they rented a house in Baghdad, within walking distance to her sister's neighborhood.

"I've missed being close to you," Mannig confided in Adriné. "I feel better raising my daughters in the city."

"You could help at the *Magazenn* like me," Adriné suggested work at Sebouh's millenary store.

Noticing how Aida and Maro played with their cousins nearby, she agreed. "My girls didn't have age-compatible cousins in Felloujeh, as they do now."

The sisters would sew, the cousins, play.

Mannig's embroidery skills, learned at the orphanage, revived her competitive spirit. Having noticed the Kouyoumdjian ladies and their society friends flaunt their gold and diamond jewelry, she resolved to show off her daughters as her jewels. From scraps and remnants gathered at the *Magazenn*, she sewed pretty matching dresses for them, always embroidering unique designs on the sleeves or the collars. She looked forward to raising her two daughters in the city. She coached them to recite short poems and sing ditties to entertain guests, also taking the time to teach the girls social graces she had learned from her husband's family at the *qasr*.

It wasn't very long before she declared to Mardiros, "I think I'm pregnant, again."

"It's about time," he said, kissing her. "It's also time to end this foolishness about working at Sebouh's store." A few days later, he said, "With a new addition to our family, we need help around the house."

Although she never questioned his finances, she surmised that hiring a servant without her consent must be a *male* thing, in line with Kouyoumdjian tradition.

"I've invited the Fessjians to live with us," he declared. "This is a big house and we can accommodate them."

Mannig had grieved at the news that Dr. Fessjian had been killed while attending to patients at a tribe in northern Iraq. But the idea of housing his widow and two daughters left her stunned.

"You're going to need assistance when the baby is born," Mardiros said. "Their Neh-Neh will help you and the baby. And their two daughters can play with ours."

Although she felt slighted that he had made the decision without consulting her, she kept quiet. After all, she had worked at Sebouh's *Magazenn* without consulting him.

Araxie, Dr. Fessjian's widow, her two young daughters and Neh-Neh, an elderly relative who had survived the Genocide, settled into their home. The noise level of an otherwise calm household rose to decibels bearable only to the four little girls, ages six to two, who seemed to enjoy fighting in the courtyard all day long.

Mannig's labor pains hushed the courtyard to an unusual calm. Neh-Neh said that she had delivered many children at the camps of surviving Armenians and a doctor was not necessary. Even so, she said to Mardiros, "for your peace of mind, you ought to bring in a professional midwife. I will assist her, and you can count on me."

Unlike her previous uncomplicated deliveries, Mannig experienced excruciating labor pains—not for a short time, but for hours that seemed to stretch toward eternity. The midwife and Neh-Neh soothed her, wiped her sweat and cooed to her no end. Mardiros played Debussy's pastoral pieces on his gramophone. A whole day later she delivered a son.

"He looks like a Setrak," Mardiros said, smiling. "I have not seen Setrak, your brother, but I'm sure he looks like him … the lucky rascal."

They baptized him Setrak at the Armenian Church in Baghdad, together with his two sisters who had not yet been baptized.

Immediately, Mannig developed apprehensions about her youngest child. He never cried for milk. She nursed him because it was too painful for her to be so heavily lactating. He didn't protest against a soiled diaper. If not for his putrid smell, she might not even have unswaddled his limbs for a bath. She longed for a baby-like response. She tickled him. Nothing. Scratched his soles but his toes remained unaffected. She wondered if he had any voice. *I ought to pinch him.* At first, she barely lifted his skin with her fingers. He didn't even grimace. Then she pinched him with force, until his skin almost bled.

He whimpered.

What joy! He feels something, after all.

He remained a constant worry. He walked at a normal age, but not as early as Aida, who walked at nine months, or Maro, who took her first steps before she was a year old. He didn't babble or make baby sounds. He was passive to sudden sounds and unaffected by lullabies. She suppressed her worries. She had heard that boys didn't grow as fast as girls. *Setrak is just taking his time*, she convinced herself. She believed he'd respond if put into jeopardy.

Shortly after he turned two years old, he uttered unintelligible words.

Aha, Mannig convinced herself, *he is just a lazy boy after all.*

Nevertheless, she felt no joy in her life. She searched deep within her spirit for the sorrows she had conquered. If she had succeeded in rising above the pain and agony of losing six members of her family, she could bandage this wound, too.

Mardiros, on the other hand, seemed oblivious to any problems that their son might have. He was constantly leaving town to work in the field, so Mannig took it for granted he hadn't had time to notice anything amiss. Secretly, she was glad he remained unaware of Setrak's problems.

However, she didn't want people to notice any oddities in her son. She took him out in his baby-carriage during the hottest period of the day when people hid themselves in cellars; she declined visiting relatives with her children; she guarded him from the Fessjians, often hinting they ought to seek another home to share.

She struggled between her pride and the reality. She didn't want her son identified as different or labeled "ugly." She hoped to prevent the likelihood of his becoming like the wind and rain throughout the city for all to observe.

She convinced herself he'd catch up with normal development in his own time. She'd teach him everything her daughters had learned naturally. She was determined to see Setrak defy the adage, "It's easier to move mountains than change a person's nature."

When Mardiros announced his new assignment to a major project outside the city of Baghdad, she cheered. "We'll all go with you," she said and breathed a sigh of relief. Here was the opportunity to be away from relatives and apart from society. Wherever they went, she'd devote her time to making her son normal.

"But they are sending me to Abu-Ghraib," he explained. "There's nothing in Abu-Ghraib."

Chapter 23

Abu Ghraib and Beyond

JUST AS MARDIROS SAID, THERE was nothing in Abu Ghraib in 1933 other than the asphalt road cutting through it from Baghdad to Amman, Transjordan, now Jordan.

"What are you supposed to do in the middle of the desert?" Mannig asked, bundling a survival kit of water, bread and dates.

"Believe it or not," he said, shaking his head, "the Irrigation Department wants to make it a paradise. Furthermore, they think *I* can do it!" He untied a tawny ribbon off a scroll and unrolled draftsman's sketches onto their dining table. She held down two corners of the translucent blueprint and he, the other two. "This, here," he lifted a hand to point, but the corner crackled to a curl.

Seeing Aida nearby, he said, "Come here. It's time for my five-year old daughter to learn a profession. Hold this corner for your Baba." Then he slid his index finger across the gloss-coated sketches and tapped on the narrowest strip of land between the Tigris and the Euphrates Rivers. "The straight driving distance from Baghdad to Felloujeh is sixty-two kilometers and *they* want to irrigate all this arid area."

"Isn't it somewhere there," Mannig teased, "where Adam and Eve lived?"

"Why do you think they said *paradise*?" He, too, chuckled, rolling the blueprint and letting Aida tie the ribbon.

Within a month, Mardiros had a structure built in Abu Ghraib to house a diesel-powered water pump, quenching the centuries-old thirst of those fallow lands. Word spread quickly among the nomads and seasonal farmers. They migrated from near and far and settled by a canal or a ditch.

Next, he incorporated a generator to produce electricity. "Tonight," he said upon returning to Baghdad long past midnight, "Abu Ghraib will be spotted by the gods!" Noticing Mannig's bewilderment, he explained. "We placed a powerful bulb at the top of a tall pole. It is lighting a spot on earth where anyone in heaven would say, '*Ah! That is good.*' "

Soon the Ministry of Agriculture established an experimental farm nearby, needing irrigation from the Euphrates River. They assigned Mardiros to build a Head Regulator to divert water to it. "This project requires all my time," he informed Mannig. "We'll be building an office large enough for me and a clerk or two. What do you think if I plan the structure to accommodate you and the children, too?"

Mannig hadn't experienced such relief in a long time. Setrak had passed his first birthday and it would become much harder for her to protect him from the long tongues she feared. "You know I will go wherever you go," she said, and then added, "as long as I have my three children and my piano."

They spent a very cold winter in the flat-roofed, one-level house in Abu Ghraib in 1934. Unpredictably, the water pipes in the bathroom and kitchen burst on the first night of below-freezing temperatures. He took any clothes or quilts Mannig could spare to wrap the exposed pipes before sunrise. One brazier of charcoal heated his home and another, his office, which was a side room with a separate entrance for the sheikhs, farmers and canal diggers who came to confer with him. A short hallway connected his office to their home. He usually worked well past Mannig's bedtime.

One day, near dawn, a crash awakened Mannig. She found him face down on the floor of the tiled bathroom. The large round metal tub used for bathing had flipped across his prostrate body, and the long-handled ladle nestled under his chin. She pulled the tub off him and nudged his shoulder.

He raised his head briefly before dropping it back down on the ladle.

"Get up! Stand up!" she insisted. He was awake, but groggy, he couldn't get up on his own. She struggled to help the dizzy man onto his knees and then onto the shower stool.

With wide eyes, she wiped his bloody face. "Abu-Zainab will drive you to Baghdad," she said and dashed out into the light of early dawn. Standing on her toes to see above the mud-brick fence between their home and the settled Bedouin workers, she yelled, "Abu-Zainab! You must take the *Effendi* to the hospital."

Abu Zainab, the lead spokesman for the laborers, dwelt in a tent with his family. Barely awake, he instantly obliged. "May Allah care for you, *khatoon*," he said, giving Mannig a worried look upon seeing blood everywhere. He let Mardiros lean on him, and the two hobbled out. He helped Mardiros get settled into the back seat of the car then hopped into the driver's seat of the government owned brown Ford. "It is a good thing the *Effendi* taught me how to drive."

Shortly after midday, Mardiros returned home wearing no bandages. He smiled at Mannig, only to hear her scream, "What happened to your teeth?"

"They're g-gone!" he nearly sobbed—his stuttering made him even less coherent.

"Light to your eyes, khatoon," Abu Zainab said. "The *Doctore* prescribed aspirin and soup. In-sha-Allah, it won't take many days before he gets a set of false teeth."

Mardiros fumed. "Imagine, I'll live with dentures for the rest of my life, and I'm not even forty-three years old!"

"What did you say?" Mannig asked.

"The Doctore predicted he would have trouble with his speech," Abu Zainab said, and then smiled. "The *Effendi* won't be yelling at the *fellaheen* for a while, either."

"Or doing office work," Mannig said. "He will rest."

"I'll see that nobody comes to see him about their problems," Abu Zainab promised.

Mardiros waved his hand, dismissing their comments. He faced the two and slurred his words. "Can I have coffee?" and walked straight into his office.

She poured a demitasse of the Turkish coffee for him and another for her. "What happened to you last night?"

"I d-don't really remember," he stammered. "Dr. Kurdian and Abu-Zainab put things together and we surmised I was poisoned …." He stopped when he saw Mannig's face go white. "Wait, wait! Let me finish. *We* think … the culprit was my negligence. I was extremely cold in the office last night. So I added a few charcoal chunks onto the brazier. With the cold wind howling across the desert and the windows rattling their bones, I ignored the danger of burning the fresh coal chunks."

"Oh, no! And the fumes filled your office?"

"Thank God the door to your hallway was closed. Otherwise, the carbon monoxide would have filled the bedrooms …. *Vye*! The children!"

"Did you faint at your desk?" she asked.

"I must have … but then I must have gone into the bathroom. I remember being dizzy …. I slipped down. I fell on my face …. You know the rest."

She nodded. "So you can't eat regular food for a while. I better see what pureed meals I can concoct for all of us."

Whatever she prepared, he consumed without complaint. Spending more time in his family's quarters, he realized how Mannig had to do without city conveniences. He asked the government to build a separate house for his family.

A new white brick house rose up across the big lawn from his office, the second of only two buildings in Abu Ghraib. Seeing how quickly the poplar trees edging the lawn were growing, he planted eucalyptus trees as a buffer between the asphalt road and his residence. A grape arbor soon became a playground for the children.

The supply of hot and cold running water in the kitchen and bathroom made them feel as if they were living in a modern house. Well, the "hot" water was a desert phenomenon.

Mardiros set up a hundred-gallon aluminum tank on the roof, with water pipes running to the kitchen and bathroom. He assigned two *fellaheen* to lug buckets of water from the canal to the roof and fill up the tank daily. Sun and gravity did the rest.

Before sunrise, Jasmiyeh, Abu-Zainab's teenage number-two wife—Muslims allow a man four wives at a time, provided each has her own domicile—filled up the large *ibriq*, the water-storage jug in the kitchen. A wooden pedestal held the thirty-gallon earthen container in place. Mannig added a measure of chlorine into it before the water dripped from the jug's cone-shaped bottom into a porcelain bowl. A metal ladle hung from the pedestal, allowing anyone who wished to take a cool and safe drink.

A healthy farm surrounded their new house. Watermelon and cantaloupes were brought in, week after week, during the six or more months of summer. Lining the floor of a long corridor, they became an obstacle course for the children's games—that is, when they weren't sneaking into the watermelon fields, cracking a watermelon here and there to see if it were red enough to taste its juicy center.

Just outside the kitchen, eggplant, zucchini and okra plants provided vegetables for everyone in Abu Ghraib. Experimental potatoes provided the main ingredient of unique recipes. Chickens and turkeys roamed the desert but roosted at night along the mud-brick fence, delighting the children, who discovered eggs here and there, fresh or rotten.

For red meat, Mardiros devised a schedule for slaughtering lambs. Mannig liked the liver and Mardiros a leg; the remainder of the carcass, along with the wool, head and feet were distributed among the families of his workers.

It suited Mardiros fine to provide for his family with the continuous support of the Arabs. He took pride in this symbiotic relationship with the nomads and conducted all government affairs with this mutual benefit in mind.

Mannig, too, appreciated this lifestyle. She spent hours playing the piano, learning new and complicated sheet music. With the windows wide open, her melodies wafted beyond the desert sands. Mardiros and the children soon became accustomed to her repertoire. They knew the end was near when she'd shift to a more poignant mood for Debussy's *"La fille aux cheveux de lin."* That was the first piece she had memorized and now, the last one she played before she flipped the piano lid closed to prevent dust from settling between the keys.

Realizing that Aida was interested in music, Mannig became her daughter's piano teacher. *Never a student in school, but always a teacher.* While Aida practiced without being coaxed, Maro seldom approached the piano on her own. Setrak, on the other hand, preferred playing with his Bedouin buddies.

The lack of a formal school for her children was the one element Mannig missed in her otherwise contented lifestyle. "Would you buy a few easy books?" she asked Mardiros, who was on his way to Baghdad for some government meetings. "The least I can do is teach the children how to read and write in Armenian."

He returned home that night, loaded with educational materials. "The principal at the Armenian school in Baghdad recommended you start with some of these books." He stacked them in order of difficulty on the card table in the living room. "I brought a few for me," he said, holding up textbooks for English and arithmetic. "Of course, you could teach these, too, but I want to have some fun, myself."

Chapter 24

The Taming of Mannig

THE NEXT DAY, REGULAR SCHOOLING began for the children. Also began a new phase to Mannig's education—not the reading or writing kind, either—but becoming the "hostess of the desert." Friends and relatives in Baghdad drove over to see this *blooming* Abu Ghraib. Naturally, they stayed for lunch, tea or supper, conditioning Mannig to always be prepared for guests. The first time Mardiros' bachelor friends drove over to play Bridge, she served desert truffles, which had been dug up, rinsed of soil and delivered by the *fellaheen*. "These are like mushrooms," one farmer had explained.

"So they might be poisonous?" She pulled her hands away.

"*La, wa-Allah!*" Abu Zainab explained. "We haven't died yet. My wife always cooks with them."

The first time Mannig prepared them—steamed and then doused in olive oil and lemon juice—she consumed them herself in private. *If they are poisonous, I'll be the only victim, not my family.* She loved the taste, but monitored her condition. When there were no ill effects, she began concocting recipes using the desert fungi. The Bridge buddies raved about the delicacy and reprimanded her if she didn't serve them on their next visit.

Short for a fourth, they convinced Mannig to join them at the card table. She found it interesting to observe the competition among the men. She bid for contracts and enjoyed the opportunity to speak English, even if it were limited to the bidding of suits. She practiced on her own and solicited the expertise of Mardiros, who made it a daily ritual to play Bridge for Two after the children went to bed. Very quickly, she became a formidable partner, not only with friends but with the government dignitaries who befriended them. She enjoyed playing cards on the lawn in the evenings in the so-called "middle of the desert."

"If you had a tennis court," suggested a British engineer, also working for the Iraqi Irrigation Department, "I'd bring my wife for a game of doubles with the two of you." He spread the sports page of the *Daily Mirror* on the linen cloth of the table Mannig had set for their meal on the lawn. "See those Wimbledon female contenders? My wife bought a white skirt for tennis just like," he read the subtitle, "Gussie Moran. A skirt just like hers."

While Mannig read the comics in the *Daily Mirror* left behind, Mardiros dug into his textbooks for instructions on how to undertake his new, exotic project—a tennis court. Within a month, the *fellaheen* spread clay for the court. Mardiros took a special trip to Baghdad to hunt for a net, rackets and balls. He finally succeeded in finding them at a sports store that catered to Europeans.

As soon as the *fellaheen* fastened the green net across the midriff of the playfield, he handed Mannig her racket and said, "Let's smash some balls."

"I don't know how," Mannig said, surprising even herself. She didn't normally admit to ignorance.

"I'm not familiar with this game, either," Mardiros said, holding up a book on sports. "This chapter on 'tennis' will be our instructor."

"You've been an athlete," she continued, "so you can easily play. My orphanage was not exactly a playground."

"I hate to see the court remain idle ...." he began, only to be interrupted by Mannig, who took the racket and stood at one end of the court. He tossed a ball to her. She hit it so hard, it flew into the *middle of the desert*. He stood by the net and yelled at the girls. "Aida! Maro! Go get the ball. Why do you think we're allowing you to watch?" The girls had to spend too much time chasing balls, so Mardiros' next project became erecting a net high enough to stop a ball from flying out of bounds.

The couple played almost every evening, before dusk, and their three children became their "ball boys."

Whenever Britishers visited, they made a foursome, prompting Mannig to sew a white skirt for herself to go with Mardiros' white slacks and sports shirt. Seeing how Mannig sewed without a pattern or a sewing machine, he surprised her with a Singer sewing machine, encased in a cabinet with pedals and a cutting platform. She was so touched by his thoughtfulness that she spent more time sewing than on her piano. She sewed curtains and tablecloths, but mostly clothing for her children, who were outgrowing everything faster than she realized. She outfitted them in red-and-white plaid costumes especially for the tennis court. To hide a multitude of mismatched seams, she threaded elastic onto the cuffs of the sleeves as wells as the cuffs of the shorts. To her

The piano tuner with the three Kouyoumdjian children: Setrak on trike, Aida in innertube, and Maro standing. Abu Ghraib, 1934.

satisfaction, the children looked professional when collecting balls for the dignitaries. She watched her two daughters and son chase the balls, bringing color onto the otherwise tawny surface of the clay-surfaced court.

"Our new king," Mardiros said, one evening, "has built a summer hideout for himself a few kilometers from us. In fact, I saw his yellow convertible whiz by my office window."

"I wish we could have seen him," Mannig said. "You're talking about King Ghazi, right?" After he nodded, she continued, "It was so exciting to meet his father, King Faisal, in Felloujeh when he stopped by for tea."

"Well, this king doesn't spend time drinking tea," Mardiros guffawed. "He is building a great nation. He's a visionary. I just received details about a new commission. The Irrigation Department is beginning a grand project at Habbaniyeh."

Mannig waited anxiously for him to elaborate further concerning their royal neighbor in the middle of the desert. Instead he added, "I'll be in charge of building the Head Regulator. It's not far from here. I'll commute daily, like I used to when we lived in Baghdad."

Suspecting the King would perhaps drive by on the asphalt again, Mannig planned walks along the road with her children, dressed in matching outfits. Setrak loved the road most, racing his trike on the smooth asphalt. Every now and then a car would appear on the horizon. She'd collect her children and their pet pup, Blackie, and they'd huddle on the dirt shoulder, waving as the vehicle drove by.

On one occasion, the yellow car loomed ahead. As usual, she collected the children on the shoulder of the road waiting for it to go by.

The convertible stopped close to them. Blackie barked. The chauffeur—no, the King—scooted up in the driver's seat. "What are you people doing in the middle of the desert?"

Mannig, pointed to the Abu Ghraib oasis and grinned. "We live here, Your Majesty."

"*Wa'allah!*" he chortled. "You must be the engineer's family." He slithered back onto his seat and drove west toward Felloujeh, the children still waving. Half an hour later, Mannig was startled to hear several gunshots coming from the direction the king's car had gone. "Let's go home," she said, herding the children back, Blackie in tow. Before they left the asphalt road onto the path to Abu Ghraib, the yellow convertible reappeared, whizzing by—the King holding the legs of several desert-quails. He smiled with the pride of a little boy displaying his trophies.

The children waved. Blackie barked.

The children waved to the king many more times over the next three years. On the occasions Mardiros walked with the children, he, too, waved.

Mannig dressed the girls in pretty dresses and urged them to accompany Setrak on his bike, but she stayed apart. She prompted them to wave but made sure to stay inconspicuous herself out of respect for the Bedouin female tradition.

"A major event is coming up," Mardiros said to Mannig, sipping on his cognac after supper. It was a hot summer evening and the coolest place was on their front porch facing the lawn. Tall poles made the area bright as day until the electric generator was turned off for the night. "On August sixth," Mardiros continued, "we're opening the gates of Habbaniyeh. The king will cut the ribbon and then the gates will rise, releasing the Euphrates water into the irrigation canals. It will be an historic event."

"Can we all attend?" Mannig asked.

"It's not that kind of occasion." Mardiros tried to be realistic about the event. "There will only be men at the dam; a few Sheikhs and many farmers—those who will benefit from this project and those who worked on it. That's all. I suppose the King will have his security guards there. It's not a party. There won't be any fanfare, I'm sure."

Mannig couldn't get over the fact that the king would be attending. "So, he is making a special trip?"

"Yes, but it's just ceremonial. He does this sort of thing all over the country."

Nevertheless, Mannig thought, *he is coming our way. We must do something special for him.* Having seen in a journal a photograph of the Queen of England accepting a bunch of colorful daisies from a little girl, she asked, "Will there be flowers for him?"

"What flowers?"

"Perhaps someone ought to present flowers to the King," she suggested.

Mardiros gave her a pensive look. "That's a good idea. I'll assign someone to be responsible for the flowers ... and to make the presentation. I'll be too busy for such things."

Mannig showed him the *Daily Mirror* and pointed to the little girl handing over a bouquet to the Queen of England. "What about Aida? She could give him the flowers."

After another pensive moment, he said, "That's appropriate. The eldest child of the resident engineer presenting flowers to the king. They don't call me *Abu-Aida* for nothing." A man was sometimes referred to as father of his first child's name. "I'll take Aida and the flowers in the car with me to the site on Wednesday."

Jubilant at the prospect of her daughter's close encounter with royalty, Mannig went to work first thing in the morning. She sewed a new dress for Aida from a piece of a blue-green plaid taffeta she had saved for such an occasion. She fashioned a pleated skirt, knee-high, and stitched it to a fitted bodice. Going through her box of remnants, she picked out a piece of white georgette and made a frilly apron, belted in the back—*apropos to serving the king.* She remembered how her nieces in Felloujeh had rehearsed royal decorum before they entertained King Faisal for tea. Mannig's biggest mission became to teach Aida how to rise to the occasion. She coached her to smile and curtsy not once or twice, but throughout the day. Anytime she and Mardiros were present, she made Aida smile and curtsy. Mannig focused all her energy into infusing gentility into the eight-year-old tomboy Aida.

The day before April 8, 1936, Mannig sent Abu Zainab to Baghdad to buy a bouquet of flowers, which she placed in a jug of water in the back seat of Mardiros' car. Early the next morning, she helped Aida into her new dress, black patent-leather shoes and white anklets. She carefully tied the white apron with a gorgeous bow in the back. She sized up her daughter front and back. *She looks the part.* She kissed her. "Don't forget to smile and curtsy."

Mardiros, too, was dressed elegantly in a khaki suit, shirt, and tie—which matched his hazel eyes, tanned face and graying hair.

"You're my handsome prince," she said with a wink, "and Aida is a princess."

"Start the car," Mardiros instructed Abu Zainab. "Today, you are my chauffeur." He winked at Mannig. "What message does *Your Majesty* send to the King?"

"Tell him 'Hi'!"

Chapter 25

Flowers for the King

"That was the hottest day, ever!" Mardiros said, flopping on the divan, disheveled. Sweat ran profusely down his earlobes and spine, staining armpits, neck and back.

After blotting his forehead, Mannig replaced his sopping wet khaki handkerchief with a soft linen napkin. She picked up one of the hand fans—made of woven dried palm tree fronds, stacked in a basket—and fanned him.

"Give it to me," he said, annoyed by her pampering.

Before selecting a fan for herself, she picked a child-size one for Aida and, seeing Maro and Setrak chase each other into the parlor, stopped them. "It's too hot for games. Sit down. Here's your fan, and yours." Then, she fanned herself vigorously. "It's been very hot here, too."

Knowing how anxious Mannig was about the dedication of the Head Regulator at Habbaniyeh, Mardiros said, "If I had something cool to drink, I'd have the energy to tell you about our day and the newly born Lake."

She offered him *Laban*, yoghurt diluted with water. "This is the best of all thirst quenchers," she said, "but if you want lemonade, I've made a fresh pitcher—it, too, is by the water jug."

He shook his head, "Give *Laban* to Aida, too. Her day was probably even hotter than mine." He consumed the refreshing drink in one gulp. "Aaah!" he slurped, wiping the edges of his mouth. "Abu Zainab said she fell asleep in the car—not just once but several times. The car must have been like a *toneer*." He meant a clay oven set in a pit.

"I was very hot, Mamma," Aida said. "He opened the windows, but the seat stayed hot. I got out. That was hotter. Abu Zainab opened the doors; he told me to sit on the step of the back seat."

"So, did she give him the flowers?" Mannig fanned her daughter, something she never did.

"The king was late," Mardiros said, after a belch. "Actually, he was late by more than two hours. Everyone was restless, wondering even if he would come at all. A lot of political grumblings heated the environment even more. I don't know if the gossip was due to the heat of the noonday sun, or if it has been simmering within their tents. Sheikh Abbas blamed the king's delay on his newly acquired British 'snobbishness.' Sheikh Hamid said it was due to wearing a crown."

He sipped half of the second glass of *Laban*. "We should have *Laban* at such occasions," he said, swallowing the last drop. "We didn't have any shade, and the vast hordes of people blocked any breezes from the desert. I should have had a shed erected … a few palm tree branches might have prevented a plethora of complaints. Next time, *in-sha-Allah*."

"Did Aida give him the flowers?"

"Yes, yes!" Mardiros said. "She d-d-did. She did. They were the one c-c-colorful thing in that desolate desert—that is, when it eventually happened. The worst behavior was exhibited by the Britishers who were assigned to be present at the dedication. They stood apart, more restless than us, making snide remarks. One even said, 'You can't expect an Arab to be civilized—why would their king be prompt?' "

Mannig looked at her husband, aghast. "I hope no one heard him."

"A whisper is heard throughout the desert."

Both lowered their heads in contemplation.

Mannig broke the silence. "Aida, did the king say anything when he took your flowers?"

Aida shrugged her shoulders.

"I think, the king must have been delighted," Mardiros said. "He was smiling all the time. He even bent down to her level—he might have said something. I couldn't tell. He put his hand on your head, Aida, right?"

Aida nodded.

"Did he say anything?"

She shook her head. "I don't remember. It was very hot. I thought it was Abu Zainab awakening me, '*Aida, Aida. It's time. Let's go.*' "

"Did you curtsy? Did you smile?"

"Um, um … I was looking down," Aida sniffled.

"How did you give him the flowers?"

"I forgot them in the car," Aida stammered. "Abu Zainab awakened me and told me to follow him. Then I went back. Pulled them out of the bucket. The water was hot. They didn't stand up. I had to carry them in my arms. My

Mardiros wrote: "A Historical Snapshot: Opening Ceremony of Abu-Ghraib Head Regulator (8 klms south of Felloujeh Town) on the left bank of the river EUPHRATES, when Aida, daughter of Mardiros Kouyoumdjian, the Resident Engineer of the Project, presented a bouquet of beautiful flowers to the late King Ghazi of Iraq in April, 1936. This head regulator is regulating the supply of water for an area of sixty thousand hectares and linking the Euphrates water with that of the Tigris on the outskirts of Baghdad."

front got wet. When I saw him, I gave them to him … to the king—I think he was the king."

"Yes, yes … that was the king," Mardiros said. "You gave the flowers to the king. I saw you. He smiled, and then he patted your head."

Mannig relaxed in her seat. She sipped lemonade, Maro and Setrak playing with toys by her side. "I wish I had been there to see it all."

Mardiros lit a cigarette and closed his eyes. "Actually, you were lucky not to be exposed to that desert sun." He crossed one leg up and untied his black patent leather shoes. He kicked them off. "A-a-ah!" He bent down to pull off his sweat-soaked, knee-high socks and lost his balance, rolling down on his side.

"*Baba-a-a-a!*" Four frightened voices echoed throughout the parlor. Mannig dropped to her knees. "Are you ill? Aida—go get Abu Zainab to drive Baba to Baghdad …."

"No, no!" Mardiros said, "I'm fine ... I got dizzy for a second. I still feel that sun on my skin."

"Do you suppose you got sunstroke?"

"No, no .... I'm fine, just tired," Mardiros dismissed her concern.

"King or no king, etiquette m'etiquette," Mannig hissed. "Next time, you keep your toppy on your head. But right now, you need a cold shower." She interrupted her own suggestion. "The water will run hot at this time. Let me see .... I can get you a bucket of cold water from our drinking jug." She dashed into the hallway.

A few ladles of cold water over his body, followed by a belated afternoon nap, revived Mardiros to his normal self. After a light supper of watermelon, bread and cheese, he dragged his chaise-lounge onto the lawn so he could watch the children.

Like monkeys, they climbed up and down, down and up the green-painted grapevine arbor surrounding the lawn.

Mannig joined her husband for their evening ritual, which was to sit and be refreshed by the cool desert breeze.

"I do want to know more about your day with the king," Mannig began. "Did he drive his convertible, or ...."

"I think so. Maybe Abbosh took a picture."

"Abbosh?"

"Can you believe that? Yes, Abbosh—our valet in Felloujeh. He's become the Royal photographer! Someone said that his photography shop in Baghdad is very popular."

"Now, I can't wait to see those pictures," Mannig said. "When will that be?"

"Don't be in so much of a rush. Besides, when you see them, you will know how better off you were here than with us."

"Comfortwise, yes," Mannig sighed, "but a-a-ah, to be so near the king."

"The local Mullahs were present." Mardiros enumerated both the Shia and Sunni sects who sent equal numbers of representatives. Also present were a Kurdish chief and several sheikhs, whose lands or migration patterns would be affected by the creation of the vast and shallow Lake Habbaniyeh. But this was an important day for the *fellaheen*," he elaborated. "They were jubilant. How they kissed the king's hand, thanking him for the water that their parched territories deserved! That was quite a sight. After the king cut the ribbon, and the gates were raised ... oh, the first splash of the gushing waters! The people's roar was worth every degree of the day's heat. Don't worry, I'll drive you there sometime to show you Lake Habbaniyeh."

"Can we swim in the lake, Baba?" Aida asked as she dangled from the eaves of the arbor.

Mardiros cocked his head, pensive. "I think so. One of the British engineers was talking about the lake as a recreational site for the RAF installation, which is nearby. Yes, yes. The lake is shallow enough to be warm for swimming. It won't be long before we go on a picnic there and then we can all swim .... Well," he looked at Mannig teasingly, "maybe not really swim, but at least wade into it. I was amazed how blue the water in the lake looked."

"You're making me eager to see Abbosh's pictures," Mannig said, and then reminded the children that it was their bedtime. "Don't forget to brush your teeth and use the toilet before you climb to the roof. Your beds ought to be nice and cool by now."

The couple sat in silence, watching the children dawdle on the way to the house.

Mannig broke the silence. "When will we see those pictures? Pictures first? Or a picnic at the site?"

"I have no idea," Mardiros blew his nose. "Abbosh was so slow doing his job; slow moving his tripod in front of, behind, or beside the ribbons. Every time he relocated the camera, it would take him ages to properly set the blackout cloth tunnel. And then he'd poke his head inside that tunnel, doing this or that ... must have been suffo-ca-ting." Mardiros began to cough. He himself felt suffocated. He could not inhale enough air, even less exhale. "I have a headache ...." The color drained from his face and his eyes rolled up in his head. He doubled over in his chaise.

"Abu Zainab?" Mannig let out a guttural scream across the cool night air. "Hurry! You must drive the *Effendi* to Baghdad. Abu Zaina-a-a-b?"

"Laban, Anyone?" Circa 1923. Eldorado Photo, Baghdad

Chapter 26

Trite Concerns

"You had a minor heart attack," Dr. Kurdian told Mardiros. "Extensive exposure to the sun and dehydration may have caused it. Otherwise, your heart is fine. I won't tell you to stop what you're doing, but you ought to cut back on your work in the open desert."

Mannig's pleading eyes prompted Mardiros to agree. "All right. Next time I see the Minister of the Irrigation Department, I'll ask him for a different assignment."

Content for now that Mardiros had promised the doctor to return for a checkup the following month, Mannig didn't stare at him while he drove to Abu Ghraib. In order to hide any worry over his physical condition, he would keep his expression placid, she surmised.

"I'm as normal as any man in his forties," he informed Mannig after his follow-up visit with the physician. "I celebrated the good news with the Kouyoumdjians in Baghdad, but I have a surprise for you."

From his jacket pocket he removed a stuffed envelope. "Abbosh gave me the photographs of King Ghazi at Lake Habbaniyeh." He flipped from one black-and-white picture to another as if dealing a hand of Bridge. Mannig peeked over his shoulder—almost all the exposures were of the *sheikhs* and *mullahs,* while a horde of spectators surrounded the king.

"The king's khaki suit is similar to yours," Mannig said, picking up the first full-figure photo of the king, "except for the band of ribbons-of-valor on his jacket."

"I probably should have worn my black suit like the dignitaries," Mardiros said, shaking his head. "I'll know what to do next time."

"Oh! Here's Aida!" Mannig exclaimed. "Aida come, see your picture. This one shows your back...." She shuffled through the rest of the photos. "Isn't there another one of her? What's the matter with that Abbosh? He only took snapshots of the faces of those sheikhs. Didn't he notice Aida was the one and only girl amid the Arabs? He should have gone around the king and pointed his camera at her face, too."

"At least he got one picture of the presentation," Mardiros said.

"Oh, no!" Mannig gagged as she took a closer look at the photo of Aida. "The belt—it's not at your waist! Aida! I told you to straighten your skirt …. I told you to pull up the apron belt in the back. What happened to the beautiful bow I had tied just before you left? Woe! Your head—it's hanging so low you could have smelled his shoes. What was the matter with you? It was one little thing for you to do—to look at him and smile. You're so hunched over …. You must like to gaze at sand and dirt. You could have caught the glint in his majesty's eyes, which is visible even behind his pilot's glasses."

Aida sniffled, tears glistening on her long lashes. "I forgot. It was too hot, and …."

"It's over and done," Mardiros interrupted, winking at Mannig. "Let's sit and enjoy this cool evening in Abu Ghraib."

Chastened, Mannig composed herself. "You've never failed me before. That's all …." Then, abruptly, she stopped berating her daughter. "*Amahn!*" She sighed and put her hand on her mouth to shush herself.

"What? What?" Mardiros asked, leaning over the picture in her hand.

"I hope no one looks at this picture—closely," she whispered. "Do you see her hair? What a horrible cut! More like steps coming down—layer after distinct layer from the top of her head to her neck. *Vye! Vye!* My poor child! I can't ever forgive myself." She hugged Aida. "It's entirely my fault—not yours. Mine, alone. I was the one who gave you that horrible haircut. Just this once I should have taken you to a coiffeur in Baghdad. I never visualized Abbosh would snap a picture of your back … such a closeup, to boot." She squirmed, puckered her lips and repeated. "I'll know what to do next time."

Mardiros set a rectangular wooden contraption on the table. "Vahram gave this to me," he said, pulling a chair and sitting down facing it. He turned a knob on a crude, homemade battery-operated radio. "He's building radios at his office at the Baghdad Electric and Power Station. When I stopped to see Toros and Hermine to tell them my good news about my health, he gave theirs to me as a gift. It worked well in his house. Let's see if I can pick up something here." He cocked his ear toward the radio, only to jerk away from the static, which was so dense that it blocked out any human voices or music. "According to Vahram, we would be able to hear a symphony being played live, in Vienna! No need for discs or gramophones, any longer. Come here children. You are witnessing advanced science."

On his next trip to Baghdad, Mardiros bought a Blaupunkt radio. "Nothing

Family Portrait at Abu Ghraib, 1936.
Left to right: Mardiros, Setrak, Maro, Aida, Mannig, and Blackie.

wrong with Vahram's product, but this German-made radio is superior. It will give us timely news of what's happening in Europe, supposedly without as much static."

Every evening, he glued his ears to the Blaupunkt, switching stations from Sofia to Valencia to Bucharest, picking up an occasional English broadcast from *BBC*. "There are a lot of rumors about Hitler," he said one evening and pinned a map of Europe on the wall next to the radio. "He is causing trouble over there. By the time we read about the successes of that madman's schemes in the *Daily Mirror*, it will be old news. This radio will keep us instantly abreast of his moves."

The radio did keep them well informed. The news about King Ghazi's accidental death was swift to reach every ear in the wide Iraqi desert. The radio announcer was somber and to the point:

His Majesty, King Ghazi, was killed in a car crash near the Palace.

The man's voice faded, while mournful music of the flute-like *nay* and the cylindrical clay and goat-hide drum *tabla* interrupted the static.

"His Majesty died instantly." The man's voice trickled across the radio waves.

"I don't believe it!" Mardiros jumped to his feet. "Not in his car. In his biplane, maybe; they are risky vehicles. But in a car? No, no! It was n-n-not an *accident* ...." he stammered. "They k-k-killed him. They wanted him out of their way. Just because the man was a Nazi sympathizer .... The British didn't like that. I'm sure they killed him."

Mannig tried to shush him, warning him to keep his opinions to himself. "Fine!" He almost yelled at her. "Fine—I won't say it out loud. But I know the truth. The Britishers have never told the truth, and they won't this time, either. They killed him. The Arabs of the desert don't have to hear me, either. They know it themselves. The king was murdered!"

A day later, he was still fuming. Mannig couldn't block her ears anymore. She knew he needed someone to hear him out—better her than some British supervisor who might retaliate against him. She could keep his thoughts private, and he needed to vent them.

"The heir apparent is only four years old," Mardiros said, two days later. "The boy can't ascend to the throne until he is eighteen, so they've appointed Abdul Ilah, his uncle on his mother's side, to be the Regent. That Abdul Ilah is their man. In the meantime, we shall be governed by ... well, it will actually be Nuri el-Said, the Prime Minister. All in all, I can only conclude," Mardiros blew his nose, "that the British have won again. They've got their man where they want him."

He drew the curtains in the parlor and carefully tuned the Blaupunkt to *BBC*. "Hitler has invaded Poland," he said.

"What is *invade*, Baba?" he heard Aida ask. After he explained, he noticed her wanting to ask another question.

"Where is Poland?" she asked.

"Come here—to this map," he said, pointing to Poland on the blue map pinned to the wall. While tracing the area with his finger, he stopped to think. "I have a better idea .... Go ask Mama if she can spare some yarn and a few pins."

"What's all this for?" Mannig said, bringing in her sewing basket.

"We're going to have a geography lesson," he said and posted several red push pins around Germany's boundaries. "Let me see now .... Hitler today took Poland, so I need to move these pins in Eastern Germany farther East." He wound the black yarn around the pins to make a frame. "Aida, it may be too late for you to learn about Poland because as of today, it doesn't exist. It has become part of Germany. I wonder what's next?"

"Will Hitler *invade* us, too?" Aida asked.

Mardiros shrugged his shoulders and Mannig took the children for their bedtime stories. From then on, beginning in 1939, Mardiros secretly listened to the *BBC* late at night after his family went to bed. He turned off the lights and drew the curtains shut. Might Germany's boundaries expand as far east as Iraq?

Chapter 27

A Vagabond Life

Upon returning to Abu Ghraib after meetings with the higher-ups in Baghdad, Mardiros said, "They assigned me to Kut—a future site for a dam."

Worried about his heart tolerating exposure to another desert setting, Mannig stopped fanning herself. Before she opened her mouth to remind him of the doctor's warning, he continued, "Just as I promised Dr. Kurdian, I declined to be the engineer for the project. I did agree to negotiate with Sheikh Bashrawi over his territory."

Delighted she didn't need to nag him, she asked, "Where's Kut? I've never heard of it."

"It's sixty kilometers southeast of Baghdad." He showed it to her on an enlarged map of Iraq, sketched by the Irrigation Department. "It's on the Tigris. I don't know much about that part of our country." He unlatched his leather valise and took out several brochures and a book. "These ought to help me get oriented before I begin my work. They've told me about the Persian influence in that region—it being close to our border with Iran and so forth."

"Is that good or bad?"

"I don't really know," Mardiros said. "Most of the Arabs apparently speak Farsi and cook Persian style. One of these papers is supposed to teach me a few words in their language, which ought to facilitate my conversations with the Sheikh."

"You learn languages fast," Mannig reassured him. "You already know five, so why not a sixth?" She chuckled and added, "I'll keep the children's ruckus under control so you can do your homework."

"It's a short assignment," he said, "a month, at best. I'm wondering if it is even necessary to relocate the whole family there?"

The two sat in silence, gazing at each other thoughtfully.

Unable to visualize living apart from him with the three children, Mannig suggested they stay with the family of her sister and her husband, who spent their summers at their farmhouse in Abu Sidara. Mardiros often drove his family to Sebouh's farm, an hour away, and Sebouh brought his to Abu Ghraib. "The children love to be with their cousins," Mannig said, without revealing her real intent, which was to have more time to assess Adriné's behavior. Mannig had noticed during recent visits that she had not been herself. "They can ride horses and picnic in the fields, swim in the irrigation canal by the pumphouse. It's beneficial for the cousins to live together for a while."

"Yes, yes, yes!" The children cheered. "When can we go?"

Mardiros' one-month stint in Kut provided excitement for the cousins in Abu Sidara, and heartbreak, too. Older than Mannig's children, Adriné's won horse races and hopscotch contests. Setrak often cried when he lost while Maro pouted and quit. Aida, at least, occasionally won in card games. All seven of them sprawled in the breezeway during the hottest part of the day to play *Fish* or *Trump*—sometimes even at night, settling on one of their beds on the roof, relying on the large, luminous tropical moon. To everyone's dismay, Aida often won the prize for a free stub at the cinema in Baghdad. When the cousins ganged up on Aida, Maro and Setrak sided with her, causing a ruckus and occasional hair pulling. It became a big chore for the adults to referee, making Mannig feel awkward as a guest in her sister's domain.

When Mardiros completed his contract in Kut, he was assigned to another short-term job, eventually establishing the pattern of becoming a roving engineer. Mannig convinced him that the children needed both parents no matter where or for how long. The end of 1939 heralded the start of a new professional routine for Mardiros and a nomadic lifestyle for his family.

After Kut, wherever Mardiros' assignment took him, Mannig went along with her three children and the piano. She adjusted to the locale and cherished the new experiences, which many city folks were never exposed to. She capitalized on the uniqueness of each place and familiarized herself with its nuances.

Visits from friends and dignitaries continued to provide pleasant interruptions in Mannig's routine. She soon became the hostess of choice for the outings of their city friends and family. After Kut and over the next several years, they came in droves to enjoy a few hours in Ramadi, Hillah and Hindiyeh Barrage. They applauded her for making skillful use of the local cuisine, either in Bedouin-like settings or at elegant tables set European style.

"What's so memorable about this place?" a guest would often prompt her.

"It was like reliving the agony of my deportation trek all over again," she said, telling friends in Ramadi how the children had been inflicted with

Family Portrait Hindiyeh Barrage, 1936.
Left to right: Blackie, Aida, Mannig, Setrak, Mardiros, Maro

malaria. "I'm grateful for the medicine Quinine that saved their lives. Although I was not infected, I experienced their trauma vicariously—my skin felt the bottomless chills as much as Aida's, which shivered constantly, even under all the warm blankets I could pile on her. The next moment, my sweat dripped more profusely than Maro's, which soaked her sheets. But poor Setrak, he didn't know how to express discomfort—he just yelled … and I cringed."

She was tempted to tell them about the lice in Hilla but decided not to. Noticing how the children were constantly scratching their heads, she discovered the parasites in their hair. She had to pick one louse at a time with her fingers and scrape away the whitish eggs glued to each strand of hair with her nails.

"Come here," she'd call to one child after the other as soon as breakfast was over. "I hope I won't find any today." Her fingertips crawled on a louse-hunt across the strands of hair on each head. "Disgusting! They never die or desist!"

No matter what remedy Mannig tried or devised, she failed to eliminate the pests. She washed their hair with the locally recommended harsh soap bars. She even dared to dab their heads with kerosene. She led her three children into the open air of the roof of their apartment because of the fire hazard. She also hauled buckets of water and soap to wash the fuel out. The hot sun immediately dried the stain on the roof bricks and rain spouts. "Just the smell ought to have exterminated them," she complained to Mardiros, "but I can't get all the eggs, and they are immediately reborn."

"I know what will take care of this nuisance," Mardiros said, and led the children to the scissors of the village barber.

Mannig stood on the balcony watching her three kids scratching their heads and walking in their father's wake until they disappeared beyond the shadowy curve of the alley. The wait for their return seemed like eternity, but she instantly detected them amid the horde of pedestrians. Three bald heads shone in the noonday sun. Tears washed down her cheeks. She prayed never to see anything like it again. It brought back memories of her mother on the deportation trek and the epidemic of typhus that had killed her brother Setrak. Her mother had cut off everyone's hair, including hers, because she suspected lice spread the disease.

Mannig cried all over again, this time for her mother, who was tormented over the demise of the son who would have inherited their land and property. She could almost hear Mama's lament, in the cold tent of the refugee camp during the deportation. "Setrak was our last hope to reclaim our property. Our business. Our heritage. Our family name is vanquished forever."

Mannig wiped her tears and later thanked the Lord for providing the barber with magical scissors. "How could he cut the hair to the root?" She swiped her hand across Setrak's smooth scalp.

"Hilla is a progressive village," Mardiros said. "He used a clipper first and then shaved their heads as he shaves men's beards."

Immediately the following day, Mannig split a paisley-designed square coffee table cloth into two triangles. "One for you, Aida," she said, covering the bald head and tying the ends tightly. Then she tied the other half on Maro's head. "Setrak doesn't need a scarf. Actually, he looks boyishly cute."

Life in Hindiyeh Barrage, on the other hand, included several pleasant events. They picnicked amid the ruins of Babylon, only ten miles away; they played Bridge and tennis with their neighboring engineer, Fakhri, who was a Muslim, and Wendy, his British wife. But the high point of life in Hindiyeh Barrage was the fishing.

The resident engineer's house was separated from the dam's control tower by a lush lawn along the eastern bank of the Euphrates River. An overabundance of date palms, interspersed with seasonal fruit trees throughout, surrounded the lawn. Juicy mulberries in the spring satiated their appetites as did apricots in the summer and the figs in early fall. In addition to the plentiful fruits of the land, the river offered a glut of fish.

Every morning Mardiros assigned two employees to haul fish trapped in the locks before the date cargo-boats entered and were raised up to go north. The men cast nets—designed, hooked and repaired by their wives—and then released the daily catch on the lawn—ten to twenty *shabboot*, fresh-water salmon.

Mannig called to her children, who each had a role to play in the daily meal.

The children breathlessly waited for the fish to settle down. Then they lined them up on the grass by length. At the age of five, Setrak measured his own height by lying down on the lawn to rub shoulders with the longest catch. He never heeded his mother's scolding about soiling his clothes and hair.

After Aida and Maro struggled with the slippery fish, filing them into place, Mannig selected one medium size salmon for the family.

Mardiros distributed the rest among his employees before directing the men to lower the water level in the locks for the passenger sail boat from the upper Euphrates, which carried pilgrims going south to Kerbela—the Shia holy city in Iraq.

At the beginning of their residency in Hindiyeh Barrage, everyone loved to eat fish. Mannig prepared it with curry one day, tomato basil the next. Other times, she fried it in sesame oil or grilled it on the open fire. After reading about the nutritional value of fish, she served it daily. Mardiros accused her of being "addicted" to it and the grumbling about the absence of "real" food increased. Occasionally, Mardiros prepared his specialty—fried eggs on spinach, served with toast. "Next time, it will be your turn," he said to Aida.

At nine, Aida knew how to fix rice—puffy, tender grains glistening with butter and emitting a rich basmati aroma, everyone's favorite dish.

Mannig pondered her daughter's attempt to please her parents. *My little girl shouldn't be in a kitchen cooking like a grown-up.* Why commit her daughter to adulthood before she'd had a chance to be a child? Adulthood had been imposed upon Mannig because she was an orphan. She wondered about the origin of her own obsession with education. Her children shouldn't be hostages to a vagabond life, notwithstanding the experiences that enriched their lives.

That evening she confided in her husband. "It behooves us to settle down in Baghdad. Let's rent a house there. I'll prepare a lunch for you to take to Hindiyeh Barrage and serve a late dinner upon your return."

"You mean you've had enough fish in your lifetime?" Mardiros teased her, and then turned serious. "I suspected you'd have enough of moving from village to village, eventually."

"It's not that, as much," Mannig said. "The girls need regular schooling. Aida is well beyond the age to begin formal education and Maro is not far behind her."

"I agree," he said. "What are we going to do with Setrak?"

Mannig glanced at her husband with a contrite heart and shrugged her shoulders.

Chapter 28

Escape from Felloujeh

BEFORE THEIR RADICAL CHANGE OF lifestyle, Mardiros was appointed to Lake Habbaniyeh. Being close to Felloujeh, they moved to their house on the Peninsula, which had sat vacant since the English engineer working for the RAF-Habbaniyeh was transferred elsewhere. Ever since the end of The Great War the British maintained a base fifteen miles from the Felloujeh Bridge and used the main asphalt road that connected Baghdad to Amman, Jordan. For projects on the base they contracted many European technicians, most of whom resided in Felloujeh or Ramadi.

The warm spring of 1941 in Felloujeh emboldened the children to dip in the Euphrates River. Aida, eleven, Maro, eight and Setrak, six, rarely took off their swimsuits. They splashed and built sandcastles along a new spit formed daily by the river's flow, always under Mannig's watchful eyes. Other times, they explored the ruins of the Kouyoumdjian *Qasr*, 500 feet away. "Your cousins used to play in that courtyard," Mannig said, orienting them to her first home in Iraq. Memories of her early married life at the elegant *qasr* with the Kouyoumdjians flashed in and out. She pointed to the back wall on the second floor, part of which was still standing. "Baba's and my flat was right up there. That's where Aida was born."

"Are our cousins as crumbly as the *Qasr*?" Aida asked, with her usual childish insight.

Mannig chuckled. "Maybe they are so now—but, certainly not then." Reflecting upon her answer, she remembered how old-fashioned her relatives' thinking had been when she arrived at the *qasr* as the new bride. When Mardiros bought a pair of britches for riding a horse, one of her nieces cautioned her, "Riding astride makes women infertile." Seeing Mardiros teach her how to use a revolver and a shotgun while riding, her sisters-in-law complained about the dangers of weapons in the hands of women. But the most severe criticism came from Hanum-*Effendi*, Mardiros' mother. Sitting on the veranda that jutted out above the riverbank, she caught a glimpse of Mardiros showing Mannig how to swim. Noticing how Mannig's dress clung to her petite fifteen-year-old bodice, she stamped her cane on the floor. "No decent daughter-in-law of mine bathes in public." *What would the Hanim-Effendi say if she saw her grandchildren in the River?*

"Mamma, Mamma," Maro was pulling Mannig's skirt. "Where was *I* born?"

"In our house—where we are now," Mannig said, and then examined Setrak's face. Seeing no curiosity, she lifted his chin. "Look at me. But you, you were born in Baghdad."

"Where's Baghdad?" Maro asked.

"Baghdad is the most famous city in our country," Mannig continued. "People born there become famous. Right Setrak?" She hoped, in vain, to see his face light up. Instead, her daughters insisted on hearing more about the magical city. "It became famous during the time of Haroun al-Rashid, the great Caliph of the Abbasid Dynasty." She concluded with a tale about Ali Baba and his forty thieves, cueing the children to chant like the hero, "*Iftah ya simsim!* Open Sesame!" Setrak joined in with his sisters in the chant but would not stop until Mannig shushed him. "Enough! Enough! Ali Baba's cave is open now."

Mannig set aside a lot of time to play her piano and read. When a friend gave her Margaret Mitchell's, *Gone with the Wind*, she neglected her music. She read a chapter while the children napped during the hottest time of the day and then related her edited version. She couldn't control her emotions, however, when Scarlett returned to Tara at the end of the American Civil War and discovered her home in ruins. She often gazed with nostalgia at what was left of the Felloujeh *qasr,* between their house and the green-painted steel Bridge. "I wish I could go back to my home in Adapazar, just as Scarlett returned to hers in Tara."

The single-lane Bridge beyond the *qasr* defined the southern boundary of the Kouyoumdjian properties. It was erected soon after The Great War for military truck-and-lorry maneuverings between RAF-Habbaniyeh and Baghdad. Even though mostly donkeys and camels plodded across its asphalt surface these days, Mannig had specified a boulder between the Bridge and the *qasr*, beyond which the children could not play.

Aida dared to ignore her parents' edict.

When she found a pair of rollerskates in the back of a closet, Mardiros surmised it was another discard by the British family who resided there before them. "They didn't take the kitchen cabinet on wheels," he said, "or the

Mannig at Resident Engineer's house, Hindiyeh Barrage, 1939.

two watercolor paintings. They must not have wanted to keep these, either. Let's see how we can use them." Everyone tried the one foot first, then the pair, ending with falls and guffaws. All lost interest. Aida persisted. Soon she was swooshing back and forth on their front concrete porch—at best twenty feet long. One day she lugged the pair of skates all the way to the Bridge and skated across the smooth asphalt road and back. When Mannig overheard her tell Maro about the joyride, Mannig deprived Aida—for a whole week—of the Nestlé Chocolate Bar the children relished before bedtime.

Upon Mardiros' return home after work, Mannig got a break from being the *gendarme*, controlling the children's whereabouts. Besides an occasional swim with them, he held their attention with stories about his athletic days in college. Only after the children went to bed did he sit on the veranda to sip his cognac. He waited for Mannig to pull up a chaise-lounge beside him before divulging his insights about the workers. "There's a strong hatred against the British these days," he confided. "The English must know about this. That's the reason for the reinforcement of Indian soldiers in RAF-Habbaniyeh." A few evenings later, he elaborated, relating more hearsay about a rebellion. "The men working on my project are restless. They vehemently despise the leadership of the British-mandated Iraqi government. Some spit when they hear the word, *Englaisy*. Others curse the royal family. I don't know how they feel about people like me who are employed by the government and deal with the British."

His most troubling observation, in April of 1941, concerned Rashid Ali al-Gaylani, the ousted former Prime Minister. "He has declared his affinity to the Nazis, which seems to rally the sympathy of ninety percent of my workers, and I suspect of all the Iraqis."

Mannig listened carefully, without expressing an opinion. After all, living in a house without neighbors to commiserate with, most of her contribution to their conversations involved the children. A good listener, she took his advice always to be aware of her surroundings to heart. She relaxed when the children took their naps during the hottest hours of the day. Sitting by a window that opened on the veranda, she relished the breeze from the river. This was her reading time. She was in the middle of a chapter in *Baghdad Sketches*, a 1932 publication by Freya Stark—a British Journalist in Iraq during its formative history—when an unusual thump on the veranda put her on the alert. She jumped up, tiptoed to the wall and pressed her body flat against one of the watercolor paintings. She controlled her panting, but sensed the painting lose its hold on the nail.

Thump-thump. Thump-thump. The sound of boots approached the window.

She was tempted to close her eyes, but instead they remained so wide open that she felt the heat of the day in her eyeballs. Breathlessly, she peered out of the fluttering curtains. *Aye!* A man in army fatigues tramped his boots toward the front door. She bent down to peak at his top and saw a huge khaki turban atop his head. *Indian!*

She barely suppressed a scream. *Aye!* The painting slid down her back, crashing on the floor. She dashed toward the ceiling-to-floor bookcase, climbed on the armrest of the sofa and reached for the shotgun on a shelf. Holding her breath, she tiptoed back to the window and poked the gun barrel through the window opening. Notwithstanding the bumping sound against the window frame, she aimed it at the intruder.

Hearing the clatter, the Gurkha-Indian soldier turned around. Seeing a metallic gun barrel pointed at him, he fled from the veranda like a terrified gazelle.

Mannig suspected his flight led him back to whence he came. She dared not go out. Instead, she closed all the windows and latched them. She bolted the front door and the kitchen door. Feeling semi-calm, she praised God for guns. She had thwarted perhaps a robbery or even a murder all by herself. Still trembling, she smiled at keeping the upperhand in the near-fatal episode. A nervous smile still twitching at her eyelids, she dashed to the children's nap area. *Thank God! They slept through it.* Noiselessly, she locked their windows, too, despite trapping the stifling outdoor heat within the walls of the tightly sealed house. She switched on the ceiling fan. *At least, it will circulate the air.*

She heard a car approaching the house; then, the sound of someone running toward the house. She dashed back and picked up the shotgun again, and again peeked out the window. *I'll break the glass, if necessary!* Surprised to see Mardiros on the veranda, she unlocked the door, the gun still in her hand.

"What's that for?" He looked taken aback. "Has the revolution begun?"

With great relief, she handed it to him. With a shaky voice she told him about the intruder.

"But, it isn't even loaded!" He cranked the shotgun in half, revealing an empty barrel.

Mannig didn't know whether to cry or, again, thank the Lord for having escaped harm. "Why are you home earlier than usual?" she asked, less out of curiosity than to erase the incident from her thoughts.

"We don't have time now," he said. "We must pack. And be quick. Just two suitcases—one for us and one for the children."

"Why? What's happening?"

"I'll explain later, in the car. We must leave immediately."

"Where are we going? Is there danger? How about the shotgun?"

He revealed his revolver inside his shirt. "We'll d-d-drive to B-Baghdad," Mardiros stammered, throwing a pair of slacks into his suitcase. He stared at his books—with a pained expression, he shook his head. He ignored the record albums as well, but he unplugged the radio and picked it up. "I think this will fit in at the bottom of the car trunk before I load the suitcases."

Mannig was filling the children's suitcase when he returned. He latched his suitcase. "Let's go."

Mannig carefully slid a small black velvet pouch inside a leg of Setrak's spare trousers. *That's a safe place for Hanum-Effendi's heirloom jewelry.* She latched the suitcase.

Mardiros picked it up. "Come on. This should be all. Let's go."

The sun had set and the sky promised a moonless night. The mullah of Felloujeh had long finished his eventide chant. A few lights beamed from the homes across the Euphrates. After tightly strapping the suitcases to the back of his car, he handed the children colored rock-candy. "Don't eat them until I tell you," he said and cranked the windows up—one as far up as it could go. "Should have had it fixed by now," he mumbled to himself. Noiselessly closing the back door, he scooted into the driver's seat and looked at Mannig. "There's nothing to worry about," he whispered, "but it might be wise to cover your hair."

Already a nervous wreck over the speed of their packing and loading into the car, she let out a guttural sigh. "With what? I didn't pack a scarf."

"Here," he said, pulling out his khaki handkerchief. He turned the key and started the engine, cringing at the loud rotary sound. "Mr. Ford should invent silent cars!" he complained.

Mannig wanted to know more about this urgency but the hanky kept her occupied while he drove across the bridge. Its corners were too short to be tied under her chin. She slinked her fingers across her head and pulled out two bobby-pins that held her hair in a bun. She clasped each on a corner of his hanky and pinned them above her ears.

After crossing the bridge, Mardiros took his first long breath. He shifted into first gear and throttled down the main road out of Felloujeh, now short on pedestrians. He breathed in short gulps. Once beyond the boundaries of the village, he inhaled a lungful of air and shifted to third, pressing on the gas pedal. On the empty asphalt road toward Baghdad, he finally turned on his lights.

"Can we eat the candy?" Maro asked from the backseat.

"No!" Mardiros yelled. "I'll tell you when."

"But Setrak is eating his," both Aida and Maro whined.

"Setrak!" Mardiros yelled so loudly that it startled everyone. "Give me back the candy."

Setrak recoiled in his seat, hiding his hands behind his back.

"Setrak! I don't want to stop the car and spank you!" Mardiros yelled.

"Shush!" Mannig nudged him. "He doesn't understand. Just let him be a boy."

They had hardly settled the candy issue when Mardiros reduced the speed of the car.

"What's the matter?" Mannig pulled herself up to see what was ahead. She then stared at her window. "Mardiros! I see the silhouettes of many people on my side."

"Children," Mardiros commanded under his breath. "Eat your candy NOW! One at a time. Don't speak! Don't make a sound!" He leaned forward and gazed ahead—as straight as the light beams of the car. He slowed down even more, braking to a near stop. The farther he drove, the more figures appeared in the headlights. Clad in Bedouin garb, bullet-belts strapped against their chests, they blocked the car's path, their palms slapping the hood and the sides of the car.

"Wuggiff! Wuggiff! Halt! Stop!"

Chapter 29

The 1941 coup d'état

Mardiros's ashen face and clenched jaw frightened Mannig. His hazel eyes stared straight ahead into the stream of the headlights. He shifted his feet, stepping on the brake while keeping his right foot on the gas pedal.

Bedouin Arabs surrounded the car like bees clinging to their hive. Bullet-belts strapped to their chests and revolvers in hand, they pounded on the windows. Finding the doors locked, one Bedou struck a match and lit a kerosene lantern held by another. He brought it close to Mardiros's window, halfway open.

His blood-shot eyes scrutinized the driver, then the passengers.

A second Bedou poked his gun through the backseat window that was stuck half open. The other raised the lantern, light flooding across the children's faces.

"*La, wallah. Bess atfaal.* No, my God. Just children." He yelled back to his buddy accomplices.

Mannig held her breath. The man would focus on her next. She tightened the knot of the hanky, puckered her lips and purposely raised her chin up to accentuate her prominent nose. Never before had she taken pride in inheriting an Armenian profile. By looking as ugly, dirty and disheveled as possible, she had avoided being violated on the deportation trek. The Ottoman gendarmes, goading a herd of surviving Armenians across the Iraqi desert, had targeted the pretty orphans for their evening pleasure. Her sister, Adriné, was among those raped. The bunch of ragged refugees learned to smear their faces with soot, dirt and even feces, hoping to escape the ravages of the soldiers in whose control they found themselves.

The man outside Mannig's window glanced at her then shifted his lantern, light streaming onto her lap and feet in search of hidden weapons.

"I don't see guns," he shouted back, just as another Bedou, his mouth muffled inside a checkered *keffiyeh,* was yelling at Mardiros, "Get out! Hands up!"

Glancing at the revolver strapped to Mardiros' belt Mannig pulled on his sleeve. "Don't be foolish. There are hundreds of them." Her words faded away as they left her mouth.

In a flash, Mardiros swung his door open, jolting the Bedou backwards.

Guttural warnings rose in the desert with the cocking of shotguns and a mass thrust toward the car.

Mardiros was being shoved back into his seat. He raised both hands, "No gun."

"What's the problem?" A husky voice rose above all babblings. "It's just a car …. Can't you manage even one car?"

The assailants held their peace and cleared a path for, seemingly, their leader.

Both Mannig and Mardiros were breathing hard.

Gargantuan in size among his fellow men, their chief swaggered ahead. A flashlight in his hand, he clicked it on at Mardiros.

Both Mannig and Mardiros closed their eyes.

"Get out!" he shouted, but then he scrutinized Mardiros' face. "*La, wa'allah!* It's The *Effendi*!" he added, as if apologizing, surprising not only Mardiros and Mannig, but causing an enormous sigh of regret among his warriors. "Where are you going, *Matruloze Effendi*?"

Hearing Mardiros' name butchered evoked both comfort and fear in Mannig. Arabs who had farmed for the Kouyoumdjians concocted characteristic labels for the hard-to-remember names. Khosrof, for example was *Khubuz*—meaning bread or dispenser of wealth—a title befitting the eldest in the family. Mardiros was *Matruloze*, meaning a machine gun because of the way he yelled at the workmen.

Mardiros was once spared by a band of marauders who also recognized him as *Matruloze* when he was escorting a wagon of supplies for the orphans. Another time, however, he had escaped the bullet when his nephew, mistaken for *Matruloze*, was shot. What would his fate be now?

"*Salaam*, Jabbar," Mardiros returned the greeting while casually pressing on the clutch, ready to drive away. "I'm taking my family to Baghdad. Why are you and your tribe out in the middle of the night?"

"We're gearing up for a *thawra*," he said, "a revolution. Tonight may be the hour for the first shot. I'm waiting for the word. We're going to get rid of the king. We're going to kick Nuri Al-Said out. We are going to nationalize the oil companies and stop making deals with the British. We're going to own our

Mannig at Hindiyeh Barrage, 1940.

Republic." He swung around to face his followers and fired a bullet into the sky. "We're going to own our Republic."

His followers echoed his exuberance. "Our Republic!"

Mannig sensed as much energy as anxiety in their posturing. "Let's go!" she urged Mardiros.

"*Salaam*, Jabbar," Mardiros stuck his neck out his window. "I must leave for the children's sake. They are tired."

Jabbar slapped the top of the car. "*Imshee!*" He scooted him off.

The car wheels rolled at a slower rate than the Bedouin pulled their figures away from the beaming lights, and yet, in a few minutes the desert became as empty as it had been before their encounter with Jabbar.

No one spoke. The children fell asleep. The only sound for the next ten minutes was the tires lapping the asphalt.

Mannig broke the silence. "What was that all about?"

"Had we delayed our departure from Felloujeh," Mardiros said, wiping his forehead, "we might have gotten trapped." He reached for her hand. "We'll be fine in Baghdad. You're a good sport. Flexibility is the best policy these days."

The coup d'état of April, 1941, that Jabbar, the rebel, was jubilating over was initiated and led by Al-Gaylani. "The former prime minister must have declared his sympathy with the pro-Nazi movement," Mardiros said in a staccato voice. "He's been disgruntled ever since his political party was denied legitimacy. I wouldn't be surprised if the British don't counterattack the locals …. Felloujeh will be in the crossfire and we, the innocent victims." He looked at the speedometer and said, "Before the hour's end, we ought to be in Baghdad."

Mannig glared straight ahead and hoped Mardiros knew what he was doing.

After half-an-hour's driving Mardiros broke the silence. "We must be nearing Abu Ghraib … somewhere to your right, behind those trees. Can you believe how this desert spot in the middle of nowhere has bloomed?"

"I'd like to see the changes sometime," Mannig whispered just to say something.

"We should be able to," he said. "It's only thirty miles from Baghdad, but not right away. I think that Al-Gaylani, the rascal revolutionary, is taking advantage of the Nazi successes in northern Africa. He must assume Rommel will conquer Libya and Egypt, and that his next conquest will be Iraq. He probably thinks the Germans will be on our lands before we drive into Baghdad," he laughed.

They arrived in Baghdad in the middle of the night to find the street lights out and nary a pedestrian in sight. "I hope we're not the only car chugging along." He drove without apparent apprehension around the first and second round-about before crossing the Tigris at the southern bridge. "The statue of the king on his horse hasn't been desecrated yet," he said with relief and veered left onto Al-Rashid Street, the main thoroughfare meandering along the east bank of the river. "I hope Sebouh will open the door at this hour of the night."

He parked the car on the desolate street below the apartment complex where Sebouh and Adriné lived. Mannig carried Setrak and Mardiros, Maro. Aida, who was awake, followed her parents through the archway and into the courtyard. While Mannig climbed the two flights of stairs, trying to keep a steady pace, Mardiros rushed up and knocked on Adriné's door. Hearing no motion within, he kept knocking gently, as if worried about waking the neighbors.

As soon as Mannig could set Setrak down, she pounded on the door. "Sebouh! Adriné! Open the door. It's us."

Chapter 30

A Fireball in the Sky

It became quite a prison for two families to manage themselves in a three-bedroom apartment. Luckily, it was the beginning of summer. Seven children between the ages five and sixteen and four adults aged thirty-seven to fifty-three slept on the roof at nights—the only time of relief from the cousins' squabbling and the effects of one hundred degree temperatures. On the roof, refreshing night breezes wafted from a sky spangled with stars. Traffic sounds off Al-Rashid Street melted away at sunset. Gazing at the sky became the best therapy, allowing each of them distraction from private thoughts of pain or resentment.

Initially, the cousins were ecstatic to be together. They played cards, and cards and more cards. Eventually, every game ended in shouting. At first, the parents refereed. Then they threatened to take the cards away, leaving only dominos, which could hardly hold their attention.

The war compelled the closure of the Baghdadi schools. Adriné's four children, under orders from their father, occupied themselves with their Arabic textbooks. The vocabulary of algebra, literature or physics was not familiar to Mannig's children, who were not only younger than their cousins but had never been enrolled in a regular school. Story books for non-adults were not common in most homes. The parents often staked out different territories for each child when a few hours seemed to appease their immediate needs. Even so, they found themselves constantly reprimanding the cousins, who squabbled over the legitimacy of the winner of a card game.

One evening the cousins booted out Aida for winning the game of *Trumps* several times in a row. She barged out of the living room, glad to depart the blacked-out room. A dark cloth covered the sheer curtains just as one concealed the glass of the balcony door. The city power station shut down at dusk and residents were ordered to buffer any light streaming from their homes in case of airraids by British airplanes. Disgusted with her cousins' accusations, Aida dashed upstairs to the roof and plopped down onto her bed. *I'll tie the mosquito net to its posts later.*

She gazed straight up at the Big Dipper. It mattered not that she couldn't identify brilliant clusters in the sky, as could *those* cousins, who told all kinds of fascinating stories. She focused upon the many shooting stars, some of which traveled so far that they seemed to touch her own horizon. The moonless sky was in the mood to entertain its audience, helping her to forget her cousins' ill treatment.

Enticed by the silent sky, she barely noticed the whirring sound of a plane flying at a faint distance. The silent sky of stars lured her into space travel.

Without warning, a great ball of fire suddenly hung above her bed.

In a flash, she screamed and was jolted to her feet. She sprinted down the stairs, yelling, stumbling, and yelling even louder, "The end of the world is here! The end of the world is beginning!"

Everyone, adults and children, gathered around her. Just the sight of Aida's ashen face nailed them in place.

"Calm down!" Mardiros shouted from the parlor, interrupting his backgammon game with Sebouh. He walked into the hallway, Sebouh in tow. "What is this all about?"

"It's like the Bible says," Aida panted, barely able to breathe. "The end of the world has started …. There's a big fireball in the sky …."

Some dashed to the outside windows, others through the balcony doors, to peek past the blankets that hung as black-out blockers.

"Ooooooooh!"

The night as bright as day confirmed Aida's panic.

Mardiros and Sebouh dashed up to the roof.

All hesitated at the base of the stairs—fearful, anxious or confused.

The sound of footsteps making a quick descent increased everyone's apprehension.

"It's just a flare," Mardiros said as he caught his breath. He and Sebouh headed for the parlor, but not back to their game. They glued their ears to the radio for announcements. The Baghdadi Radio Station interrupted its regular programming of that hour.

The men sat down.

The station was silent.

They waited.

Mardiros got up to jiggle the dial, but hearing faint sounds he raised the volume and sat back in his chair.

Suddenly, a classical piece by Beethoven blared into the parlor.

"Dial the local station," Sebouh reprimanded him. "I want to know what's going on in Baghdad, not in Vienna!"

"This IS the Baghdad Radio Station!" Mardiros almost lost his temper. "Here! You work on your useless radio!"

The static at other broadcasting stations made it impossible to learn anything. They decided to hit Al-Rashid Street, where someone who was out and about might know more than they did.

"Where are you going?" Mannig called after them. "You've told us that the light in the sky is from a flare. How can you expect us to understand? Well, I don't. Are we trapped in this apartment? What else do you know? Is this going to be another 'escape from Felloujeh'? I need to prepare …."

"It's a flare. That's all we know, t-too," Mardiros stammered. "Maybe s-s-someone on the s-s-s-sidewalk can tell us s-s-something."

The two men dashed across the walkway, down the stairs and into Al-Rashid Street.

A cluster of neighborhood men, huddled together at the street corner, were analyzing the phantom noise of the airplane and the subsequent flare in the sky.

"The British planes must have dropped it to illuminate our street," one pedestrian said. But when another asked him why, he shrugged his shoulders.

Mardiros pulled Sebouh's arm. "I'll go ask the men across the street while you learn whatever the group of men at the far end of our street know."

Ten minutes later Mardiros and Sebouh regrouped. Echoes of heavy bombing in the far distance made them scurry back to the apartment. They scrambled upstairs and shared a moment of peace before going into Sebouh's apartment.

Like sentries, both Mannig and Adriné stood in the hallway, the children clustered behind them.

"We're safe here," Sebouh said while Mardiros explained that the bombing was directed at the Iraqi military installations on the outskirts of Baghdad. "There's nothing to fear."

Nevertheless five-year-old Setrak clung to Mannig's skirt.

"They won't bomb the civilians," Mardiros assured everyone. "Mosques or residential enclaves are safe, too. The British pilots are well-known for hitting their targets, and only their targets."

Sebouh moved forward and looked at the huddled children. "We've solved the puzzle. You don't have to be afraid, anymore," he said. Addressing his own four teenagers, he added, "It only means that the schools will remain closed for a little while longer. There won't be time for final exams this year, either."

Before he finished explaining, the kids yelled, "Goooooooood!" only to be shushed by the adults.

After a two-week period of constantly refereeing the children's activities, Mannig complained to Mardiros, "This 'skirmish' between the Iraqi army and the British—as you call this war—is not ending in a day or two. Encroaching on Adrine's family for more than ten days is unhealthy."

"All right," he announced a few days later, "I found a bungalow we can rent for a while."

Mannig couldn't wait to move into the two-bedroom house on the other side of the Tigris River. They settled into a so-called furnished house with a large yard, surrounded by a fence. She relished the open space around her. At first sight, she wondered if she ought to complain about the scanty bedding—cots, ordinary camping cots. The cooking facilities, which consisted of a single hot plate on a stone-top table next to a sink, appeared extremely cumbersome. "At least we have running water," she consoled herself.

Seeing an apple tree in the yard, she picked a couple of near-red applets and stewed them with raisins, dried apricots, sugar and a hint of cinnamon. She served the compote with cooked rice, laced with crispy sautéed vermicelli noodles. Everyone devoured her new recipe. Was it that tasty, she wondered, or were they starving? She concluded the real reason for their appreciation must be the ambiance—eating on the porch felt like a picnic.

At night, Mannig delighted at their remoteness from the hustle and bustle of Al-Rashid Street. One look at Mardiros, glued to his Blaupunkt radio in absolute concentration, also confirmed they had made the right choice by moving out.

She lay on her cot for the night, quite content.

The rattling of the rickety doors and flimsy windows of the bungalow awakened them that very first night in their new home.

A huge roiling cloud of smoke filled the sky above them after continuous bombing nearby.

Mardiros, in his pajamas, dashed out and into the street where all the neighborhood men were huddled in a quandary.

Even before the men could speculate about the source of the sound, airplanes zoomed from the East, disrupting the sleepy night air with heavy bombing.

"They're bombing the Railroad Station!" The men shouted to one another. "Allah! Be with us …. Tie the hands of the enemy. Make them miss our homes."

Enemy? The British, of course.

Had Mardiros, unwittingly, entrapped his family in the crossfire? He should have investigated the location of this bungalow. He would never forgive himself if anything should happen to them now. How futile to have assumed a sense of superiority for having rescued his family from a battle in Felloujeh, only a fortnight ago.

Mannig sensed her obvious mistake, too. Adriné's apartment with its traffic noise and crowded quarters seemed like a haven now.

"The bombing will resume again tonight," Mardiros said. "I did not know that the houses in this area were so close to the Railroad Station. The Allied Forces are flying over from Habbaniyeh to decapitate transportation facilities. They've decided to bomb them at night. First they attacked the military barracks, now they intend to paralyze all means of transportation."

The couple sensed the risk they'd be taking if they stayed. "We'll lose two months' rent if we move somewhere else," Mardiros murmured. "I paid for the first and last months, and I won't be paid myself for another two weeks."

"We must return to Adriné's apartment," Mannig decided.

"The British are experts at hitting specific targets," he assured her. "The railroads are their target and those lines will be the only scenes of destruction."

"We are too close to those lines," Mannig said. "No one will spend a peaceful night here."

"The British know what they are doing," he assured her.

"I believe you, but since I calm the fears of the children, I want to move."

"This house shouldn't be left unoccupied," Mardiros said. "We're responsible for its contents against looting."

"Maybe we ought to spend the days here and return to Adriné's at night."

"In that case," Mardiros whispered, "I think, I will spend the nights here."

During the next month, Mannig followed a daily ritual, back and forth from their bungalow to her sister's flat. She collected her three children at Adriné's, even before breakfast, and led them down Al-Rashid Street carrying a basket—a butcher's knife stowed in its bottom, covered with a towel. This refugee-like routine reminded her of her childhood in Adapazar when the Ottoman authorities had decreed that all Armenian residents must relinquish their personal weapons. Not owning any guns, her family felt safe. Haji-doo, her grandmother, however, feared that when the gendarmes searched their home for weapons they might confiscate her kitchen cutlery. By hiding their best butcher's knife inside a heap of cool ashes in their brick baking oven, she prevented it from being confiscated. Her mother lugged along that very same knife throughout the deportation trek. Mannig remembered Mama slicing *basturma*, dried meat, for a meager sandwich. And then again, she used it to hack off the children's hair, hoping to thwart the growth of lice.

Mannig packed her butcher's knife for good measure. She would use it as a weapon, if threatened. She didn't expect problems at all, but felt safer to have it while walking down Al-Rashid Street on her way from Adriné's home to hers, across the River Tigris.

The knife came in handy one morning when she passed by a baker on their way to the bungalow for the day. She bought a *Sammoon,* European-style loaf of bread. Instead of breaking the bastone into chunks, she retrieved her butcher's knife and sliced pieces for the children and one for her. They nibbled on their way to their bungalow. "I relish that first bite," she reminded the children each time. "Besides its cardamom flavor, its crispy crust tantalizes my pallet."

The daily walk from Adrine's flat in the mornings took over an hour, but Mardiros always drove them to Adrine's after supper, where his family spent the night. He then returned to the bungalow. Having no garage, he drove his car inside the fenced yard.

Hoping for official reports on his Blaupunkt, he switched it on. Beethoven continued to blare. He wished the composer had not composed so many pieces. Then he prayed for the Iraqi Information Department to run out of the maestro's repertoire or better still, to throw all their records against the wall. Having no alternative stations to dial to, he switched it off.

He fell asleep for the night.

At midnight, a boom startled him.

Chapter 31

Settling in Baghdad

MARDIROS, TOO, WORRIED ABOUT THE proximity of the bungalow to the Baghdad Railway Station. Should the British planes miss their target by a few blocks, they would annihilate everything in the neighborhood. *The RAF are precise*—his head said—*but the pilots are human*—was his heart's hollow reply.

The next day, he informed Mannig that he was off to hunt for a house closer to downtown Baghdad. Still assuming that their stay in Baghdad would be temporary, he rented a brick house with a large courtyard close to the King Faisal I Bridge of the Tigris River. After signing a rental lease for two months, he was glad to learn that several of the neighbors were Armenian. *Mannig would like that,* he thought.

Indeed, Mannig preferred to be independent in her own home. She loved her sister, Adriné, but had found it hard to watch how Sebouh, her husband treated her without civility. He often belittled her in front of his children and blamed her for wasting food with her experimental recipes using different staples and vegetables. He preferred his standard meals of rice and stew. He also insisted that she and their four children take off their good clothes as soon as they came home and don their old rags. "Why waste fashion at home?" To Mannig, he was a miser and Adriné was not the only one to suffer from his caprices. His three beautiful teenage daughters were seen wearing the same pink coats with black velvet collars, winter after winter.

Mannig was tempted to fight with her brother-in-law for treating his own family like paupers, but as a guest in his house she was compelled to keep quiet. She was determined to speak her mind in due course.

She cherished her independence in her new house and was immediately convinced of the advantages of living in civilization. "Mardiros *Jahn*," she addressed her husband after supper while the two lounged in the courtyard, "shouldn't we consider settling in Baghdad?"

"The Irrigation Department will not assign me to a desk job yet," he said, sipping the last of his Turkish coffee and lighting a Camel, the new rage in Baghdad for smokers. "I may be fifty-one years old but I still have a lot of field potential in me. They need my services until such time as they find better skilled engineers. These days, I can commute between Baghdad and Habbaniyeh. It would be out of the question for them to send me to Kirkuk or Basra."

The couple didn't resolve the issue that evening, but the more Mannig thought about it during the day, the more determined she became. "While we are waiting for your next assignment," she said, "let's salvage our things in Felloujeh—whatever we can. I know I want my piano."

Mardiros borrowed the government lorry that Friday, his day off, and drove to Felloujeh. He returned to Baghdad with a lorry-full of stuff, mostly unusable, including the ripped books. "I'll find someone to restore some of my treasures," he moaned, holding the gold-edged pages of the complete set of Alexandre Dumas.

"You also brought our carpets?" she asked upon seeing the burlap rolled rugs that Mardiros had stored in Kaloust's *qasr* for the summer. "Didn't they loot his place?"

"No, no. The Felloujeh people wouldn't do such vile things," he said, wiping his forehead. "It was the Gurkha Indian soldiers who violated our house …. They were working for the British Military and did some fighting for them during the Gaylani insurgency. So when that one short war was over, upon their retreat from Baghdad back to Habbaniyeh, they apparently noticed our house on the peninsula by itself and raided it. The scum bums ruined my books and photographs and chopped up anything they couldn't carry out with them."

"You will find someone to restore my piano, too, won't you?" Mannig brushed her hand over the scored walnut cover of the keys.

Feeling guilty for the expense of transporting an *axed* piano, Mannig questioned her own selfishness, especially after the repairman installed a new set of keys and a few strings. She refrained from complaining, even though the piano didn't sound like it used to. *The children will need music lessons soon,* she rationalized, *and I will be their teacher.* After all, she had taught them reading and writing throughout their travels during the last ten years.

"Aida is almost ten years old," she confronted Mardiros a few weeks later. "She should be enrolled in a regular school. I've taught her everything I know. The older the children grow, the less adequate I feel about teaching them anything. You know I haven't even attended school myself!"

"Come, come, Mannig!" Mardiros said. "The orphanage gave you a far better education than the fancy private schools that all my sisters-in-law graduated from. You've amazed me with your self-determination to learn on your own. You've tutored yourself in English and French, and let's not forget the piano. Yes, you had a few lessons, but you practiced and practiced and kept us and all the Kouyoumdjians at the *Qasr* enthralled. I think you can compete in, and win, any contest."

"That's not the point," she said. "If it were only a question of giving piano lessons, then I probably could manage. But academics are beyond me. I don't feel competent to teach beyond basic mathematics. How about science? And who knows what else schools teach these days? I'm sure they need to learn how to read and write in Arabic. After all, it's the language of the country. As citizens of Iraq, they should excel in Arabic. I'm ashamed to say, I can barely speak it. Also, you are too busy yourself to spend any time with them."

A few days later, she brought up the subject of settling down in Baghdad. "Maybe I am selfish," she said. "I need to stay in one place, myself. I like Baghdad. I like talking with other Armenians. I like the social gatherings with the Kouyoumdjians. Don't you enjoy being with your relatives more often than once in a while?"

Mardiros refrained from expressing an opinion, although he listened with an open mind. His job was their priority.

"Baghdad is a grand city," she said, soon after they had moved into the brick house on the west side of the Tigris River. "It has an Armenian Church and a school on the other side of the river. But the *Agoomp*, the Armenian social club, is on our side."

By the end of the week, she hoped for a decision. "Look at your brothers," she said. "They've sold their shares in Felloujeh and settled in Baghdad. Visiting them in their independent homes and meeting so many of their new friends makes me envious. I've missed social life. During our last ten years of gallivanting throughout the Iraqi deserts, I can count the times we've socialized with people like us on one hand. I've missed dancing at parties and dressing up at ladies' teas. You go to work every day and face new challenges and people; you don't seem to crave getting together with friends. I think, I'm almost glad that Iraq was involved in a war, albeit for only five weeks. I got to live in a city and now I appreciate its lifestyle."

Mardiros' silence didn't mean that he was ignoring his wife's feelings. He promised to take action the next day after work.

After work never came.

He and his colleagues were urged to return home at noon and not show up at the office until further notice.

"What's happening?" He nudged a fellow engineer.

"It's going to be one hundred degrees," was the answer.

Mardiros knew that answer meant more than the weather. He drove straight home and warned Mannig. "Something political is brewing …. I can't figure out what it is yet. Have you heard anything from our neighbors?"

Mannig shook her head but then gave the matter some thought. "Maybe I'll learn something this evening." After a light supper of watermelon, cheese and bread, she walked out the front door with a broom and swept the steps that led to their house. Uncharacteristically, she continued an airy sweep of the leaves and debris down the dirt street. She sprayed water with a hose to settle the dust. Immediately after that, she brought out a couple of chaise lounges and sat in one, a book in Armenian in her hand.

When the children ran to join their mother, Mardiros grabbed them. "Today, I want you out of sight. So go to the roof and get to bed. Do you understand?"

They knew Baba meant what he said. Maro and Setrak followed Aida, their oldest sibling, her head lowered in disappointment. Once on the roof, Aida poked her chin over the railing, and seeing Baba still in the courtyard monitoring the children's ascent, quickly pulled back, lest he yell a loud threat.

Within a few minutes, he saw how the neighboring women, clad in black *abayas*—the traditional Arab caftan-style black garb that hung from the top of the head to the ankles—flocked and squatted near Mannig. She greeted them saying, "I'm glad you are here this evening. I've seen some of you gathered around your homes, and I wanted to be like you."

"My man told me this morning," one woman began the chatter, "that he might stay at the *souq* later than usual."

"Mine, too," another squatter interrupted her. "Something terrible is brewing in the bazaar and he thought it wise to keep vigil over his *Subbah-Silver* store."

Mardiros quietly retreated to the parlor and turned on his Blaupunkt. He wanted to hear the woman's statement confirmed. Not getting even a signal, he slapped its side in disgust. "I'll be back soon," he said to Mannig, as he stepped out and past the cackling women, who instantly held still, stunned by his sudden exit.

He returned within thirty minutes. "You better go back to your homes," he said to the women, who were still hanging around. "The talk at the café by the bridge is troubling. The Jewish stores in the *souq* are being ransacked."

As the covey of abaya-clad women stood up to leave, Mannig raised the book in her hand. "We're not Jewish …. We are Armenians. See? I'm reading a book in Armenian."

Chapter 32

The Thieves of Baghdad

Mardiros returned home before noon the next morning. "S-s-s-something terrible happened last night," he stammered upon seeing Mannig in the hallway, on her way to the *souq*. "You mustn't go anywhere. We will eat whatever we have."

She put her shopping bag on the counter and headed directly to the kitchen. After looking inside the cylindrical coffee grinder, she said, "There's enough powdered coffee. I can brew some." Without waiting for his response, she turned on the gas stove to boil water in a *jazwa,* enough for two demitasse cups of Turkish coffee.

"Thieves! Thieves!" he continued. "What do you expect from the people of Baghdad? Eh? The Thief of Baghdad may be a fictional tale of the *Arabian Nights,* but these days, our city has become a nest for him and his kind."

He lamented for the good old days—when all ethnic groups had worked together throughout history—back to the times when Islam was first introduced to the Babylonians, and later on to the Greek, Armenian and Jewish civilians. "Everyone befriended their neighbors and played together," he fumed. "People tolerated any idiosyncrasies and traditions of ethnic groups. So, I don't understand how they have become strangers overnight—not just strangers, but enemies. More so, savages."

He was convinced that the Gaylani influence of Fascism had aroused sentiments suppressed in the general population. The night before, they had stopped showing respect for the Jewish merchants or their successful businesses. They broke into the Jewish stores in the *souq* and the upscale retailers on Al-Rashid Street, stealing radios, refrigerators, air conditioners and everything else they could get their hands on, whether or not they knew what they confiscated.

"Didn't the police stop the riot?" Mannig asked. "I thought some merchants had hired their own guards. Where were they?"

"Ha! You're picturing a civilized uprising. Apparently, it was a mob mentality. Once they were unleashed, everyone grabbed his loot." Mardiros sat for a long time, thinking quietly. "I don't like what's happening to our people. Those looters must have had an exaggerated sense of their own privilege in their own country. Today they're getting even by getting something for nothing. At this rate, tomorrow they will be after human flesh. I'm not comfortable in my birthplace anymore. The opportunities for our children are dim."

Mannig worried about her husband's physical condition more than his concern about the future. If his anxiety continued, he could have another heart attack. "Stop predicting what's going to happen," she insisted. "We're fine and the children will be fine, too. I think you need some rest and perhaps no more cigarettes."

Still puffing, he said, "All right! I shall rest."

Unfamiliar voices awakened him. He peeked inside the parlor but didn't recognize the heavyset lady sipping from a demitasse of coffee with Mannig. Across from them, Aida and a girl of the same age sat on a divan.

Hearing him, Mannig said, "Mardiros. Come and meet Diggin Tatyossian, our neighbor from one street up. We met at the *souq* earlier."

"Very honored to meet Armenian neighbors," Mardiros said, shaking her hand. "I thought I knew all of us in Baghdad. Are you new?"

The lady laughed so hard her stomach rippled. "We are old Baghdadi Armenians. You can't find a people who are anymore ancient than us in this town. We go back to the birth of Armenia. In fact, we speak Arabic better than the Arabs themselves. Even our native language has its own dialect."

Mardiros had already detected the lady's usage of Arabic words incorporated into her Armenian grammar. "And this must be your daughter?" He went to shake hands with the girl sitting tidily next to Aida.

"Lala is my youngest daughter," the lady said. "We enrolled her at the American School for Girls last year and I'm wondering if your daughter will be attending the same school."

Both Mannig and Mardiros exchanged a curious look, wondering whether she had actually said *American*.

"The American School is the best in Baghdad," the lady continued. "Better than the French *Ma Soeur*."

"How about the Armenian School?" Mardiros asked. "Isn't it functional anymore?"

"Oh, it is. But it is not the best. They emphasize Armenia and its history."

Both Mannig and Mardiros looked at each other again as if Diggin Tatyossian was doing their thinking for them about their children's education.

After a lengthy discussion about who among the neighbors went to what school, Mannig said, "We ought to send Aida to Lala's school."

"Since our chauffeur drives Lala there every day," Diggin Tatyossian said, "He could pick her up at the same time."

"I don't want to inconvenience you," Mardiros said. "Aida can walk to school."

"But the American School for Girls is across the bridge and fifteen miles away, past Al-Rashid Street."

Knowing that Mardiros wouldn't be stationed in Baghdad all the time and so couldn't drive Aida, Mannig was in a quandary. She really wanted to send their daughter to an American educational institution. After all, her own mother, who had perished on the deportation trek, had attended an American School in Adapazar. Mannig felt a tug at her heartstrings. This would provide a link to her past.

Calling Mardiros' attention to how the two girls carried on a chitchat of their own, she whispered, "I think the girls themselves would want to be together. Diggin Tatyossian has noticed their friendship, too. She is very kind to offer a ride."

Mardiros thought a minute. "And when I'm not on an assignment, I myself will drive the two girls. We will take turns."

"Barone Mardiros," Diggin Tatyossian said, changing her tone and looking him in the eye, "do you know exactly what took place last night? I can't wait until my husband returns home this evening to tell me. But I think a lot of ugly things happened during the night."

"That's what I heard, too," he said in a somber voice. "It must be the winds of war of 1941. I think the fighting in Europe has corrupted our citizenry. Fascism has taken hold of the Arab spirit. Once a society adopts a dogma, it seeks out the opportunity to show its fangs. That's what happened in the marketplace last night. The townspeople were influenced by the idea that *what Jews own actually belongs to the people*. So by midnight, all the Jewish stores were raided and any merchandize they could grab became their own property. Shop after shop, they tore off the front doors and looted anything and everything and hauled it all to their homes. I heard some Armenian stores were mistakenly looted, too."

"Yes, yes," Diggin Tatyossian said. "Our chauffeur's cousin has a store for mirrors, and he found every piece smashed to smithereens."

"My biggest fear is," Mardiros said just before Diggin Tatyossian rose to leave, "that the looting of the Jewish stores is just the beginning. At their next opportunity, their thirst to annihilate the Semitic race will surge forth—"

"That's too much," Mannig interrupted him. "They can't eliminate a race, especially their own race. The Arabs themselves are Semitic, too."

"They're not concerned with technicalities," Mardiros dismissed Mannig's comment. "If they want to get rid of the Jews, they'll find an excuse to massacre them."

Mannig refused to perpetuate gloomy predictions and the only way she could was to say what she knew. "The Arabs wouldn't do that …. Remember how they saved the Armenian orphans? In fact, you yourself were involved. I wouldn't be here if they hadn't gone out of their way searching for stray orphans in the desert after the Turks massacred us."

"I agree with both of you," Diggin Tatyossian said. "I can't imagine the Arabs hurting us. We've lived on these lands for centuries, and no harm has come to us. But my husband fears something is brewing in the midst of the people."

"The politics of Europe always influences the Middle East," Mardiros seemed to want the last word, and the two ladies glanced at each other to let it be.

Diggin Tatyossian rose to leave and, seeing her daughter Lala talking intimately with Aida, repeated that the two girls should be enrolled at the same school. "Besides playing with each other," she said, "the girls can do their homework together."

The following day—on Friday, his day off—Mardiros suggested that Mannig accompany him to this American School for Girls and enroll Aida. After crossing the King Faisal I Bridge across the Tigris, he veered southward on Al-Rashid Street. For ten miles, they passed a parade of upscale shops and department stores, their doors crushed and merchandise gone.

"I'm glad Aida doesn't have to walk this way," Mannig whispered. "But what happens if Lala can't go to school one day?"

"When that time comes," Mardiros assured her, "these places will be rebuilt. The British are in control of the government again, and soon people will forget how our town was shamed because of the Nazi influence."

Within half an hour, he was driving in the eastern wing of Baghdad. He screeched his brakes to a halt next to a gated, three-level brick building. The sign on the fence said, in Arabic, *El-Madressa el-Americanya l'il Benaat* and below it in English, The American School for Girls.

"The school is too far from our house," Mannig thought out loud, as she followed Mardiros up the front steps and into the office, their three children in tow.

Mrs. Thompson, the founder and principal of the kindergarten-through-high-school welcomed them into her office. She was elderly, with white hair, set in a bun. Looking at Setrak, she immediately said, "We don't accept boys. This school is only for girls."

"Actually," Mardiros apologized, "we're here to register our eldest daughter only."

"Is it because of the tuition?" she asked, looking at Maro. "We give special rates to siblings."

"But she hasn't learned to read and write Armenian yet," Mannig protested in English.

"Oh!" Mrs. Thompson showed her surprise. "Both of you speak English? Judging from your name, I thought you were Armenian."

"We are," Mardiros claimed proudly, "we also speak English and French."

"Of course! Of course!" Mrs. Thompson mumbled. "I just wanted you to know that if you wish your children to learn Armenian, you should enroll them at the Armenian Church school." She sounded very stern, expecting the couple to depart.

Both Mardiros and Mannig already knew those facts. What they didn't know was the steps to register their child into the school.

"Our curriculum is defined by the government," the principal explained. "The pupils here study all subjects in Arabic—beginning in first grade. In the fourth grade, they are introduced to English which, in the early grades, is limited to the alphabet and simple songs. We want them to sing English songs at our weekly assemblies. By the time the successful students graduate, they will be competent enough in Arabic to pass the required government examinations for graduating seniors. In addition to that, they will be able to express themselves in English to non-Arabic speakers and understand most of what is spoken in the movies. Any questions?"

The couple might have come up with a question or two, but at that moment they wanted assurance that this stern lady would accept Aida as one of her students.

"Since she hasn't attended school before," Mrs. Thompson said, "I must test her knowledge and decide on her grade level."

She handed Aida a book in Arabic to read.

Aida stuttered on the first few words, but eventually felt comfortable enough to read without sounding out the letters individually, deciphering the total sound of the word at once.

"That's a fourth-level text," Mrs. Thompson said. "Let me hear you read English."

Aida glanced at the Dick and Jane book and zoomed through the pages.

"Good!" the principal said. "That's better than sixth grade. How old is she?"

"She will be twelve at the end of this year," Mannig said.

"I'm inclined to sign her up for the sixth grade. What do you say?"

"But her Arabic reading was not good," Mardiros objected. "Won't she have problems in an upper grade?"

Chapter 33

Echoes of the War

Aida's first year of commuting to school with Lala was mutually satisfactory at the beginning. Soon Aida became involved in music, art and sports. Outside of the required curriculum, sport sessions met before the school bell rang—music or art, after school was dismissed. On those days, she walked home, or if she had ten fils, she'd cross the Tigris River in a *belem*, the local commercial rowboats for passengers.

"Did you learn anything new?" the oarsman who had befriended her would ask as soon as he dipped the oars into the swift and murky current.

"Nothing special in English," Aida would say almost every time. "In Arabic, we read something about Iraq."

"What can be special about this place?" His sarcasm was obvious even to ten-year-old Aida, who immediately wanted to speak out on behalf of the school of her parents' choice.

"Did you know that Baghdad is a very old place?" she quizzed him.

"Why do you think our main street is called Al-Rashid?" he snickered.

Aida raised her shoulders defensively.

"I suppose they don't teach historical landmarks, anymore," he sighed. "It was named for Haroun al-Rashid, our most famous Caliph of the Abbasid Dynasty. He made Baghdad a mecca for scholarship. People came from all over the world to attend our schools and universities."

She wanted to remind him about how these days, the top students traveled to Europe or America for their higher education. She decided not to argue. Instead, she whispered, "Next year, I'll probably go to a different school."

Attending another school didn't happen immediately, even though Aida breezed through fourth grade, receiving accolades from teachers and students. When Mrs. Thompson, the principal of the American School for Girls, recommended that she skip fifth grade, Mardiros asked Aida her wishes. She preferred to stay in the same grade with her friends, including Lala.

Upon Maro's registration the following year as a first grader, Mannig consulted her husband. "We can't depend much longer on the generosity of Lala's family to drive our children." Since they only rented their house, they could easily rent another across the Tigris to be within easy walking distance of the children's school.

Bustan al-Khass, meaning Garden of Lettuce, was a newly developing suburb in Southern Baghdad and within walking distance of most private schools. Mardiros purchased a corner lot and committed all his spare time to supervising the builders and the contractors. While their residence was going up, he realized the property was large enough to build more than one structure. As soon as the family moved into the finished house, he oversaw the completion of an adjacent second one, separated by a common wall and a shared yard fence. He rented the vacant and larger residence to what he had assumed was a widow and her daughters.

Both Aida and Maro walked to the American School for Girls. Their house was close enough to return home for lunch and take a rest before attending non-academic sessions from three to five in the afternoon.

During these naptimes, the sisters, now teenagers, bonded. "Do you hear the neighbors?" Maro asked, her ears glued to the common brick wall between their bedroom and the neighbor's.

Aida hopped onto her sister's bed and glued her ears to the wall, too.

"Boom! Boom! Boom!" Aida mimicked the rhythm of an Arabic song. "They are having fun, the girls are laughing …. There's music, too. It's an Um-Kalthoom disc. Maybe they're doing the belly dance. Imagine, a night-time event at this hour."

"Let's turn on our radio," Maro suggested, "and practice the jitterbug."

"Mama won't let us," Aida cautioned her. "If we can't actually nap, we're supposed to read …."

Setrak tiptoed into his sisters' bedroom. "Don't tell Mom I skipped naptime," he begged. "I want to see the pretty girls coming and going." He went to the window and peeked past the curtains.

Both sisters jumped up to see what he was talking about. "I don't see any girls," Maro said, "but two men are going in …."

"What men?"

"I don't know … men in suits getting out of their chauffeur-driven Cadillac. Now here comes a Rolls Royce …. They're hurrying through the neighbor's gate …."

To Mannig's chagrin, the tenant of their second house was a madam, operating a brothel for elite employees of the government. She couldn't wait

Aida, Mannig, and Maro at Hindiyeh Barrage, 1947.

till the weekend to confront her husband. She called him—an extravagant expense during those times of war. Mardiros had just been appointed as the resident engineer in Hindiyeh Barrage, a two hours' drive. He commuted home on weekends only. Of course, he had no idea about the lady or her profession, even though he had questioned the renter's generous offer for the year's rent. The madam had flattered him with her compliments about his great architectural talent for having built "no less than a grand mansion," saying that her circle of friends considered that it worth ten times more than what he planned to charge.

If only he had not assumed that some people simply had a distorted idea of grandeur … or was her praise just a ploy?

It took "grand" doings to finally make the madam vacate the premises. She used her powerful nocturnal clients to sue him. Mardiros countersued her with the backing of the higher-ups in the Irrigation Department. He was glad he didn't have to resort to appeal to Nuri-el-Said, the prime minister—a regular bridge partner—even though he was tempted to bring it up one evening during a game on his porch.

It took a year for the brothel to be vacated, and another year before Mannig could breathe freely when someone rang their doorbell. Strange cars and a variety of men—some in native robes and a keffiyeh, others in western suits—had to be shooed away at all hours of the day. For a whole year, she forbade the girls to flaunt their youthfulness in the neighborhood.

With the lack of rent money and high prices for commodities during WWII, Mannig resorted to her childhood/orphan pragmatism. The weekly cleaning woman was dismissed, and she did her own daily shopping at the *souq*.

When they received an invitation to a garden wedding for Margot, one of the Kouyoumdjian cousins who would be marrying a Britisher, the family was in a quandary. Buying an appropriate gift would be too costly, considering that the family was expected to give items such as refrigerators, ovens or summer vacations at a resort. They decided to remove one of their own chandeliers, polish the metal and clean the ornate crystal glass as their contribution to the newlyweds.

Instead of store-bought clothes, Mannig sewed the dresses for her growing teenage daughters and a pair of stylish cloche hats made of white organdy. She re-fashioned one of her gowns for herself and altered her husband's tuxedo trousers to fit his expanding waistline.

The compliments she received from relatives for the girls' dresses affirmed her sense of style. She kept her family attired with panache. Since the children's parties always included parents, she noticed the attention her daughters received from foreigner-guests—American, English and French. She was delighted to see the two girls flanked by non-Armenians, especially when the attention came from American young men, married or single.

Instead of enduring the WWII austerity prevalent throughout the free world, Iraq had become a playground for the Western Powers, as was apparent at Margot's wedding. American, French and British military and diplomatic personnel attracted the admiration of the locals, and from then on, they were included in any and all parties, private or public.

At one such party, the family met the personnel of the USIS. The director was enchanted with their family and extended a casual invitation to them to visit his office. The office being within the bounds of downtown Baghdad, more accessible to pedestrians than cars, Mannig didn't attempt to visit the premises.

Aida and Maro did. The office was air-conditioned and books and the latest issues of American magazines were easily accessible. They spent many hours there and became acquainted with all their personnel—local and American. It was on such an occasion that Aida seized the opportunity to apply for a Fulbright Scholarship.

The whole family participated in filling out the forms. There were many, some requiring the signatures of the higher-ups in the government, such as the Minister of Education.

Chapter 34

Departures

AIDA SEEMED NOT TO BE going anywhere, soon.
For two years, Mannig and her whole family anxiously awaited to bid Aida farewell to the United States, where she would receive her degree in higher education. September of 1950 and 1951 came and went and there was absolutely no news to cheer anyone. Watching her daughter's disappointment each September made Mannig suffer most, especially when Aida was invited to farewell parties for friends who left Iraq for the United States.

Mannig left Baghdad and joined her husband in Hindiyeh Barrage, where he had been appointed the resident engineer.

Almost unexpectedly, Aida's luck changed.

What a grandiose change!

In September of 1952, she received a telephone call from Mr. Hayden Boswell, the director of the United States Information Service (locally identified as USIS). Unable to pronounce either her first or last name, he managed to say, before he hung up the receiver, "Can you come to my office right away?"

Aida was tongue-tied. It didn't matter how he butchered her name. She couldn't contain her excitement at having received a call from a prestigious officer representing America. "It will take me an hour to get there," she whispered. "Is that okay?"

"Yes, yes," he said. "We're open until six."

Breathlessly she dashed out, glad that there was no one at home to whom she needed to explain her sudden departure. She didn't want to raise their hopes.

A tall, lanky young man in his twenties, Hayden Boswell extended his hand and congratulated her. "I'm delighted to inform you that you have been granted a Fulbright Scholarship."

Fulbright? She hoped they hadn't assumed her to be anything but a bright student. Apparently realizing her bewilderment, he explained that Fulbright was the name of a senator from Arkansas who had initiated the idea of a student exchange program.

Of course all her relatives and friends heard about Aida's award and tacitly assumed that because Aida was *fully bright*, she deserved a totally sponsored grant. What more would a student of her caliber be granted than a full scholarship to go to Washington—D.C., that is? No matter how many times Aida tried to set them straight, explaining that the University of Washington was actually in Seattle, nearly 3,000 miles west of Washington, D.C., they bragged about how their compatriot was so smart that she was being sent to the capital of the United States.

Thus, on the morning of her departure, all of Aida's relatives and friends, nearly 200 of them, went to the airport to bid her farewell.

Mannig never realized how difficult it would be to see her oldest child leave home. Her only wish and hope was her daughter's happiness. Watching Aida exude joy at the airport satisfied her that her daughter was doing the right thing, until it was time to kiss her family goodbye. The boisterous crowd acted as one entity—the floodgates broke and the herd of friends and relatives who had come to bid her bon voyage burst into tears.

Just before Aida boarded the plane at the Baghdad Airport, her immediate family was allowed onto the tarmac. As one clan, they trotted up to the steps of the British airline, BOAC. Once again, Aida made the rounds, kissing her family members, one after the other. When it was her mother's turn, Mannig barely let her face touch Aida's—lest her daughter's tears breach her own emotional barriers.

After Aida's departure, Mannig found solace in her second daughter, Maro. Maro, although three years younger than Aida, had bonded with her sister as if they were twins. She had a lighter complexion and hair but otherwise was almost a duplicate of her older sister. The sisters often socialized apart from each other, yet seemed to give the same answers to questions neither of them had heard before. Often, acquaintances couldn't identify Aida from Maro. To avoid embarrassment, they addressed each as *Aida-Maro,* especially when they dressed alike—thanks to Mannig's expertise.

Mannig had become her daughters' seamstress with great enthusiasm. Having grown up in orphanage uniforms, she was deprived of such frivolities during her childhood. When she married Mardiros, the orphanage's wealthy benefactor, she ventured to visit her sister, Adriné, at her in-laws' dressmaking shop and acquired the skills of a seemstress. She sewed anything

Maro, Mannig, Aida. Baghdad, 1948.

and everything the girls wanted. Often, after seeing a movie with Betty Grable or Rita Hayworth, the sisters would describe a dress in the movie they'd love to have. Mannig would listen carefully to their description of the style, buy the material and design her own patterns to suit the girls' taste. The three seemed happy about the arrangement and the tradition continued until Aida packed her trunk and left for the USA.

Within six months of Maro's graduation from high school, she received a scholarship from Columbia College, in Columbia, South Carolina. The departure of Mannig's second daughter, Maro, impacted her with unequalled sadness. Mannig felt lonely and abandoned. She persevered, trying to maintain a happy family life with her husband and son, Setrak, but a sense of utter desolation became rooted in her heart.

She missed the camaraderie she had developed with her two daughters.

As soon as the girls had become young ladies, they had shared their daily activities with her. She anxiously awaited their return from school, when she would prepare Turkish coffee for the three of them. Sitting with them on the porch, she would listen to their stories about what had happened in school, at the youth club and after parties. She relished the fun and excitement of youth—much of which she had never experienced. After all, she'd been merely fifteen years old when she married Mardiros, the bachelor benefactor of her orphanage. She often felt as if she had missed a vibrant part of growing up.

Soon after Maro's departure, both Mannig and Mardiros sought an opportunity to send their son, Setrak, to another country lest he, an idle young man, be inducted into the Iraqi army and be deployed to fight the Iranians.

They appealed to a close friend, Roupen Ter-Minassian, who had been educated in Germany and was working for a German company in Baghdad at that time. Roupen was able to obtain a visa for Setrak to leave Iraq to attend the Heidelberg University on a work/study program in 1964. Setrak became a resident of Basel, Switzerland, across the river from Heidelberg. In 1967, he immigrated to the U.S. and worked for the Bellevue School District in the State of Washington for twenty-eight years.

Setrak passed on in 2005 and was cremated and buried near Mannig at Sunset Cemetery in Bellevue, Washington.

Three years after her children's departure, Mannig made a bold decision. She convinced her husband she ought to travel to the United States to witness their daughters' graduations from their respective universities. Then, on their way back home, the three of them would visit Setrak.

Finances and visa requirements took another year, but finally Mannig was on her way to the United States.

She took the Nairn Bus out of Baghdad, to Beirut, Lebanon. After spending a week there, she embarked on a small ship to Genoa, Italy.

The instant she boarded the S.S. "Independence" to sail from Genoa to New York, she knew how she'd feel upon stepping onto the soil of the New World. The memory of that feeling would remain as fresh as if she were experiencing it for the first time whenever she reminisced.

Was she really going to the New World? *How amazing!* she had thought at departure time.

She always dreamed of being in New York, but never believed her dreams would come true. But it was true! Would miracles never cease? She had geared herself up for the voyage.

Hordes of people crowded the pier of the Italian city of Genoa to see the beautiful ship and bid their relatives and friends a *bon voyage*. They looked up, laughing and talking loudly, shouting to one another over and above the din.

The day was bright and warm, and more and more people gathered on the pier. No one came for her, of course. She was a stranger in transit. Nevertheless, she was so happy and excited she found herself laughing and shouting and pushing people, just like the rest of the voyagers.

This farewell scene was already exciting enough, but it reached its height when an American steward brought along a big box of colored streamers. Lots of them. He distributed them among the passengers to be thrown to the people on the pier. The paper trail formed a rainbow-like bridge, uniting the passengers with their friends—this, for the last time before they sailed.

They were all just like children, jumping and shouting and pulling the streamers from each other's heads or hands. At the same time, the huge ship's siren blared.

Tea following an official ceremony after a ribbon cutting in Baghdad, 1951. Left to Right: Maro, a friend Hermine Ter-Minassian, Mannig, Aida, Rouben Ter-Minassian (Hermine's husband).

Mannig felt exhilarated. The slow departure hurled her into the aura of a different world—a world so gay and carefree, her heart filled with hope for a confident future.

Fascinated, she sensed being in a different world already. The discipline on an American ship seemed perfect to her, with the passengers all lined up, about six hundred in tourist class, to hand over their passports. She was amazed at how, unlike crowds in Baghdad, these people stayed in an orderly line.

Soon, their dining cards were distributed, and dinner-partners assigned according to their ages. She admired the way they arranged everything for passengers to have a good time. She noticed that for Americans, having a good time and amusing themselves was most important.

She relished dinner—scrumptious and plentiful—served at tables with white linen and china. An unlimited quantity of red wine was poured into crystal goblets. If this was the style for the tourists' section, she wondered, how much more elaborate could the meals be at the first and second classes? It boggled her mind even though she had experienced extreme affluence living with her husband's rich family soon after she was married. The evening suppers with the Kouyoumdjians at the *Qasr* in Felloujeh perhaps topped ambassadorial functions at that time.

During her first meal aboard, she saw a small jug of milk on the table. She had heard that the milk in America was very safe and delicious. She snatched up the jug and poured it into her glass. She took a sip. *Yuck*! Thick and very rich. She simply could not drink it. Just then, the dining room steward saw her and said, "No, no, lady. That's cream for the coffee, not milk. It will make you sick."

She was very much embarassed, but tried not to think about it. Instead, she decided to appreciate everything and enjoy the present.

The fellow passengers at her table, two men and one lady, were surprised when they heard she was from Baghdad. They seemed very happy to have a table partner from a distant country and never ceased to ask her all sorts of questions, most of which seemed ridiculous to her especially, when they wondered about Ali Baba and His Forty Thieves.

After finishing her very enjoyable dinner, she left the table. While leaving the dining room, a man seated at another table swung around his chair and reached for her hand. "Hey, beautiful!" he said with a big smile. "I think I know you."

Mannig gave him a quizzical look.

"I do not remember where I have seen you," he went on, fondling her fingers, "but I'm sure I can figure it out. Will you wait for me in the sitting room? I will join you there shortly."

She was very much surprised and momentarily flattered but decided not to wait for him. She just didn't care for his attitude. She suspected that was just his way of making friends.

She was so happy, as it was, she didn't want anything else. Blessings of all blessings, she was on her way to America. She could hardly believe she would soon be with her daughters.

Just those thoughts exhilarated her. She went to her cabin, excited and very tired. She wanted to be alone with her memories.

That very first night, she thought and thought and remembered everything. She prayed to God, thanking Him for allowing her to be on her way to see her daughters again. It had been four years.

Epilogue

FOR SIX MONTHS, MANNIG EXPERIENCED the United States her own way. Whatever she had been told about America never reached the glorious images she gathered herself. Traveling in a Greyhound Bus, she traversed the Southern States, across California and Oregon, with a final destination of Seattle, Washington. She analyzed everything she saw and often made her recommendations for its improvement—if not to her traveling seat-mates, at least in her thoughts.

The United States was heaven on earth.

Upon her return to Baghdad, she convinced her husband that America was a land for people like them. "We should live in America at least during our old age."

He agreed.

Through the regular channels, he applied for the appropriate papers. His and Mannig's names were listed on a quota system—a process that for Iraqi citizens might take a lifetime. Meanwhile, Aida, now a U.S. citizen and a resident of Washington state, appealed to Senator Magnuson, who introduced a bill in Congress on their behalf.

By the time the visa was issued, Mardiros had had a heart attack and passed away. He was seventy-three. Mannig buried him at the cemetery of the Armenian Church in Baghdad, Iraq.

Now fifty-seven years old, Mannig packed two suitcases—the limit a citizen was allowed to take out of Iraq—taking $100.00 in cash in her pocket for emergencies on route.

After a three-month sea voyage, she arrived in Charleston, South Carolina. Maro, her second daughter, her growing family and the community of Lexington, a suburb of Columbia, welcomed her with open arms. She relished the Southern hospitality for two months before she moved to Seattle, Washington, to be with her oldest daughter, Aida and her growing family.

Mannig was immediately hired by the University of Washington to tutor graduate students in exotic languages. After instructing her students in Arabic, Turkish and Armenian for several years, she retired to Mercer Island to be near Aida and her family.

She made her mark with several senior-citizen organizations in Seattle. Dr. Stanley Chapple of the University of Washington included her in his ensemble, *Musicians Emeritus,* giving Mannig the opportunity to play the piano at venues in Seattle and Bellevue. She was on the guest program at the local Rotary, Kiwanis, Chamber of Commerce and other community organizations.

Since her retirement income from Social Security was a mere $200 per month and $74 from the State Retirement Program, she lived in a low-income housing unit for retirees. In spite of her meager allowance, she had accumulated $20,000 in savings by the time of her death in 1984.

She was seventy-nine—that is, if we believe the birth certificate they devised for her at the orphanage.

She never complained about anything except the tragedy of not being able to come to the United States as a young person. She often murmured, "In America, I could have become somebody."

In her humility, she discounted her own achievements.

That was Mannig.

At Seattle's First Hill Stimson/Green Mansion, musicians prepare to rehearse a string ensemble. Mannig, their pianist, is seated at the far right.

Mardiros, 1947.

Mannig, 1948.

Mannig, 1950.

Mannig, 1964.

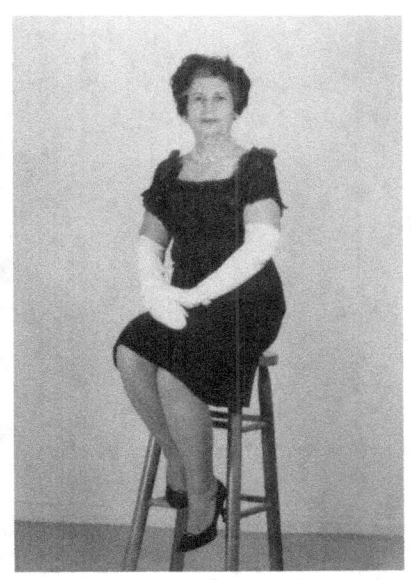
Mannig, 1967.

Glossary

abaya = outer robe (Arabic)
Abdul Karim Qassim = revolutionary leader of Iraq in 1952 (Arabic)
Agha = title for nobility (Turkish)
Agoomp = club-house (Armenian)
Ahkh! = exclamation of pain/loss (Universal)
Allah-u-Akbar = God is great (Arabic)
Amahn! = exclamation for surprise (Armenian)
ambar = rice harvested in the Ambar region (Arabic)
Aqqal wa keffiyeh = head-band and kerchief (Arabic)
arabana = horse-drawn carriage (Arabic)
bahce = orchard (Turkish)
Bedou = Singular for Bedouin (Arabic)
belem = rowboat (Arabic)
bess atfaal = only children! (Arabic)
boghcha = orchard or a carrier-scarf (Turkish)
chai-khana = tea house (Arabic)
Diedie & Mokor = nicknames for uncle and aunt (Armenian)
Der Hayr = Holy Father—for addressing a priest (Armenian)
dizhdasheh = tunic—usually for men (Arabic)
doctore = doctor/physician (Arabic)
Ahlen = welcome! (Arabic)
Englaizy = English (Arabic)
etiquette-m'etiquette = dismissing politeness (Armenian)
fellaheen = farmers/peasants (Arabic)
gawad = traitor/fucker (Arabic)
gel bunaya = come here (Turkish)
ghee = clarified butter (British)
ghoorabia = butter cookies (Middle Eastern)
gozleri guzel = beautiful eyes (Turkish)
guffa = round fishing boat (Arabic)

haleeb = milk (Arabic)
ibriq = water jug (Arabic)
iftah ya simsim = Open Sesame! (Arabic)
Imshee = Scat! Gitt! Go! (Arabic)
In-sha-Allah = God willing (Arabic)
jabbar = rebel (Arabic)
jahleh = young girl- immature (Arabic)
Jahn = endearing label (Armenian)
jamhuriya = republic (Arabic)
jamil = beautiful (male) (Arabic)
jamileh = beautiful (feminine) (Arabic)
Jasmiyeh = maid in Baghdad (female name)
jazwa = Turkish-coffee brewing pot (Arabic)
khara = shit/feces (Arabic)
Khatoon = lady/matron (Arabic/Turkish)
khubuz = bread (Arabic)
kubbeh = dish made of bulghur and ground meat(Armenian/Arabic)
la wa'allah = No, my God! (Arabic)
Laa = No! (Arabic)
labni = buttermilk (Lebanese)
laban = yoghurt (Arabic)
lorry/lorries = military truck/s (British)
Ma'a salaam = with peace (good-bye) (Arabic)
Mabrook = congratulations (Arabic)
Mannig = pronounced: maan-nig (Armenian)
Mardiros = pronounced:maar-dee-rohss (Armenian)
Matruloze = machine gun (Nickname for Mardiros)
moderne and *modelle* = acquired from the French for modern and model (Armenian)
Moudeer = director (Arabic)
mu'edhin = chanter from the minaret (Arabic)
mu-sharif = I'm honored (Arabic)
napththalene = the poison used in moth balls
nargeeleh = hukka/water-pipe/hubble-bubble (Arabic)
nye = flute-like musical instrument (Bedouin)
odaar = alien/foreigner/outsider (Armenian)
Quaimaquam = mayor (Turkish)
qasr = castle/palace (Arabic)
Ra-iis belediyeh = mayor/chief of town (Arabic)
saboon = soap (Arabic)
Sajadah = small carpet (Turkish)

salaam = peace (Arabic)
Sayid = Mister/Master (Arabic)
shabboot = fresh water salmon (Arabic)
Shia = Islam sect/partisans of Ali (Arabic)
Shukran Jezeelan = extreme thanks (Arabic)
simit = pretzel-like snack (Turkish/Arabic)
souq = marketplace/bazaar (Arabic)
Subbah-silver = Subbah sect's silver craft (Arabic)
Sunni = Islam sect/partisans of tradition (Arabic)
tahn = buttermilk (Armenian)
tasse = metallic cup with handle (Armenian/French)
tass = metallic cup with handle (Arabic)
tdabuul = cylindrical-clay/goat-hide drum (Bedouin)
tennoor = bread-baking under-ground oven (Arabic)
thawra = revolution (Arabic)
Tibbets, Abbet, and McCarthy = U.S. engineering firm in Baghdad, Iraq (TAMS for short)
toneer = bread-baking clay oven (Armenian)
Um Kalthoom = Famous female vocalist (Arabic)
vorpanots = orphanage (Armenian)
Vye! = Oh, My! –Exclamation (Armenian)
wu = and (Arabic)
Y'allah = God willing (Arabic)
Ya ballad el-jamili = my city of beauty (Arabic Song)
Ya balad el-Rashidi = My town/palace of Rashid (Arabic)
Yukh! = Expletive for unpleasantness (Universal)
Zengeeneh = wealthy female (Arabic)

Who's Who

Mannig = maan-neeg, orphaned in the Armenian Genocide; at the age of 15, she married the orphanage's benefactor, twenty years her senior
Mardiros = maar-dee-rohss, Mannig's husband
Hagopig = Mannig's first born son
Aida = Mannig's oldest daughter
Maro = Mannig's youngest daughter
Setrak = Mannig's son
Adriné = Mannig's sister
Sebouh = Adriné's husband
Heranoush = Mannig's mother; also Adriné's oldest daughter
Sirarpi = Mannig's little sister; also Adriné's second daughter
Hratch = Adriné's son
Anita = Adriné's youngest daughter
Khosrof = Mardiros' second oldest brother
Sarah = Khosrof's second wife
Maggie = Khosrof's daughter by his first wife
Diran = Khosrof's son by his second wife
Armen = Khosrof's youngest son by his second wife
Sona = Khosrof's youngest daughter by his second wife
Dikran = Mardiros' second brother
Siranoush = Dikran's wife
Margo = Dikran's daughter
Toros = Dikran's twin
Hermine = Toros' wife
Vahram = Toros' oldest son
Hagop = Toros' second son
Carlo = Toros' third son
Haigo = Toros' fourth son
Karnig = Mardiros' oldest brother
Rose = Karnig's wife

Badrig = Rose's older son
Antranig = Rose's second son
Iskouhi = Rose's oldest daughter
Lizinka = Rose's second daughter
Meliné = Rose's youngest daughter
Kaloust = Mardiros' cousin in Falloujeh
Leon Kurkjian = Armenian doctor in Falloujeh
Zuwaydeh = Chief of the Irrigation Department
Berj = Tennis champion and Bridge game partner
Levon Donatossian = Daring businessman and Bridge game partner
Yeprem = Newcomer from Beirut, Lebanon and Bridge game partner
Telemaque Tutunjian = Iskouhi's husband from Egypt
Dr. Kurdian = Physician in Baghdad
Bedros Dobajian = Mannig's father, victim of the Genocide
Fareed = Valet/server/driver
Hamid = Chef at the Kouyoumdjian *qasr* in Baghdad
Sheikh Dhari = Tribal chief near Abu Ghraib
Mustafa = Assassin in Falloujeh
Diedie = Nickname for Uncle Sebouh
Mokor = Nickname for Aunt Adriné
Jasmiyeh = Day maid in Baghdad
Um Kalthoom = Famous female crooner from Egypt
Bustan al-Khass = New residential district in Baghdad
Sheikh Abbas = Chief of a nomadic tribe in Iraq
Sheikh Hamid = Chief of another nomadic tribe in Iraq
Bashrawi = Sheikh in Kut
William Wilcox = Chief engineer for Hindiyeh Barrage
Harun al-Rashid = Famous Caliph in Baghdad during the Abbasid dynasty
Rashid Ali al-Gaylani = Politician who was pro-Nazi
Nazlu = maid at the *qasr*
Fessjian = Widow and children who live in Mardiros's home
Neh-Neh = Fessjian's in-law—midwife
Jasmiyeh = Abu Zainab's second wife
Dr. Kurkjian = Falloujeh Obstetrician
Diggin Fortuna = Dr. Kurkjian's wife
Hrandt = Dr. Kurkjian's older son
Ara = Dr. Kurkjian's second son
Sita = Dr. Kurkjian's daughter
Selma = Maggie's friend in Falloujeh
Vartanoush Alianak = Siranoush's sister-in-law

What Makes an Armenian?

ARMENIANS HAVE ENDURED THE WARS between the Greco-Roman and the Persian East since the first century B.C. Warring empires looted, burned, and devastated Armenian territory, leading its people into captivity, rape, and murder. Each time, the surviving population toiled stubbornly to reconstruct what had been destroyed, as would a swallow rebuild a ruined nest. If asked, what makes an Armenian? The answer would be, "A trek."

Armenians proclaimed Christianity as the national religion of Armenia in A.D. 301, establishing precedence in the annals of the Christian Church. Surrounded by the empires of Rome and Persia, which denounced and persecuted them, Armenians prescribed their own suicide as would a scorpion sting itself when trapped in blazing fires. If asked, what makes an Armenian? The answer would be, "Faith."

Armenians invented an alphabet late in the Fourth Century. It was conceived by St. Mesrop to create a Christian literature in the mother tongue during the most critical epoch of Armenia's political existence and provided the very weapon which, by awakening nationalism, inspired and enabled the Armenian people to survive to this very day. If asked, what makes an Armenian? The answer would be, "Zeal."

Armenians saw yet another foe, the Islamic Caliphate in A.D. 644. Like fragile violets, they were plucked by gnarled hands and mangled by the merciless claws of Arab mercenaries. Never stripped of spirit, all that remained was praying to God. If asked, what makes an Armenian? The answer would be "Hope."

Armenians regained statehood during the Tenth Century, the wages of which spelled compromise. Soon compromise meant change. No Armenian would rather live than see the death of his identity. If asked, what makes an

Armenian? The answer would be, "Pride."

Armenians lost their kingdom in 1375. Since then, they have persisted to be Armenian in their own right. They have clung to their culture, traditions, and language like an iceberg (one that doesn't melt) in the North Pole. If asked, what makes an Armenian? The answer would be, "Preservation."

Armenians begot Armenians, perpetuating a conquered people. United, they failed to liberate themselves; independently, they menaced the conqueror. A people without a leader, they safeguarded themselves from falling like wheat at the edge of a scythe, by having recourse to weapons. If asked, what makes an Armenian? The answer would be, "Individuality."

Armenians became dispersed throughout their lands. Robbed of an unalienable land by the invading forces of the Mongols, Persians, Kurds, and the Ottoman Turks, they were determined to survive as a nation. Obsessed with education, they developed a talent for commerce, evolving into an elite Christian minority that catered to a needy Muslim majority. If asked, what makes an Armenian? The answer would be, "Capacity."

One and a half to 2 million Armenians perished in the first Genocide of the Twentieth Century, perpetrated by the Ottoman Turks during WWI in 1914-1918. The survivors were consumed into the Soviet Republic and endured Communism for seven decades. Unlike sheep being goaded into the slaughterhouse, they proclaimed independence and sovereignty in 1991. If asked, what makes an Armenian? The answer would be, "Fidelity."

Armenians established a Christian kingdom at the foot of Mt. Ararat. They have defended their ethnicity from mountains; they have sought refuge in the mountains; and having stood rugged like mountains, they have survived religious, political, and economic persecutions. If asked, what makes an Armenian? The answer would be, "Mt. Ararat."

A IDA KOUYOUMJIAN WAS BORN IN Felloujeh, Iraq. When she and her sister were old enough to attend school, her family moved sixty miles east to Baghdad.

In 1952 Aida won a year-long Fulbright Scholarship to the University of Washington in Seattle. As the eldest daughter, she was the first in her family to leave Baghdad. The Iraqi government, a monarchy at the time, gave her its blessing. After the year was up, Aida reapplied and stayed another four years. At the end of that period, her father warned her of unrest in Iraq and advised her to extend her stay. Aida married an American—a fellow student—but she still received deportation notices. Her politically savvy in-laws appealed her case to Senator Warren G. Magnuson, who introduced a special bill in congress allowing her to stay in the U.S.

Aida's path to citizenship was further delayed by her engineer husband's frequent moves. Finally his work allowed them to stay in Warrensburg, Missouri, for the requisite two years, thus allowing her to study and pass the citizenship exam in 1962. Her family, which now included three sons, eventually settled in Mercer Island.

After Aida's father died in 1965, she was finally able to bring her mother Mannig to this country. A year later, Aida's brother joined them. Her sister had left Baghdad in 1953, a year after Aida, and settled in South Carolina.

At the age of 69, Mannig was hired by the UW to tutor graduate students in Turkish, Armenian, and Arabic. She remained on the UW staff for seven years before retiring. Not long before her death in 1985 at the age of 79, Mannig was one of ninety survivors who attended the 70th commemoration of the Armenian Genocide in Washington, D.C.

After thirty years of teaching in public schools, Aida offered a course on

Iraq at Bellevue College. Although retired from teaching, she is still a popular speaker at schools and public service organizations. She is a former winner of the Pacific Northwest Writers' Association Prize for Non-fiction. She was also awarded first place by the Washington Association of Press Women for an editorial that appeared in the Seattle P-I.

Aida has been active in Seattle's Armenian community since her University days. After Armenia's great earthquake of 1988, she helped organize Seattle's relief effort. In 1989 she spearheaded the formation of the Armenian Cultural Association of Washington (ACA) and was elected first president of its board of directors.

Aida's first book, *Between the Two Rivers: A Story of the Armenian Genocide*, won first place (Washington State) in the National Federation of Press Women (NFPW) At-Large Communications Contest in the nonfiction: history category.

Aida has three sons, eight grandchildren and two great-grandchildren.

You can find Aida online at armenianstory.coffeetownpress.com.

www.ingramcontent.com/pod-product-compliance
Lightning Source LLC
Chambersburg PA
CBHW071156070526
44584CB00019B/2808